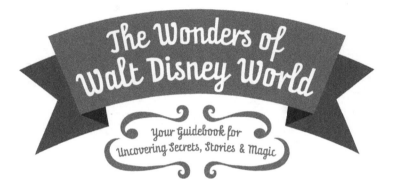

The Wonders of Walt Disney World

Your Guidebook for Uncovering Secrets, Stories & Magic

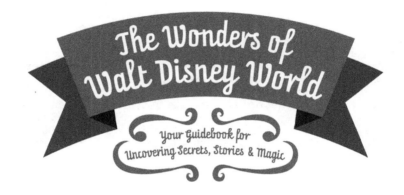

The Wonders of Walt Disney World

Your Guidebook for Uncovering Secrets, Stories & Magic

Aaron H. Goldberg

Quaker Scribe Publishing
Philadelphia, Pennsylvania

Published by Quaker Scribe Publishing
Philadelphia, Pennsylvania
quakerscribe@gmail.com

ISBN: 1733642040

ISBN 978-1-7336420-4-0

Library of Congress Control Number: 2017961261

Visit the author on the web: www.aaronhgoldberg.com

Follow Aaron Goldberg on Twitter at @aaronhgoldberg

CONTENTS

The Wonders of
Walt Disney World

Your Guidebook for
Uncovering Secrets, Stories & Magic

Introduction

Walt Disney had a dream, a dream that would revolutionize the way families vacationed and spent their free time together.

To quote the man himself, "I felt that there should be something built, some sort of amusement enterprise built, where the parents and the children could have fun together." In July 1955, that dream was realized when Disneyland debuted in Southern California.

Walt's park was such a success that folks from all over the world wanted him to replicate his Magic Kingdom in their hometowns—they even offered him free land in an attempt to lure him. About a decade later, and after much research, another Disney theme park was on the horizon.

Many cities were on the drawing board as a potential landing spot. Saint Louis came extremely close, and even the seasonal state of New York was entertained as a possibility. But Walt wanted warmth. Southern Florida had a shot for a brief moment, but ultimately, central Florida, near a little sleepy town called Orlando, won out.

On November 15, 1965, the world got what it wanted. A second Disneyland, or Disneyland East, as some people referred to it, was in the planning stages. Walt made the announcement at a press conference in Florida, and the state hasn't been the same since.

Florida wouldn't be the home to a mere reproduction of Disneyland. Walt's aspirations for this project were grandiose and extremely ambitious. As he stated during the press conference, "We have many things in mind to make this unique and different from Disneyland. It's the biggest thing we've ever tackled."

Sure, there was going to be a theme park on the property, but the "Florida Project" was going to be so much more. Walt envisioned a city of the future on his land, one that would revolutionize and culturally change the way people lived, worked, and played.

Unfortunately, most of those magical dreams Walt Disney envisioned for the more than forty square miles of land he purchased in central Florida would be nothing more than unrealized dreams. Roughly a year after the big land acquisition announcement, Walt Disney passed away, on December 15, 1966.

Best-selling author James Patterson once said, "Dreams die hard. And sometimes they don't have to die at all." Waiting in the wings to ensure that not all of his kid brother's dreams died was Roy O. Disney.

Roy was Walt's older brother, business partner, and confidant. As brilliant and creative as Walt was in entertaining the masses, Roy was equally astute and imaginative when it came to finding a way to finance his brother's wildest dreams.

Roy and Walt set out on their entertainment journey during the 1920s, oftentimes not in lockstep, but they usually found a way for their partnership to work. Now, for the first time, Roy was flying solo—the Walt Disney Company was without its creative leader at the crux of a major project. Roy did what any big brother would do: he looked out for his little brother and built the theme park on the company's land in central Florida. (For more on Roy and Walt's brotherly love, check out my other book, *Meet the Disney Brothers*. Ok, shameless plug over!)

Under Roy's guidance and tutelage, Magic Kingdom at Walt Disney World came to fruition on October 1, 1971. As Roy O. Disney stated in his dedication on October 25, 1971, the park wouldn't be Disneyland East or Disneyland part two; it would be known as Walt Disney World.

"Walt Disney World is a tribute to the philosophy and life of Walter Elias Disney...and to the talents, the dedication, and the loyalty of the entire Disney organization that made Walt Disney's dream come true. May Walt Disney World bring joy and inspiration and new knowledge to all who come to this happy place...a Magic Kingdom where the young at heart of all ages can laugh and play and learn—together. Dedicated this 25th of October 1971, Roy O. Disney."

Initially, Walt Disney World consisted primarily of Magic Kingdom. As time progressed, the more than twenty-seven thousand acres of land evolved and grew. EPCOT Center (later renamed Epcot) debuted on October 1, 1982. Next came Disney's Hollywood Studios on May 1, 1989; Disney's Typhoon Lagoon on June 1, 1989; Disney's Blizzard Beach on April 1, 1995; and finally, on Earth Day, April 22, 1998, Disney's Animal Kingdom.

Within each of these magical places are countless hidden secrets and creative details that Disney crafted for your enjoyment. What may seem like an ordinary item often has more than meets the eye—be it a hidden Mickey or a hidden fire hydrant. So let's explore the Happiest Place on Earth and scratch just below the surface to see the fun and details that lie just out of eyeshot.

Welcome to the wonders of Walt Disney World!

Aaron H. Goldberg
December 2019

Chapter One

Magic Kingdom

> *I don't want the public to see the world they live in while they're in the park. I want them to feel they're in another world.*
>
> **—Walt Disney**

You've just traveled for several minutes along the highway in the sky in one of Walt Disney World's sleek monorails, or perhaps you've earned your sea legs and cruised the Seven Seas Lagoon in a boat or ferry. Or maybe you were chauffeured via a Walt Disney World resort bus. No matter how you got here, you're about to embark on a magical day and enter Walt Disney World's Magic Kingdom.

From the moment you approach the entrance, you know you're on the cusp of something special, as you're about to be transported again, this time to several unique lands, lands that for the most part originated from the imagination of your host, Walt Disney.

As the world knows, Walt Disney was a storyteller with a penchant for perfection and detail. When Walt opened Disneyland in 1955, he set the ultimate stage for a story starring each and every person who visits one of his theme parks.

Today, at Walt Disney World, just like at Disneyland, Walt's attention to detail has been cultivated and honed by the storytellers who help to carry on his legacy, the Disney Imagineers. (The name "Imagineering/Imagineer" combines imagination with engineering.) Utilizing Walt's schematic for Disneyland, the Imagineers created a magical kingdom that is immersive and all encompassing, a living, ever-changing theater show featuring a lifelike set and background just for you, the star of the show.

While everyone's experience and participation in the "show" at the Magic Kingdom may be different, there are numerous hidden nuances that are all around and consistent for every visitor. Many of these special and obscure details are hiding in plain sight, while some of them require a bit of thought or knowledge about the setting and story being told in order to appreciate them.

Let's walk beneath the tracks of the Walt Disney World Railroad station and soak up all that is Town Square, which then leads to Main Street, USA.

As you leave your cares and worries behind and step onto **Town Square**, the first thing that may catch your eye is the color of the sidewalk—it's red. Weird; the sidewalks at home aren't usually red. Well, here in Disney's world, there can be many reasons behind the uniqueness of the object you're viewing.

The red in this case is a specific color that was selected for a couple of reasons. The main reason is this shade shows up really well in pictures. The other reason is, it makes certain colors—many in nature such as the green grass—look more vibrant. If you look at a color wheel, green and red are opposite from each other.

If you don't like the technical aspect, think of it as part of the "show." Walt and his Imagineers have rolled out the red carpet for you. Welcome to the kingdom!

Once you get past the color red, turn around and notice the train station behind you. I know, it's very easy to have the urge to take off down Main Street and immerse yourself in the lands that await you, but this book is about appreciating and uncovering the secrets and details. So before we head down the street, there are a few things to notice about the Main Street station, the Walt Disney World Railroad, and Town Square.

Climb up the stairs and venture into the station. Notice the early-1900s decor, the authentic nickelodeon against the wall, and the Mutoscopes, which allow you to crank a wheel and watch a little moving-picture show. These two pieces aren't the only things at the station that are from the early 1900s; so are the trains.

The Walt Disney World Railroad operates four authentic steam-powered narrow-gauge locomotives. The trains were built by Baldwin Locomotive Works of Philadelphia between 1916 and 1928.

Before life at Walt Disney World, they hauled sugarcane for United Railways in Yucatan, Mexico. Disney disassembled them in

Mexico and shipped them back to Tampa, Florida, in 1969, where they were restored, bolt by bolt.

Since 1971, the Walter E. Disney (Walt loved trains!), the Lilly Belle (named for Walt's wife), the Roy O. Disney (named for Walt's brother), and the Roger E. Broggie (named for the Imagineer who led the railroad project at WDW) have welcomed guests alllll aboooooboard for a twenty-minute, mile-and-a-half ride around the Magic Kingdom, making stops at Frontierland and Fantasyland before returning to Main Street.

But we're not taking the train today; we're going to walk back out of the station and grab a great bird's-eye view of the hustle and bustle of Main Street, USA. This view is usually a great opportunity to snap a pic or a selfie with the backdrop of Main Street and Cinderella Castle in the distance.

After the obligatory selfie, note the flagpole in front of you; it's kind of hard to miss. Each day at 5:00 p.m., grab yourself a dose of some good old American patriotism and watch the **Flag Retreat Ceremony.**

The Pledge of Allegiance is recited, and the flag is lowered for the evening as a guest veteran assists. It's certainly something to see and appreciate. Note: just behind the flagpole is a great tribute to the man who made WDW happen, Roy O. Disney, who's sharing his bench with Minnie Mouse.

Speaking of flags, take a look down Main Street, USA. Do you notice the American flags perched atop the buildings? Well, here's a little secret: they technically aren't American flags.

As just mentioned, the American flag must be lowered each night, according to the United States Flag Code (usflag.org). Since, logistically, this would be difficult for the cast members (Disney's name for their employees) at WDW to maintain each day and night, the flags don't have the traditional fifty stars and are therefore not in breach of the flag code.

Instead, these flags are missing a few stars and may therefore fly day and night. This little tidbit also helps to sell the authenticity of Main Street, USA, since at the time Disney is trying to portray here, our country did not have fifty states or fifty stars on the flag. Alaska became a state on January 3, 1959, and Hawaii become one on August 21, 1959.

Now, take a quick look to the left of the flagpole. You'll notice the fire station, which gives a slight wink and a nod to the number seventy-one, representing the year Walt Disney World opened. We will see a lot of numerical nods to years relevant to Disney history throughout each of the parks.

Just next to the fire station is the **Harmony Barber Shop.** Feel free to stop in and get a haircut; it's an actual working hair salon, offering haircuts for adults and children. Their specialty is "first haircuts" for children who've never received a haircut before.

Now, looking to the right of the flagpole, is **Tony's Town Square** restaurant, serving Italian cuisine. The Hotel Saratoga in New York is the influence for the exterior design and theme here.

As the story goes, this is where Lady and the Tramp shared their first kiss.

Now it's time to enter Main Street. Our first stop is adjacent to Tony's Town Square and attached to Main Street Confectionary: the **Chapeau.** Pop in and purchase a pair of those legendary Mickey ears, and before you leave, locate the old-timey phone on the wall. Pick it up and eavesdrop on a conversation. The gossip isn't juicy, but it's still a fun throwback to yesterday!

Exit through the Main Street Confectionary and venture out into the middle of the street—being careful to not get run over by a stroller or scooter. You're finally here: **Main Street, USA**, a replica of an early-1900s town that could be found anywhere across this country back in the day.

Main Street at Walt Disney World is similar to its predecessor, Main Street at Disneyland. The street is an amalgamation of Walt's own experience as a child living in Marceline, Missouri, and a town about 650 miles away, Fort Collins, Colorado.

Walt tapped artist Harper Goff, who was raised in Fort Collins, to help recreate and bring his fondness and nostalgia for "yesterday" back to life.

One can't help but notice the how realistic and detailed the buildings are. However, there is a bit of an optical illusion at work here, something called forced perspective, which is basically a set-building trick. Disney has mastered this technique, and it's on full display throughout Main Street.

As you gaze upon the buildings, they appear to be taller than they actually are. In reducing the scale of the building as it grows taller and taller—the second floor would be smaller than the first, and the third would be smaller than the second—it gives the appearance of the building being farther away. For example, the **Plaza Ice Cream Parlor** has a first-story height of twelve feet; the second story is ten feet tall, and the third story is eight feet tall.

Since we're looking up at the buildings, what's the deal with the windows advertising businesses and people's names? Well, this is Disney's tradition of honoring folks who have been important to the Disney theme parks.

As Jeff Heimbuch explains in the introduction to his book *Main Street Windows*:

> Marty Sklar said "The tradition [of the Main Street Windows] was established by Walt Disney for Disneyland Park. He personally selected the names that would be revealed on the Main Street Windows." They served roughly the same purpose as a screen credit on a film. They were acknowledgements given to employees for their work on the Park.
>
> To fit in with the motif of a small town at the turn of the century, the names couldn't just be painted on the window. Instead, everyone was given a whimsical fictional business that, in many cases, related to their contribution to the park or a hobby they enjoyed. If they were a photographer, chances are they worked for a photography company on Main Street.

If they enjoyed fly fishing, then an outdoors company would be their trade. Each Window became more imaginative than the last, allowing Walt to pay tribute to those that helped him, and to breathe life into this fictional setting.

I'll give you a few names and a little background on their windows. See if you can find them as you walk down Main Street.

Earl Vilmer, Consultant: Yucatan Engine Works. Boiler & Engine Specialists. Highest Grade Steam Power. The word *Yucatan* should sound familiar from a few pages back. Earl was a transportation superintendent at Walt Disney World. He went to Mexico to purchase the trains currently running at Magic Kingdom. He also oversaw their restoration.

Lazy M Cattle Company of Wyoming. Ron & Diane Miller & Partners. Christopher, Joanna, Tamara, Jennifer, Walter, Ronald Jr., Patrick. Ron Miller married Walt Disney's daughter Diane. Ron worked in the "family business," eventually rising to CEO of Walt Disney Productions in 1983. Their partners are their children, in birth order: Christopher, Joanna, Tamara, Jennifer, Walter, Ronald Jr., and Patrick.

Iwerks-Iwerks. Stereoscopic Cameras. Ub Iwerks, Don Iwerks. Repairs Modifications. No Two Exactly Alike. If you love Mickey Mouse, one person to thank is Ub Iwerks. Ub was the "hand behind the mouse" and helped Walt cultivate the character we know and love. Ub was an amazing artist (as we see in the early Mickey Mouse short cartoons) and a technological genius.

Walt and Ub met in 1919, and he was even an original partner in the Disney Studio. Ub eventually left the studio and sold his shares back to the Disney brothers. Years later, Ub returned to the studio along with his son, Don. The Iwerks family has left a lasting imprint on the technology the Walt Disney Company uses in their parks.

M. T. Lott. Real Estate Investments Subsidiaries. A Friend in Deeds Is a Friend Indeed. Don Tatum, President. Tomahawk Properties. Latin American Development. Ayefour Corporation.

Baylake Properties. Reedy Creek Ranch Lands. Compass East Corporation. Leave it to the Disney company to even have creative names for the shell companies they used to purchase the land for Walt Disney World. By utilizing these company names rather than having the world know it was Disney buying up the land in central Florida, they were able to keep the prices down.

M. T. Lott sounds a bit like Empty Lot; Aye Four sounds a lot like the major highway leading to Walt Disney World, I4 (Interstate Four); and Baylake Properties—well, Baylake is the lake near the Magic Kingdom behind the Contemporary Resort.

After Roy O. Disney passed away, Don Tatum assumed the role of CEO and chairman of the board. Don was CEO until 1976 and stayed on as chairman of the company until 1980. There's another window along the same lines: ***Pseudonym Real Estate Development Company.*** See if you can spot it.

Elias Disney. Contractor. Est. 1895. This window is a tribute to Walt and Roy's father, Elias. Elias worked in many professions and trades, most of them with little to no success. Elias tried his hand at farming, being a letter carrier, owning a newspaper route, having an interest in a jelly company, and working in construction and carpentry.

Dreamers & Doers Development Co. Roy O. Disney Chairman. "If We Can Dream It, We Can Do It!" This window is a bit self-explanatory; it's paying homage to the other half of the dynamic Disney duo, Walt's older brother, Roy. As we know, after Walt's death, Roy postponed his retirement to see his brother's dreams through. Roy stayed on with the company and oversaw the creation and construction of what he named Walt Disney World.

General Joe's Building Permits. General Joe's Raconteur. "Joe was a man Walt Disney was very fond of. Without Joe Potter, there would be no Walt Disney World today." This quote came from Dick Nunis, former president of Walt Disney Attractions—Dick has a window too. Actually, his name pops up on two different windows. See if you can spot them.

General Joe was an engineering genius, a graduate of West Point and MIT. In 1956 President Dwight D. Eisenhower appointed the good general (Joe was an army major general) governor of the Panama Canal Zone. During his tenure in this position, Joe was responsible for a community of over forty thousand people, along with overseeing the education, military, public health, medical care, fire and police protection, and postal system for the area.

Joe retired from the military in 1960, and by 1965, he started his "second act" as the vice-president of Florida planning for the Disney company. Joe is responsible for overseeing the construction of the infrastructure of the Magic Kingdom and developing the drainage canals across the entire property.

And in case a window on Main Street wasn't enough, next time you take one of the ferries across the Seven Seas Lagoon to the Magic Kingdom, check the name of your ferry; you may just be traveling on the *General Joe Potter*.

We've covered a few interesting windows, but you may be asking, where's Walt's window? Don't fret; Walt is obviously well represented. Next time you get your ticket scanned or use your Magic Band to gain admission to Magic Kingdom, take a good look at the train station before you enter the park.

You'll notice there's a window dead center, **Walt Disney World. Railroad Office. Keeping Dreams On Track. Walter E. Disney. Chief Engineer.**

Back on Main Street, you'll notice another window for Walt: **Open Since '71. Magic Kingdom. Casting Agency. "It Takes People To Make The Dream A Reality." Walter Elias Disney. Founder & Director Emeritus.** See if you can spot one more with Walt's name on Main Street: **Walter E. Disney Graduate School Of Design & Master Planning. Head Master Richard Irvine Dean of Design John Hench. Instructors Howard Brummitt Marvin Davis Fred Hope Vic Green Bill Martin Chuck Myall.**

One last little secret about the Main Street, USA windows. It's a bit off to the side, but look for the windows that say **Voice &**

Singing Private Lessons, Music & Dance Lessons Ballet Tap &
Waltz. Linger around this area, maybe even grab a seat for a few
minutes, and take a listen to the background.

If you were successful in finding the windows mentioning
the singing and dancing lessons, you shouldn't be too far from
the **Main Street Bakery.** Take in a deep breath. How good does
that smell? Throughout many locations and even many of the attractions themselves, Disney uses something they created called a
"Smellitizer" to play with your senses.

In July 1986, Robert McCarthy received a patent for a
"scent-emitting system," which uses a pump to launch smells up to
two hundred feet at the precise second Disney wants you to smell
something. Disney can regulate the strength and intensity of the
aroma they want you to enjoy.

Here's an interesting blurb about it from *Epcot Center Today,*
Volume 1, Number 2, 1981:

> Working with the Imagineers at WED Enterprises in Cali-
> fornia, Bob McCarthy has developed "a smellitizer machine,"
> to add the aroma of everything from an erupting volcano in
> the Universe of Energy show to the tantalizing smell of a
> barbecue or the fragrance of orange blossoms. Each will be
> keyed to a particular show scene to enhance the realism of
> experiences in the Future World and World Showcase.

> WED designers are collecting scents from suppliers all over
> the world and blending them to produce the desired effect.
> So far, more than 300 odors have been tried, but more than
> 3,000 will be tested before the final choices are made. The
> smellitizer operates like an air cannon, aiming the scent up
> to 200 feet across a room toward an exhaust system. Guests
> traveling on the moving vehicles will pass through the scene
> as the appropriate scent drifts across their path. Regulated
> by computer, the scent can be triggered for a fresh aroma
> just prior to each vehicle's arrival.

If you would like to geek out about the smellitizer, Google "US Patent 4603030 A" and read all about it.

FIG.1.

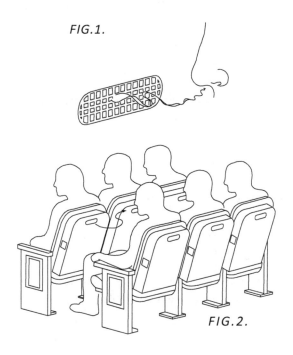

FIG.2.

I hope you enjoyed the stroll down Main Street, USA. If you did and you would like to write home about it, feel free! You can find two turn-of-the-century mail-collection boxes on loan from the United States Postal Service on Main Street. You can purchase postage stamps at the **Newsstand** at the entrance to the park.

Drop a postcard or a quick note to a friend or family member, telling them about all the fun they are missing out on. The United States Postal Service will deliver the letter to its destination.

You're now at the end of Main Street, USA, standing in something called **Central Plaza**, also known as "the hub." Big decisions are made here thousands of times a day—which way should we go?

At the hub, Magic Kingdom branches out, extending like spokes on a wheel. Which land do we whisk ourselves away to first? Do we

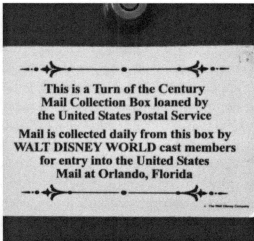

This is a Turn of the Century Mail Collection Box loaned by the United States Postal Service

Mail is collected daily from this box by WALT DISNEY WORLD cast members for entry into the United States Mail at Orlando, Florida

visit pirates or ghosts, pay a visit to Peter Pan, or battle Zurg with Buzz Lightyear? As I said, big, big decisions!

In our case, we're going to visit Buzz Lightyear and head over to Tomorrowland and work our way counterclockwise through the Magic Kingdom. But before we take a trip to the future, the past, and a few other stops in between, we have some unfinished business directly in front of us.

Standing in the shadow of Cinderella Castle is the bronze Partners statue, depicting Walt Disney holding the hand of his famous creation—and some would say alter ego—Mickey Mouse. This is another popular spot to take a photo, since you're also able to get a shot of Cinderella Castle in the background.

Speaking of the castle, let's chat for a minute or two about that beauty. Forced perspective is front and center here as well, so again, the upper part of the castle is constructed smaller than the lower portion, giving the illusion of the castle standing taller than it actually is. In keeping with Florida law, any structure above two hundred feet requires a red light at the top, so Cinderella Castle tops out at 189 feet, to avoid the light.

While it appears that the castle is constructed of bricks, quite the contrary. Lots of steel, cement, plaster, and fiberglass give the appearance of a brickwork castle, and it took roughly eighteen months to build.

There is a lot to absorb and appreciate when looking at the exterior of the castle. The lower portion resembles a fortress, and the upper section is distinctly medieval, with its inspiration coming not only from Disney's own animated version of Charles Perrault's classic fairy tale *Cinderella*, but also from the architecture of twelfth- and thirteenth-century France.

Marvel at the towers (eighteen of them) and their corresponding spires, turrets, and gargoyles. In medieval architecture, gargoyles were decorative drains for a structure; in Disney's case, the thirteen gargoyles on the castle are decorative, but not functional.

However, the clock on the castle *is* functional, allowing park goers to know what time it is. But perhaps it's also a bit more symbolic when you think back to the story of Cinderella and her limited time to enjoy the ball that evening.

Now, let's take a peek inside. Within the main castle corridor, check out the five handcrafted mosaic murals telling the tale of what else but Cinderella! The five murals are each fifteen feet high and ten feet wide and were completed by the renowned father-in-law and daughter team of Hanns and Monika Scharff.

The murals were designed by Disney artist Dorthea Redmond in Glendale, California. Redmond's painted designs were then re-drawn to life-size proportions on heavyweight paper by world-renowned mosaicist Hanns Scharff.

Scharff then divided the murals into workable sections, which were called sheets—the first mural actually consisted of fifty-five sheets. Next, came the actual mosaic work: Scharff glued the tiles in reverse (upside down and backward) on the paper sheets according to the design on the paper. The tiles consisted of hundreds of thousands of jewel-like pieces of venetian glass, made up of over 400 regular colors and 100 additional accent colors, many fused with real silver and gold.

Once the tiles were secured and in place, the mosaic was

sprayed with a water mist to prevent the glue from drying, which would have caused the mosaic to bulge and lose glass tiles. The sheets were then wrapped tightly in polyester film and shipped off to Florida from Scharff's workshop in California.

When the sheets arrived in Central Florida, they were reassembled onto the wall by pressing the reverse side of the sheets into wet plaster; next, the glue and paper backing were taken off with a sponge.

As you look at the murals, notice the faces of Cinderella's stepsisters. As Cinderella tries on the glass slipper, you'll notice one sister has a red tint, as she's "red with rage," and the other sister has a greenish tint, showing she's "green with envy." These are great subtle details in the storytelling.

A portion of the castle is also home to **Cinderella's Royal Table**, which allows for a meal with a princess in an enchanting setting. Before you go up to the second floor for your meal, via circular stairwell or elevator, look around the throne room and see if you can spot Jaq and Gus looking down at you.

Once you've reached the restaurant, look around for the more than forty coats of arms on display. Each coat of arms is an acknowledgment to a person who played a significant role at the Walt Disney Company. Reservations are *highly* recommended if you're considering dining here for breakfast, lunch, or dinner.

There's one other exclusive place to see inside Cinderella's Castle. Actually, perhaps a more appropriate word would be *elusive*, since reservations for this place are basically nonexistent.

The Cinderella Castle Suite affords those lucky enough with the opportunity to sleep like Cinderella in her dream suite. Since its debut in 2006, the only folks spending the night in this location have been contest winners or celebrities. Every so often, there have been tours available to the public to catch a glimpse of what it would be like to stay in this magical suite. A picture or two in this book wouldn't give the suite its due, so I won't even bother. Just Google it and let your daydreams and fantasies begin!

Tomorrowland

> *"There's a great big beautiful tomorrow, shining at the end of every day. There's a great big beautiful tomorrow, and tomorrow is just a dream away."*

This optimistic quote is from the song for **The Carousel of Progress**, a stage show Walt Disney created for the 1964 World's Fair—which now runs all day long in Tomorrowland at WDW.

The show tracks the progress and innovations that occurred for the average American family during the twentieth century. The Carousel of Progress was one of Walt's favorite attractions, as, at its core, it deals with advancing technology and the limitless possibilities that may be upon us in the future.

Walt loved creating and being on the cutting edge of technology; he was certainly a bit of a futurist, which is a theme he wanted to bring into his theme parks.

But even he knew portraying the future can be a Herculean task. As he once said, "The only problem with anything of tomorrow is that at the pace we're going right now, tomorrow would catch up with us before we got it built."

Presenting a land of tomorrow sounds great on paper. However, as Walt's quote suggests, a major difficulty in dabbling in the future in physical form, like at a theme park, is to portray it tangibly and realistically each and every day.

To capture the essence of the future or what technology we would use "tomorrow" would require constant updating, in an effort to keep the concept relevant for an extended period of time. This is a problem Disney ran into over the years at both Walt Disney World and Disneyland. So the theming you encounter now in Tomorrowland at WDW is a bit different from when WDW opened in 1971.

Today, you will enter a galactic spaceport of tomorrow, or,

more specifically, the future as seen from yesterday, where extra-terrestrials, humans, and robots mingle.

The theme and story line are sort of retromodern, with more of a sci-fi flair. It's a take on the early to mid-twentieth-century science fiction; think Buck Rogers or Flash Gordon meet Disney. Let's see which secrets and details we can uncover in the area.

Walking into Tomorrowland from the hub, let's head over to **Buzz Lightyear's Space Ranger Spin;** it will be on your right side. Join Buzz as he attempts to defeat the evil Zurg.

Your goal here is to use your laser gun to hit as many of the Z targets as you can. Your score will be tallied on the digital dashboard of your space cruiser. The harder the Z target is to hit, the more points you will get. Here are a few pointers to help you to become a galactic hero.

When you enter the first room, just as your laser blaster activates, quickly look down at the far side wall and see if you can spot the hidden Mickey. It's tough to spot, but there are two blue circles that make up the ears and a green circle for his head.

If you can spot him, great; if not, don't look too long, as there are some big points ahead of you.

Quickly rotate your space cruiser back toward the orangish robot and shoot the target on the inside of his left hand. Next, whip your vehicle around and hit the claw near the ceiling. These two targets are *big* points.

In the next room, zero in on the volcano that is on the back wall, right side; the highest Z is worth fifty thousand points. Try to hit that bad boy multiple times if you can.

The next high-value target you should try for is the large Zurg on the right side. Look low on him for the Z target; it's worth a hundred thousand points. Be sure to keep your best game face on, as your picture will be taken during the battle! Definitely Fastpass this attraction, as the standby times can be pretty long.

Leaving Buzz Lightyear, let's head over toward the **Astro Orbiter.** You'll see the spaceships orbiting high in the sky (about eleven revolutions a minute) among constellations and planets.

There's a lot going on around here at **Rockettower Plaza**. You can pilot a spaceship at the Astro Orbiter, grab a quick snack, or take a take a trip along the **Tomorrowland Transit Authority** in the PeopleMover, which is where we're heading.

The PeopleMover is a great attraction on many levels. It's a good opportunity to get an aerial view of Tomorrowland, you'll get off your feet for a few minutes, and, best of all, there's usually a very short wait, if any.

When the attraction first opened in July 1975, it was called the WedWay PeopleMover (WED standing for Walter Elias Disney) and was based on the PeopleMover operating at Disneyland. There are a few interesting things to notice during your ten-minute trip.

You're going to get a different view of Buzz Lightyear's Space Ranger Spin, Space Mountain (if you're lucky enough to be on the PeopleMover when Space Mountain has a breakdown, and the lights go on, you may get a cool view of the inner workings of the attraction), and of Mickey's Star Traders.

You'll even pull alongside the architectural model for Progress City, Walt Disney's original concept for Epcot and a driving motivation for the original plans for Disney's land in Florida.

As you motor along (by the way, the PeopleMover is emission free, as it runs magnetically via linear induction motors; 533 electromagnets propel the PeopleMover along its 4,574-foot track), keep a lookout for Disney's Contemporary Resort. The hotel was purposely built to be aligned as a background for Tomorrowland—a magical resort to stay in and the only hotel that allows you to walk to the Magic Kingdom.

If you listen closely during your ride, you may hear Mr. Tom Morrow being paged overhead. Yes, it's a cheesy pun on the word *tomorrow*, but it's also a nod to a character who was the operations director from a short-lived Tomorrowland attraction, *Flight to the Moon*, which was at both the Magic Kingdom and Disneyland.

Lastly, if you have a sharp eye, when you pass by the scene for a futuristic hair salon, check out the woman's belt, and you'll find a hidden Mickey.

Before we visit the Carousel of Progress and Space Mountain and then head over to Fantasyland, there are few quick things to note around the Rockettower Plaza.

Head over toward the Merchant of Venus and look for a very large round ball, known as a **Kugel Ball** or **Kugel Fountain**. This large granite ball weighing several tons is very easily moved, even by children.

Behold, the magic of physics and not Disney! According to an article titled "Physics of the Granite Sphere Fountain," from the *American Journal of Physics* (82, 1049, 2014):

> These fountains consist of a perfectly polished ball floating in a socket that fits precisely around it. The fluid that wells up around the rim of the socket is pumped into the fountain via a hole at the base. In spite of its considerable weight, the sphere is easily brought into a spinning motion. The fluid layer between the socket and sphere is very thin, thinner than a credit card which is important for any kugel on display in a public place, since it means there is no risk of children's fingers being caught under the spinning sphere.

We learned a bit about **Walt Disney's Carousel of Progress** in the beginning of this chapter, so now's a good time to actually sit down and travel through the twentieth century in about twenty minutes. I know what you're thinking: *This really isn't about tomorrow; it's more about yesterday and sort of doesn't fit the theme of Tomorrowland.*

Well, you're right, but it has

been a fan favorite for decades, and it's a twenty-minute show in an air-conditioned building—which can be a welcome treat during the hot and humid summer days at WDW.

There's rarely a long wait for the show, as it runs continuously throughout the day, and there are quite a few interesting secrets throughout, so let's head on in.

As you enter the theater, if you really want to notice some of the minute details, obviously sit closer to the stage, but there really isn't a bad seat in the house.

The show you're about to see is a bit different from the one that opened at the 1964 World's Fair in New York. The version of that show was created for the General Electric Pavilion as an effort to showcase the innovations coming from GE.

After the World's Fair, the Carousel of Progress was featured at Disneyland from July 1967 to September 1973, and finally, in January 1975, the show debuted at Walt Disney World, featuring changes from its two prior incarnations.

When the show begins, listen to the narrator, who also voices the father, John. He may sound familiar. It's Jean Shepherd, the narrator from the beloved movie *A Christmas Story* from 1983.

In the first scene, note the young girl cranking the handle on the washing machine while Mom is ironing. You won't see her again; she's unnamed, unmentioned, and unseen throughout the rest of the show!

During the 1920s scene, look out the kitchen window. If you look carefully, you'll see a sign with black letters on a white background that advertises "Herb Ryman, Attorney at Law." In 1953 Walt Disney asked Herb to sketch out his dream for a theme park. During the course of a single weekend, Herb put Walt's dreams down on paper and illustrated what would eventually come to be known as Disneyland.

In the 1940s scene, daughter Patricia pops up with a little magic during her exercise scene. As she's strapped into the shaker exercise contraption, look off to the right of it. There's a Mickey Mouse sorcerer's hat.

The final scene has a lot to take in. There's a dry-erase board on the wall next to the bulletin board. Check the saying on the board; there's often a witty message that changes from time to time, and it usually has something to do with the history of the attraction.

As for that bulletin board just mentioned, look for the message that reads "Marty Called Wants Changes." The Marty who is being referenced is the late Marty Sklar, who passed away in July 2017.

Marty was the former vice chairman and principal creative executive of Walt Disney Imagineering. A young Marty got his start at Disney just a month before Disneyland opened in 1955. He rose through the ranks, eventually becoming the creative and driving force behind much of what we find across the Disney theme parks around the world.

This little note is playing on the notion that the carousel needs some updating, since the last update to the attraction happened in the mid-1990s.

While some may say it's very dated and a bit campy, the Carousel of Progress is a fan favorite—me included! There are a few other things to look out for during the ride.

The final scene has a few hidden Mickeys, below the Christmas tree and on the mantle. Here and there you'll still a GE insignia on an appliance.

And take a good long look at John's face; maybe even snap a picture of it on your phone. John looks awfully similar to someone over at Epcot in the attraction Spaceship Earth. Pay attention during the Renaissance scene.

It also seems as though the grandmother from the Carousel of Progress is pulling double duty and moonlighting over at the Haunted Mansion.

In the first scene at the carousel, note Grandmother sitting in a chair. She's wearing a shawl, has glasses on, and has her hair parted down the middle.

When you take a trip over to the Haunted Mansion, notice that in the ballroom scene, near the fireplace, the woman sitting there looks just like the carousel's grandmother!

Get ready for blastoff! Saving one of the more popular Tomorrowland attractions for last is the 183-foot-tall **Space Mountain.** There are no huge drops or inverted loops, and it doesn't go incredibly fast (28.7 mph, give or take a tenth of a mile), compared to other coasters. But it does feature lots of quick turns and small drops that aren't expected.

This ride is all about the out-of-this-world theme and playing with your senses, as much of it is in the dark, with very little light.

The concept for Space Mountain actually dates back to the days of Walt Disney in the early 1960s. However, the ride didn't come to fruition until January 1975; the logo StarPort Seven Five makes reference to the year the attraction opened.

During the planning and creation of the attraction, Disney hired former astronaut Gordon Cooper as a consultant. Cooper was a member of the Mercury 9 and Gemini 5 missions.

Astronaut Cooper gave this ringing endorsement to the ride in the August 29, 1977, issue of People magazine: "Space Mountain is about as close as you can safely get to actually being in space." Pretty powerful words from a man who orbited the earth twenty-two times during his Gemini mission.

While you're making your way through the queue before you board your rocket, look for a destination on a galactic map entitled Disney's Hyperion Resort. The word *Hyperion* is a reference to the Disney brothers' early studio at 2719 Hyperion Avenue in Los Angeles.

The cone-shaped structure of the building has a base diameter of three hundred feet and could hold a small skyscraper in its interior, as it contains 4,508,500 cubic feet.

Another fun fact: there are two tracks, Alpha and Omega. Alpha is 3,196 feet long, and Omega is 3,186 feet long.Once you're on the ride and you're ascending a hill, look for a spaceship suspended in the middle of the room. You'll see "H-NCH (SM1975)" on it. This is a nod to legendary Imagineer John Hench, who was in charge of seeing that Space Mountain came to fruition.

This attraction is a *definite* Fastpass ride. There is almost always a lengthy wait for standby. Riders must be forty-four inches or taller, and those with back and neck problems should definitely think twice about their trip to space, as it can be a bit of an unexpectedly jarring and bumpy ride for some folks. Don't forget to smile, because you're going to have your photo taken!

A trip to outer space can definitely make you hungry. Before you leave Tomorrowland and head into the land of fantasy, stop at the **Cool Ship** and grab a quick snack. You'll find it near the Tomorrowland Speedway. Look for the red ship titled Space Rangers; it's actually a reimagineered ship from Disney's 1986 movie *Flight of the Navigator.*

Fantasyland

Welcome to the land of fantasy, fairy tales, and make-believe. Many of Disney's most beloved attractions and legendary characters reside here. There's lots of ground to cover, so let's get right to it.

When you stroll into Fantasyland from Tomorrowland, or, for that matter, when you cross from one land into the other anywhere in the Magic Kingdom, you can actually see and hear the transition. The music will start to change, as will the decor, and before you know it, you're immersed in a new land.

We are approaching Fantasyland from Tomorrowland, for the convenience of keeping things linear in the book, but many folks prefer to reach Fantasyland by going straight down Main Street, USA, going through the hub, seeing the castle, and arriving smack dab in the middle of Fantasyland.

Going this route puts you in the original portion of the land, which is complete with some of the favorite attractions that are synonymous with a Disney theme park. Taking this route is perfectly fine and logical.

Over the years, Fantasyland has expanded and evolved to become more than what you see immediately around Cinderella's Castle.

The land even received two new castles in recent years, Beast's Castle and Prince Eric's Castle, but we aren't there just yet. Let's continue our stroll from Tomorrowland into Fantasyland. We will roll past the **Mad Tea Party**; feel free to stop and spin for a bit, and then head off to the right, and you'll see the sign for the **Storybook Circus**. Go in and give your regards to Dumbo and Goofy.

As a sort of subsection of Fantasyland, this area is themed around Dumbo and a "big top" or circus atmosphere—just note the animal footprints and peanuts scattered on the ground as you stroll the area.

The first ride on the right as you enter is **Dumbo the Flying Elephant**, a tame ride that gives you a quick spin and allows riders to control their own elevation.

Notice there are two Dumbo rides side by side, which is unprecedented for a Disney theme park. Watch as one attraction moves clockwise and the other counterclockwise.

Approaching the ride near the entrance, look down on the concrete for a hidden Mickey or two. Guests waiting to ride Dumbo will be entertained with the covered and interactive queue, which should be very entertaining for the kiddies!

Next to Dumbo is the **Barnstormer Featuring the Great Goofini**, a quick little coaster featuring Goofy. As you approach the ride, look at the massive sign that says "The Barnstormer"; below the sign is a fake ticket booth. Check out the right and left sides of the ticket booth window. See the gold-colored fancy scroll work? There you have two hidden Mickeys.

If you decide to ride the attraction, as you disembark, look left for a set of skis in a barrel. These are symbolic of Goofy's attempt at skiing.

In the 1940s, Goofy had a string of cartoon shorts that showed his less-than-stellar skills at many things. In his how-to series, he tried baseball, horseback riding, fishing, golf, football, and, of course, skiing.

Before leaving the Storybook Circus, pay a visit to **Pete's Silly Sideshow**, which features a character meet and greet. Interesting little history about Pete: he's sometimes known as Peg-Leg Pete and is technically the longest-running continuous Disney character, debuting in 1925 in the Disney short *Alice Solves a Puzzle*.

After hanging with some characters, feel free to cool off at the **Casey JR Splash 'N' Soak Station**, or grab a souvenir or treat at *Big Top Souvenirs*. Look down at the floor as you stroll through the big top and note the detailed and themed flooring.

We are going to exit this area where we came in and walk toward the right, where you see the boulders and **Prince Eric's Castle**—a second castle in Fantasyland.

Get ready to for your visit with Ariel and hear how she met her prince in **Under the Sea—Journey of the Little Mermaid**. As you enter the attraction, you're entering via "low tide" into the caverns beneath the castle. As you walk the outside queue, you'll notice waterfalls, shells, and some hidden secrets as you make your way into the ride.

There are a few neat interactive features to keep you interested and entertained. As you venture deeper into the queue, be sure to notice the elaborate artwork on the ceiling of the rotunda. The murals are telling stories of hidden legends of the sea, most notably the lore of sea monsters.

Go ahead and board your clamshell. As you go under the sea, you are entertained by 183 characters throughout the ride, of which 128 are featured in the "under the sea" scene. The biggest character of them all is Ursula; she measures seven and a half feet tall and twelve feet wide.

Both inside and outside the ride, there are more than twenty thousand real and artificial plants. Some of them make a great background to hide a Mickey.

As you enter the scene where Sebastian is singing "Under the Sea," look for the purple coral that are grouped together to form Mickey's head. It's on the right side of the wall, stuck on a rock near a line of singing and dancing fish.

After you say your good-byes to Ariel and walk back into the park, look across the way for the Disney Vacation Club building. There will be a hanging sign that says H Goff Cartography, and below that sign will be a smaller sign for the DVC (Disney Vacation Club).

Above the sign that says H Goff is a sun, a moon, and a globe; this makes up a hidden Mickey. Who is H. Goff? Well, the last name should sound a bit familiar, if you think back to Main Street, USA. Harper Goff helped Walt create Main Street, conceptually. A little more magic in the details!

Still facing the H Goff sign, start heading right and see if you can find that goon Gaston from the movie *Beauty and the Beast*. Keep walking along until you see the fountain featuring Gaston and LeFou. Check the back of the statue; look near the water line. There's a nice little hidden Mickey imprint in the rock he's standing on.

As you look around the area, you'll see **Gaston's Tavern, Bonjour! Village Gifts**, and **Maurice's Amazing Popping Machine.** The popping machine is themed to look like something Maurice, Belle's father, created.

As you can imagine, over in **Gaston's Tavern,** it's Gaston, Gaston, and more Gaston. His ego is front and center in this joint, along with a mighty large portrait of the man himself. Lots of antlers, animal heads, and machismo adorn the walls of this French lodge.

Take a look at the score on the dart game; naturally, Gaston is winning. The theme is very cool and detailed throughout this area of the park. Even the outdoor drinking fountains in this area are themed appropriately. However, one can only take so much Gaston. Now it's time visit with Belle and Beast.

High in the sky is **Beast's Castle** (castle number three in the Magic Kingdom). It's not as detailed and large as Cinderella's, but this beauty does have 115 windows. Go in and grab a bite to eat at the **Be Our Guest Restaurant**. This is an incredibly detailed restaurant, serving a fast, casual/quick breakfast, lunch, and dinner.

It offers American and French cuisine in three very creative dining atmospheres: the Grand Ballroom, the West Wing, and the Castle Gallery. Each room offers its own magical experience.

Despite its being dark and mysterious, *don't* stay out of the West Wing! Much like Gaston's Tavern, there is a pretty large portrait hanging on the wall. However, this one isn't quite as jovial as Gaston's.

The Beast slashed this photo in a fit of rage. Watch as a petal drops from the enchanted rose. You'll notice the portrait will change, and Beast's other face will appear briefly.

The Grand Ballroom is so grandiose, it's as if the story truly came to life. The chandelier (it's twelve feet tall and eleven feet wide and features eighty-four candles and a hundred jewels) and gothic arches on the twenty-foot ceiling are remarkable. Be sure to watch the snow fall on the French countryside through the eighteen-foot-tall arched picture windows.

In the Castle Gallery, the nearly seven-foot-tall rotating music box featuring Belle and Beast dancing is the real focal point of the room. If you take a look up above the dancing duo, there's a stained-glass rose chandelier.

It's all about the details throughout this restaurant. The Imagineers went above and beyond to sell the theming here, from the portraits and tapestries along the walls featuring some of the other characters in the story to the beautiful mosaic above the front door to the restaurant. Everything really helps to sell the story of *Beauty and the Beast*. And don't forget to try the gray stuff; it's delicious (seriously)!

As you leave the restaurant, you can't but help notice the Seven Dwarfs mine train whoosh on by. This is our next stop. Follow the track all the way down and turn left at the corner. Walk to the entrance of the **Seven Dwarfs Mine Train**.

When you walk through the Enchanted Forest that leads to the attraction, watch for footprints of forest creatures, large and small, and the impressions of sticks, stones, and acorns embedded in the dirt path.

This attraction may be new to Fantasyland, having debuted in May 2014, but the characters in the story are anything but. Disney's first full-length animated feature film was *Snow White and the Seven Dwarfs*.

The premiere was held at the Carthay Circle Theatre in Hollywood on December 21, 1937. Time for a shameless plug: check out my other book, *The Disney Story*, and read all about the premiere from the news stories of the day.

Snow White was a huge risk for the studio. There was a lot of time and money invested in the picture and not a lot of faith in the film being successful or profitable—except for Walt; he believed.

Obviously, the film debuted, and, as the saying goes, the rest is history. *Snow White* was a huge success on many levels and propelled the studio into bigger and more adventurous enterprises, so it's only fitting that Snow White has a presence at the Disney parks.

As noted earlier, this attraction debuted in 2014; however, this wasn't Snow White's first appearance in Fantasyland. When the park opened in October 1971, Snow White's Scary Adventure was one of the original attractions, and now it's part of the park's history.

The ride was located in what is now the **Princess Fairytale Hall**, located in the Castle Courtyard. Hop on over and meet and greet a princess or two at the Fairytale Hall. There are many details and special thematic princess touches throughout the area, including an elegant glass slipper.

Today, remnants of the original ride survive at the Seven Dwarfs Mine Train. See if you can spot the two vultures sitting at the top of the mine train's first lift. As the mine cars pull out of the load area, they'll travel up the track to the top of the mountain, where a jib crane sits, topped by two vultures. These two critters originally appeared in Snow White's Scary Adventures.

There's more to this attraction than just a couple of vultures making an encore appearance. The queue is quite interactive and amusing. Get ready to sort and wash gemstones.

At the first interactive station, Doc's note will explain the jewel-washing game. As the jewels flow by in a wooden trough or sluice, you can touch and drag them into a tray on the side of the sluice, matching them by color and shape. The trough is about fifteen feet long and is accessible from both sides.

At the third interactive station in the queue, "Vault" is carved into the wooden crosspiece or lintel above the doorway. This is a reference to the scene in the film where Dopey opens the vault and throws in a bag of gems and then locks the door with a key. For safekeeping, Dopey hangs the key to the vault on a peg next to the door. The key hangs on a peg next to the entrance to the vault in the queue as well.

While you're working with your gems, listen carefully to the music in the queue. You'll hear the song "Music in Your Soup."

This song and the scene it accompanied was animated by legendary Disney animator Ward Kimball but was cut from the original movie. Ward worked for nearly a year on the scene, and it finally gets its due.

The rest of the time spent in Fantasyland will be back over near Cinderella's Castle, so start to head that way. Walk toward the castle, and let's stop at the **Prince Charming Regal Carousel** for a ride atop a royal steed.

As the old-fashioned organ plays and the nearly twenty-three hundred glimmering lights shine down upon the ninety ornate hand-carved and hand-painted horses (seventy-two were original, and Disney added eighteen antique horses to the carousel), check out the eighteen hand-painted vignettes of the story of Cinderella on the inner rounding board above the horses.

While the story of Cinderella may be a fairy tale, everything about this carousel is authentic. Constructed in 1917 by the Philadelphia Toboggan Company, it was originally known as the Liberty Carousel and made its home at Belle Island Park in Detroit, Michigan.

In 1967 Disney rescued it from Olympic Park in Maplewood, New Jersey, and reconditioned it, and it's been home in the Magic Kingdom since 1971.

After your spin with Cinderella is complete, see if you're the one to claim the throne of England by removing the **Sword in the Stone**, located just next to the carousel.

According to the 1963 Disney movie of the same name, based on the 1938 book, also with the same name, "According to legend, only someone with honor, decency and inner strength can claim the throne of England—by pulling out the enchanted sword that lies locked in a massive stone."

You may not have been able to remove the sword from the stone, but that's OK, as you're about to notice something very cool, something that dabbles in pop culture lore and urban mythology.

Often, when people talk about the Magic Kingdom, they will

say, "Hey, did you know there are secret corridors underneath?" or "Did you know there are underground tunnels throughout the park?"

For those who don't know, yes, there is an underground corridor, and they are referred to as Utilidors, short for utility corridors. Technically, the Magic Kingdom that we see and visit is on the second floor. The Utilidors are ground level.

If you've been to WDW many times or you already know the whole story with the first level and the second level, just bear with me for a minute.

For those who aren't familiar with it, here's the deal with the Utilidors: they serve a very valuable function in the park. They basically keep some of the less-than-Disneyesque park operations out of sight. The area is home to a vacuum system for trash removal, electrical operations, food prep, costuming, and cast-member services.

There is one other major purpose to having it: direct access to each land. Characters dressed in their "land"-specific garb won't have to traverse the park, walking through lands they shouldn't be in, ruining the setting Disney works so hard to portray.

Over the years, the myths and legends of what is going on down there have taken on a life of their own. There really isn't anything magical or spectacular down there, so don't attempt to gain access. People have tried, some successfully, some unsuccessfully; either way you're trespassing, and that's a big no-no, so please don't go spelunking at Walt Disney World!

That said, I'm going to show you an example of this whole first-floor, second-floor thing at the Magic Kingdom. If you've been to Walt Disney World often, you've probably seen or experienced this many times, but for whatever reason, a lot of people don't make this connection, though it's hiding in plain sight.

As you leave the carousel, go into the **Pinocchio Village Haus**, the restaurant next to ***it's a small world***. Now look for the grouping of windows to the left that look out over the load area of "it's a small world." Do you see the folks walking into the attraction?

They are walking in from park level, the level you are currently standing on. They're walking into the attraction and then descending a ramp and boarding a boat to set sail on the happiest cruise that ever sailed.

The boat and the ride itself are technically the first floor, roughly the same level the Utilidors are found on. Pretty cool, huh? And sort of obvious, right? I guess only if you're looking for it.

It's definitely one of the things most people aren't paying attention to. A special thanks to retired Imagineer Tom Morris for confirming for me that this is the same level as the Utilidors.

If you can't wait until the next time you visit the park to see this, here are a few photos of what I'm talking about. There's also an artist's rendering of the Utilidors. This map may not be exact or the most recent, but it's pretty close to what's going on down there.

One last thing about subterranean Walt Disney World: a few pages back, we spoke about the secrets and magic at Cinderella's castle. Above park level there's the suite and restaurant, but there's also something below the castle.

THE UTILIDORS

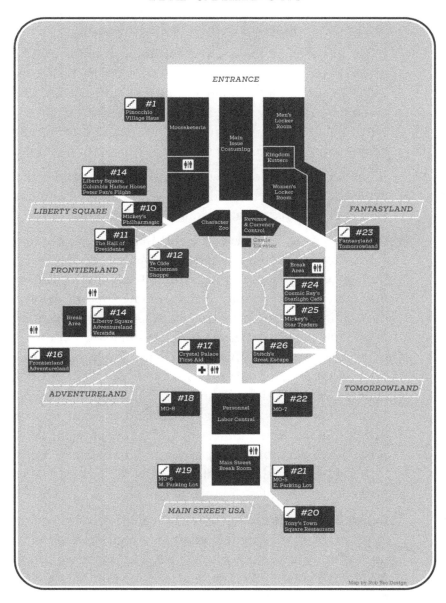

On December 27, 2010, the *New York Times* ran an interesting story titled "Disney Tackles Major Theme Park Problem: Lines." Here are a few interesting tidbits from the story:

> [Disney] has spent the last year outfitting an underground nerve center to address that most low-tech of problems, the wait. Located under Cinderella Castle the new center uses video cameras, computer programs, digital park maps and other whiz-bang tools to spot gridlock before it forms and deploy countermeasures in real time.
>
> In one corner, employees watch flat-screen televisions that depict various attractions in green, yellow and red outlines, with the colors representing wait-time gradations.
>
> If Pirates of the Caribbean, the ride that sends people on a spirited voyage through the Spanish Main, suddenly blinks from green to yellow, the center might respond by alerting managers to launch more boats. Another option involves dispatching Captain Jack Sparrow or Goofy or one of their pals to the queue to entertain people as they wait. "It's about being nimble and quickly noticing that, 'Hey, let's make sure there is some relief out there for those people,'" said Phil Holmes, vice president of the Magic Kingdom, the flagship Disney World park. What if Fantasyland is swamped with people but adjacent Tomorrowland has plenty of elbow room? The operations center can route a mini parade called "Move it! Shake it! Celebrate it!" into the less-populated pocket to siphon guests in that direction.
>
> Other technicians in the command center monitor restaurants, perhaps spotting that additional registers need to be opened or dispatching greeters to hand out menus to people waiting to order. "These moments add up until they collectively help the entire park," Mr. Holmes said.
>
> In recent years, according to Disney research, the average Magic Kingdom visitor has had time for only nine rides—out

of more than 40—because of lengthy waits and crowded walkways and restaurants. In the last few months, however, the operations center has managed to make enough nips and tucks to lift that average to 10.

Pretty interesting stuff. So, we just saw a little hidden magic involving **it's a small world**. Here are a few more details to notice. Inside the attraction, check out the large, elaborate clock near the load and unload area; it comes to life every fifteen minutes.

During your ten-minute cruise of the world, sailing the Seven Seaways Waterway, you'll see many of the children of the world (nearly three hundred of them dressed in the traditional garb of their cultures and countries) by traveling to all seven continents.

Follow along as you visit some of the children from the British Isles, Western Europe, Eastern Europe, the Middle East, Asia, Africa, Antarctica, South America, Australia, and the South Pacific Islands. Disney created this attraction and its famous song for UNICEF, the United Nations Children's Fund, for the 1964–65 New York World's Fair. It was sponsored by Pepsi.

As you exit the attraction, look at the large pink poles acting as supports for the front façade. It looks like a giant jousting lance, which goes along with the medieval faire theme in this area of the park.

Head out across the walkway toward **Peter Pan's Flight**, but don't go in just yet. Here are a few magical details for you, one by the entrance, the other by the exit.

If you're facing the entrance to the ride, look up at the sign that says Peter Pan's Flight. You'll see Peter and his crew in the clouds. Take a good look at Peter Pan; notice he's standing on a cloud in the shape of a hidden Mickey. Now head over toward the exit of the ride.

As folks are leaving the attraction, notice the brown barrel against the wall of the building. The barrel reads "Fire Chief Richard LePere Jr. Lost Boys Fire Brigade."

Underneath this barrel is a fire hydrant, and Richard LePere

Jr. is the Reedy Creek Emergency Services fire chief (you may see RCID, Reedy Creek Improvement District, on certain things such as manhole covers around Disney property; this is the name of the governing body for the land of Walt Disney World), a very witty wink and nod to the man who helps to keep Walt Disney World safe.

Your flight over London on Peter Pan's Flight is a definite Fastpass attraction. The lines are consistently long all day, every day. If you do opt for standby, the queue is very interactive. Disney sprinkled lots of pixie dust around; you'll even get to catch a glimpse of Tinkerbell.

Before we leave Fantasyland and head into Liberty Square, catercorner from Peter Pan's Flight is **Rapunzel Tower** and a group of restrooms. Go over and look around the garden; see if you can find Pascal, Rapunzel's little friend. There should be ten little chameleons to find in this area.

Liberty Square

As you pass Rapunzel's Tower and exit Fantasyland, welcome to Colonial America.

Compared with the other lands in the Magic Kingdom, there aren't a large number of attractions to ride, but there's still much to see and appreciate here. Strolling through this part of the park, think of the setting as life in the original thirteen colonies. Towns such as Boston, Massachusetts, or Philadelphia, Pennsylvania, should come to mind. Both cities have specifically left a significant impression on Liberty Square at Walt Disney World.

Philadelphia is home to the Liberty Bell. Liberty Square at WDW has a Liberty Bell too; it's not the genuine bell, obviously, but a beautiful replica.

Go take a look at it, adjacent to the **Liberty Tree Tavern**, a tavern that gives a good representation of an establishment one might have found in Boston during this era.

While we're talking about the Liberty Tree Tavern, there are a few interesting details to see there. Note the thirteen lanterns hanging in the tree out front of the restaurant, symbolizing America's original thirteen colonies.

From the moment you walk in the door and meet with the "town crier" to arrange for seating, everything seems very authentic. The detailed architecture, from the wooden floors to the authentic-looking colonial glass in the windows, makes dining here a really unique experience.

When your table is ready, you're going to be seated in one of the historical rooms themed around some pretty important people from the early history of America.

Benjamin Franklin is very visible, as is the kite in his room. Betsy Ross is synonymous with the country's flag, so it's no surprise that there's one on display.

See the tricornered hat hanging on the wall in the first couple's room, George and Martha Washington? Perhaps that hat was George's?

The John Paul Jones room has a very nautical feel, as he was a naval commander.

Paul Revere, who was a silversmith by trade, has some tools necessary for his work in the room. Can you spot some items of significance in the Thomas Jefferson room?

As you walk around Liberty Square, watch where you step. Do you see the brownish pavement running down the center of the walkway throughout this land? Well, this is representative of the waste and rubbish of the town.

Back in the colonial days, it was very common for the residents of the town to discard their waste and garbage right there in the center of their street.

While we are on the wonderful subject of waste, there is a story floating around, in books and on the web, regarding the restrooms in Liberty Square.

You may notice that there aren't any stand-alone restrooms in the entire land, and the only ones available are deep in the backs of the restaurants, so technically, they aren't a part of Liberty Square, as that area is actually in another land.

Now, as this story or rumor goes, this was done intentionally, as there were no modern bathrooms in colonial days, and Disney wanted to stay true to their theme and really keep this authentic to the time period.

I posed this question to retired Imagineer Tom Morris. (I've included a brief bio of Tom in the appendix, since his name will pop up a few more times in the book.) Here's Tom's response: "They probably figured the ones in Adventureland/Frontierland and Fantasyland were close enough. I don't think theming was an issue because the same would apply to Frontierland and all the others except Tomorrowland."

Interesting notion, since we do find stand-alone modern bathrooms in those other areas of the park. These can be seen if you follow the "poop trail" toward Frontierland, which actually leads you right into a shortcut to a bathroom in Adventureland.

We've explored some of the secrets of Liberty Square, and now, for you **Haunted Mansion** fans, the time has finally come. Let's visit the once-abandoned estate in Liberty Square. *Once-abandoned*, you ask? Well, of course, it's now inhabited by 999 ghosts.

This beloved attraction (which even inspired a movie, starring Eddie Murphy, released in 2003) has so much magic and mystery, it's easy to see why so many folks rank this ride as one of their favorites.

This is an attraction for which it can be very easy to ruin the magic by explaining some of the secrets, tricks, and illusions, so I'm going to try to steer totally clear of the magic behind the mansion and focus on some of the details that are just on the surface—and there are lots of them.

For the most part, I'm not going to delve into too many things to look out for during the actual ride, for a few reasons. First, it's dark. Second, it can move pretty quickly, and there is a lot to see all around you, so just sit back and enjoy the ride—but don't forget to see if you can spot the grandmother from the Carousel of Progress sitting in her chair in the ballroom scene!

That said, there are some spoilers ahead in regard to the actual story line of the attraction. If you've never experienced the attraction before and you want to go in fresh, come back to this section after you've experienced it. Some of the information here will help you to appreciate the attraction even more.

Before we go in and visit with our ghost host, here's a little background on the setting and how the mansion ended up in Liberty Square.

The concept for the attraction was years in the making over at Disneyland. Unfortunately, the passing of Walt Disney complicated and delayed the arrival of the mansion at that park until 1969, when it finally made its debut.

As Disney was building the version for Disneyland, they knew the Haunted Mansion would also be a part of Walt Disney World, so as they decided to create duplicates of everything simultaneously and put the components for WDW into storage until they were needed in Florida.

Two major differences between the Disneyland version and the WDW version are the outside facade and the location within the parks.

At Disneyland, the setting is New Orleans Square, and the exterior is a Southern-style mansion. This wouldn't work for Walt Disney World, as there wasn't going to be a New Orleans Square.

Former Imagineer and author Jason Surrell explains in his wonderful book *The Haunted Mansion, Imagineering a Disney Classic*:

> This geographical shift led Imagineers to New York's lower Hudson River Valley, the ancestral home of Sleepy Hollow and the Headless Horseman, and they were inspired by the region's stately old manor houses, in which English, Dutch, and German settlers would gather by the fireside and spin tales of the supernatural such as those by Washington Irving.
>
> So the Haunted Mansion was transformed from an antebellum, Southern mansion into a Dutch Gothic-style manor house to fit in with its new Colonial surroundings. The final design incorporated a number of strong gothic elements typical of pre-Revolutionary New York's lower Hudson River Valley, including arches thrusting upward into the sky, large stone foundations, and cornerstones, and the stone brickwork common to the English Tudor style.
>
> This particular style of architecture is referred to as Perpendicular Style for its use of strong vertical lines, which enhance the sense that the Mansion is towering above you, tall and forbidding. The style was chosen precisely because Imagineers wanted the Mansion's exterior to look a bit scarier than the Disneyland original.

Sounds like the illusion of forced perspective seen elsewhere in the park.

Let's take a look around before we enter the attraction. As you pass through the gates of the estate, you'll notice a hearse with an invisible horse—which is a great spot to snap a photo.

Now, this isn't just any old hearse; it was actually used in the 1965 John Wayne movie *The Sons of Katie Elder*. Look down at the ground, and you'll find a few horseshoe prints, where the horse is "standing."

The queue for the Haunted Mansion is quite interactive and filled with creative nuances, along with witty references to those who contributed to the attraction, both real and make-believe.

As you move along through the queue, you're faced with two options: make your way into the mansion or take the scenic route and go through the cemetery. Since this book is all about the details and magic, you know which way to go—cemetery, of course!

First up, come meet the family: Bertie, Aunt Florence, Uncle Jacob, the twins, and Cousin Maude. This greedy group killed one another in an attempt to inherit the family fortune.

If you read the script and follow the clues on each monument, you can try to figure out the murder mystery.

Spoiler! Here's "who offed who": Bertie was shot by Aunt Florence; he was a big-game hunter, so that's only fitting! Aunt Florence was killed by the twins. Uncle Jacob was poisoned by Bertie. The twins were killed by Cousin Maude—no relation to Bea Arthur—who was, in turn, killed by Uncle Jacob.

The next stop in the graveyard is the large crypt of the composer. The sides of the crypt have interactive musical instruments; go ahead and give them a touch.

When you look at the pipe organ, it will look a little similar to an organ in the ballroom scene. Also, the brand of the organ is a Ravenscroft. It just so happens that Thurl Ravenscroft voices Uncle Theodore inside the mansion. He was also the voice of Tony the Tiger for the breakfast cereal Frosted Flakes, and he can be heard at Pirates of the Caribbean as well.

Naturally, every cemetery has tombstones. Check out a few of the names when you pass them. Each one is a tribute to one of the folks who worked to bring you the Haunted Mansion.

Here are a few notables: "In Memory Of Our Patriarch, Dear Departed Grandpa Marc." This is for Marc Davis; more on Marc in a page or two when we get to the story line.

When you get to the mausoleum, look for the inscription "Farewell Forever. Mister Frees, Your Voice will Carry on The Breeze." This is a reference to Paul Frees, the voice of your Ghost Host through the attraction.

Next up, and you can't miss this one, the Captain's Crypt. When you're inside the load area of the attraction, look along the walls. See if you can spot the captain's portrait; he's wearing the same hat that is perched atop this crypt.

Moving right along, we find the final resting place of Prudence Pock. As the story goes, "Prudence Pock She Died, Tis Said From Writer's Block." Go ahead and push some of the books back into their shelf when they slide out.

As you continue past Prudence and make your way to the front door of the manor, you'll notice another family plot to the left.

Again, the tombstones have witty sayings and are a show of appreciation, Disney style, for those who helped create the attraction.

Watch the headstone of Madame Leota, as she's definitely watching you! You'll encounter Madame Leota once again during the séance scene.

As I mentioned previously, I'm not going to examine and dissect the ride itself too much. But I will give you a bit of background on the story line and a random fun fact here and there. For example, when you're in the foyer scene, the fireplace in the foyer is actually an air conditioning duct!

What you actually see and experience today is an amalgamation of two creative geniuses—and their creative differences. Marc Davis (you remember, Grandpa Marc) and Claude Coats worked together very successfully on Pirates of the Caribbean (which we will visit soon in Adventureland).

However, their collaboration didn't go as smoothly on the Haunted Mansion. Gone was Walt Disney, to manage and be the final decision maker for attractions.

It boiled down to this: should the attraction be truly scary or more whimsical and humorous? Coats wanted scary, and Davis wanted more humor.

Ultimately, having more humor than horror prevailed—there's much more to this backstory, and Surrell's book goes into great detail if you're interested in all things Haunted Mansion. It's an excellent tribute and read.

Quoting from page 32 of Surrell's book:

Though not as intricately constructed as a Shakespearean play, a story exists. In fact, Imagineering legend and Disneyland veteran Tony Baxter believes that, in combining the seemingly divergent work of Marc Davis and Claude Coats inadvertently gave the Haunted Mansion a fairly solid three-act structure.

In Act One, which begins slowly and ominously in the Foyer, guests anticipate the appearance of the happy haunts, and experience poltergeist activity and unseen spirits.

Madame Leota provides the curtain that separates Act One and Act Two. The medium conjures up the spirits and encourages them to materialize, which they promptly do in the swinging wake in the Grand Hall and Attic.

The descent from the attic window into the Graveyard takes guests into Act Three, in which they are completely surrounded by the ghosts who are enjoying the manic intensity of a graveyard jamboree. Finally, one of three hitchhiking ghosts materializes beside guests in their Doom Buggy before the exit.

Yes, that's kind of a deep for analysis for an attraction that is supposed to be a haunted house. Obviously, if you've never ridden the ride before, don't pay that much attention to the overall theme and the whole act one, two, and three; appreciate it for what it is.

The attraction we experience today has even more of a story line than what was originally featured at the Haunted Mansion. The decade of the 2000s brought forth a new backstory, which featured a ghostly bride, Constance Hatchaway; you'll meet her in the attic scene, where her plot unfolds.

As the story goes, Constance had a few marriages. Lucky husband number one was Ambrose Harper. Victim, er, hubby number two was Frank Banks. Husband number three was Marquis De-Doom, number four was Reginald Caine, and, last but not least, number five was George Hightower.

As you move through this scene, you'll see the wedding photos and gifts actually tell the story of Constance. She basically stays the same, but her husbands change. With all the visual stimuli and dim lighting, you're bound to miss some of the details.

As Constance progresses through her five marriages, her

wedding dress doesn't change much, but her jewelry does. Note the strands of pearls she's wearing; with each new husband comes a new strand, and she ends up with five strands of pearls.

Constance is a bit of a social climber and keeps "marrying up" financially. Eventually, before you exit the scene, you'll have the pleasure of meeting the blushing bride. She's the gal with the axe in her hands!

Also, be on the lookout for the hat rack with five hats hanging from it, a hat for each of her husbands. Some of these details are hard to see, so it may take you a few trips to absorb it all.

As you exit the attraction and walk back outside to the park, look to the left, and you'll see a few more witty epitaphs on the wall.

If you're so inclined, as you leave the Haunted Mansion, you can pop into the shop **Memento Mori** and buy some Haunted Mansion–themed merchandise. The backstory with the shop is also quite interesting.

Madame Leota was a fortune teller or psychic, and she fled Salem, Massachusetts, to avoid persecution during the Salem witch trials.

She set up shop in a town in the Hudson Valley and named it Memento Mori, which in Latin actually means "remember that you must die," a nice use of the verbiage. Be sure to purchase a "memento" at the shop!

Leaving the Haunted Mansion in our rearview, we will walk toward the center of Liberty Square. As you approach the Liberty Square Market, turn left and walk toward the **Hall of Presidents**.

Whichever side of the presidential aisle you favor, you'll be sure to find some historically important and genuine presidential memorabilia before you take in the audio-animatronic show featuring the presidents of the United States.

If you're not that interested in politics but wish to brush up on your American history, next to the Hall of Presidents is **The Muppets Present...Great Moments in American History**. It's a cute, quick outdoor show featuring all your favorite Muppets.

One last thing before you leave this little area. See if you can spot two interesting signs. Look around the area of Ye Olde Christmas Shoppe, where it's Christmas 365 days a year.

Can you spot the heart-shaped sign that reads Kepple Est. 1779? This sign pays homage to Kepple Disney, Walt and Roy's grandfather.

Another interesting one to spot is closer to the Columbia Harbour House. Look for several hands in hands.

What does this emblem mean? According to the National Museum of American History:

> Beginning in the 1750s, some American insurance companies issued metal fire marks to policyholders to signify that their property was insured against fire damage. The fire marks bore the name and/or symbol of the insurer, and some included the customer's policy number. The company

or agent would then affix the mark to the policyholder's home or business. For owners the mark served as proof of insurance and a deterrent against arson. For insurance companies the mark served as a form of advertising, and alerted volunteer firefighters that the property was insured.

The Philadelphia Contributionship for the Insurance of Houses from Loss by Fire issued this fire mark around 1802. The fire mark consists of the company's symbol cast in lead showing four hands clasped at the wrist attached to a shield-shaped wooden backing.

The Philadelphia Contributionship was established in 1752, becoming the first successful fire insurance company in America. Benjamin Franklin was one of its founding members. The Contributionship began as a mutual insurance company and this concept is represented by its "Hand in Hand" fire mark. The Philadelphia Contributionship is still in operation. (http://americanhistory.si.edu/collections/search/object/nmah_1341505)

Great authenticity abounds again, by Disney. That's going to wrap up Liberty Square, and we are going to head back toward the Rivers of America, make a left, and mosey on past the Liberty Tree Tavern and enter Frontierland.

Frontierland

> *Here we experience the story of our country's past...the colorful drama of Frontier America in the exciting days of the covered wagon and the stage coach...the advent of the railroad...and the romantic riverboat. Frontierland is a tribute to the faith, courage and ingenuity of the pioneers who blazed the trails across America.*
>
> **—Walt Disney, July 17, 1955**

The quote above is from Walt's dedication of Frontierland at Disneyland, and it's still very much applicable to Frontierland in Walt Disney World, so let's head west, literally.

Frontierland is a western-themed land that happens to also be on the western side of Magic Kingdom. Along the way, we're going to encounter a few prospectors and pioneers—but don't be surprised if we encounter a few musical bears, hares, and foxes too!

As we enter from Liberty Square, note the stream that runs between Liberty Square and Frontierland; it is supposed to represent the Mississippi River and its division between east and west. Go ahead and try your hand at the Frontierland **Shootin' Arcade**. See how quick your draw is or how sharp your eyes are. Do you see the hidden Mickey? Look to the left of the tombstone of Ol' Tom Hubbard. Note the shape of the cactus; you'll see it forms the three shapes of a hidden Mickey.

Put down your gun and walk over to the rustic log cabin, Grizzly Hall. As you leave the Shootin' Arcade, watch your step, as Disney was really going for authenticity here when they constructed raised wooden sidewalks just like in the Wild Wild West. This was done purposely back in the day so men wouldn't get their boots dirty and women would keep their dresses clean.

Grizzly Hall is home to the **Country Bear Jamboree.** Starring Big Al, Liver Lips McGrowl, and the triplets, Bunny, Bubble, and Beulah Bear. (Wait, a bear named Bunny?) There's even a character named Teddi Barra. She isn't related to baseball legend Yogi Berra but gets her name from silent screen film actress Theda Bara. The inspiration for Teddi's character, however, comes from screen legend Mae West. These are a few of the critters who bring you a country-western, knee-slappin' good time!

A few interesting tidbits about this big bear hoedown. The concept for this attraction was originally created for a ski resort Disney planned to construct during the mid-1960s on a parcel of land called Mineral King, in the Sequoia National Forest in California.

One of the Imagineers working on the project was Marc Davis. Marc was working on character designs and storyboard sketches and would often cover his office walls with his work.

The book *Walt Disney Imagineering* recounts a memorable moment that happened one afternoon:

> One day, as Walt so often did, he stopped in to see what Marc was up to. From literally hundreds of pinned up sketches, he immediately singled one out that featured a bear playing the tuba, and began to laugh hysterically. He told Marc, between guffaws, that he "really had a winner here with these musical bears." As Walt began to leave the office, he turned and said, "Good-bye, Marc." This took the artist by surprise as Walt never said good-bye, but rather, always said "so long" or "see ya." Walt died a few days later. Marc believes this was the last time Walt ever had a good laugh.

Disney's plan for the ski resort never came to fruition on the land, but what did make it past the drawing board was the concept of a show featuring musical bears. But the show would be in a much warmer climate, Walt Disney World.

The Country Bear Jamboree is cute and nostalgic feeling, so feel free to clap along as eighteen hillbilly bears entertain you with a country-western flair for sixteen minutes.

This show is one of the last attractions Walt Disney personally worked on before he passed away. The Jamboree was even the inspiration for the 2002 movie *The Country Bears*. If you look at the reviews and ratings on imdb.com, clearly folks like the show at WDW better!

If you decide to take in the show, look above the stage. There is a profile picture of the Bears' founder, Ursus H. Bear, 1848–1928. It may be hard to see, but look really closely at the top of the frame around the photo of Ursus. See the hidden Mickey made up of the two scrolls above the circle?

Some call the Country Bear Jamboree "the wildest show in the wilderness," but musical bears are only so much fun and excitement. So let's leave and go find the "wildest *ride* in the wilderness."

Walking toward the end of Frontierland, you'll pass Splash Mountain on your left and the **Rivers of America** on your right.

If you're so inclined, hop aboard a raft, float across to **Tom Sawyer Island**, and enjoy a self-guided tour of an area inspired by the tales of Mark Twain. There isn't a lot to do on the island, but if you get close to the creaking of the rotating gears of Harper's Mill, you may actually hear the song "Down by the Old Mill Stream." The island offers some really good views of **Big Thunder Mountain Railroad**, which is where we are headed now.

Big Thunder Mountain Railroad is set in the Southwest during the Gold Rush era, in the fictional mining town of Tumbleweed. As the legend went, the 2.5-acre site and the 197-foot-tall mountain is full of gold. The train ride winds around a majestic mountain, waterfalls, landslides, and hairpin turns through 2,780 feet of track.

When creating the attraction, to guarantee authenticity, Imagineers scoured ghost towns in search of cogwheels, buckets, ore carts, and mining gear.

It took years of planning, hundreds of rock makers, tons of

steel and concrete, and four thousand gallons of paint to create the nearly two-hundred-foot mountain. Big Thunder Mountain Railroad is also the very first ride where Disney used a computer to design and create the track.

Big Thunder Mountain is brainchild of now-retired Imagineer Tony Baxter. Tony gave an interesting interview to Disney historian Didier Ghez at Disneyland Paris on May 31, 1995. Let's hear what Tony had to say about the creation of Big Thunder:

> I started to work with the Monument Valley rock work from Utah and figuring out how to build a train that would look like the train was built *after* the rocks.
>
> You go to the parks in Europe and it is like they put rocks around the train: the train was there first and then rocks grew around the train! This does not make any sense. The challenge was to make it look like the rocks were there and to make it find its way through the rocks to make it look like not a roller-coaster but like a real adventure. I guess I did a really good job out of it, because they [Disney] all thought: we are going to do it.
>
> As luck would have it, *Space Mountain* came first, because of the tremendous interest in the space program and WDW's close proximity to Cape. *Space Mountain* opened in 1974 and *Big Thunder* did not come in Florida before 1980. Even though I finished it in 1974, we put it away for a while and then brought it back 6 years later.

In 2012 Big Thunder Mountain Railroad received a new backstory, and it pays homage to Tony Baxter. As the story goes, from the Disney Parks blog:

> Barnabas T. Bullion is the founder and president of the Big Thunder Mining Company. The longtime mining magnate comes from a powerful East Coast family and considers gold to be his very birthright by virtue of his oddly appropriate name; in fact, he considers the ultimate gold strike to

be his destiny.

And that is why he is having so much trouble with Big Thunder Mountain. According to superstitious locals, Big Thunder Mountain is very protective of the gold it holds within, and the unfortunate soul who attempts to mine its riches is destined to fail. And so far that prophecy is coming to pass.

The mine has been plagued by mysterious forces and natural disasters ever since. And yet the Big Thunder Mining Co. is still in operation. In fact, Bullion is discovering new veins of gold and digging new shafts every day, offering a closer look at the Big Thunder mining operation than ever before. But a word to the wise for anyone attempting to visit the mountain: watch out for runaway trains.

In addition to a refreshed backstory, the attraction also received an updated and interactive queue. As you mosey through the attraction waiting to board your train, you move from the mining office to the explosives magazine room. There's some fun interactive stuff to do here.

Then head on through to the foreman's post, where you can actually take a look down into the mine. As you go through the ventilation room, take a look at the name of the equipment used to make the miners' air safe to breathe. The large piece of machinery is called "AutoCanary, Air Quality Analyzer," which is an obvious reference to the old practice of bringing a canary into a mine to detect when the air becomes too toxic.

See if you can spot the painting of Barnabas T. Bullion. He looks a lot like Tony Baxter! Lots of legends and lore here at Big Thunder Mountain Railroad, but there's one fact that is neither legend nor lore: this ride may help you pass a kidney stone—seriously!

The October 2016 *Journal of the American Osteopathic Association* included a paper entitled "Validation of a Functional Pyelocalyceal Renal Model for the Evaluation of Renal Calculi Passage While Riding a Roller Coaster."

The physician who authored the paper found that he had patients on vacation who had passed their kidney stones after riding Big Thunder Mountain Railroad.

The good doctor noted that research published in other countries indicated similar success when patients bungee jumped or rode other roller coasters. Dr. Wartinger received permission from Disney to test his hypothesis. What he found was twenty-three out of thirty-six kidney stones were passed when riding in the rear of the car of Big Thunder Mountain Railroad. Pretty wild stuff!

And as the saying from the ride goes, "Hang on to them hats and glasses because this here's the wildest ride in the wilderness!" That legendary spiel from the attraction is voiced by the late character actor Dallas McKennon. Dallas also voices Benjamin Franklin over at Epcot's American Adventure.

Let's move from one railroad to another. Adjacent to Big Thunder Mountain Railroad is the Walt Disney World Railroad, Frontierland station. If your feet are tired and you're looking for a leisurely way to get to the front of the park, hop aboard.

But before you do that, look around the train station. See if you can find the poster on the wall offering a $1,000 reward for B. H. Stevens; it says to contact a US Marshal.

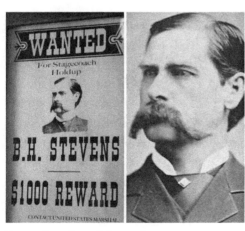

Well, upon further examination of the picture of B. H. Stevens, it appears it's actually Wyatt Earp, who was a deputy sheriff and deputy town marshal from Tombstone, Arizona, and was a part of the gunfight at the O.K. Corral. Check the pictures I've included; very creative, witty stuff here!

Zip a dee doo dah, we're on our way to **Splash Mountain**, which is next to the Frontierland train station and will be our last attraction in Frontierland.

First things first: you're going to get wet, as you're about to have a musical adventure with about a hundred talking, singing, and dancing animatronic critters and about 950,000 gallons of water!

Why are you going to get wet? Well, you're going to experience a few drops and then take a trip down a five-story waterfall in a log, fifty-two and one-half feet, to be exact, and at a forty-five-degree angle, which has you going about forty miles per hour.

Sitting in the front, you're probably going to get soaked; in the back, definitely wet, but probably not as bad as the front passengers. If you're nervous about the liquid factor, at the main entrance of the ride are some lockers to stow your dry goods. But fret not, Disney thought this one out—should you be splashed by the mountain, the water shouldn't stain your clothing or bother your skin. Disney uses Bromine in the water here, which isn't as harsh as chlorine.

Br'er Fox, Br'er Bear, Br'er Rabbit, and a slew of other characters and animals are going to show you their Southern hospitality and have you clapping and singing to the songs from the Disney film *Song of the South*, which premiered in 1946 and is the inspiration for this attraction.

The movie is based on the Uncle Remus stories by Joel Chandler Harris. Disney adapted the stories and combined animation with live action to tell the tales. The hit song "Zip-a-Dee-Doo-Dah" won the 1947 Academy Award for Best Song. You'll hear it during your ride. What you won't see or hear, just about anywhere, is the actual movie itself. The film has a story line and characters that are considered racist and offensive toward African Americans.

How did an attraction like this come to be at Walt Disney World? Tony Baxter's influence is seen within the park again. Quoting from the same interview about Big Thunder Mountain Railroad:

> The idea for *Splash Mountain* popped into my head as I was

driving to work. Dick Nunis who was the Chairman of DL and WDW had always nagged me, saying: "Why don't we do a water ride? All the other parks have one." I said: "That is why we are not doing one...Because all the other parks have one, it would seem as if Disney were copying."

So I am driving my car and the idea sparked and I thought: "I know, we are going to do a water ride to please Dick." The final element was the impending closure of *America Sings*. They were going to throw away all those characters and someone said, "*Song of the South* looks a lot like *America Sings*." So we got out some of the original model sheets from *Song of the South* and I found some characters that were not used in the movie, that I would swear were done by Marc Davis, because they just look like the possums and all the characters that were in *America Sings*.

We knew we only had to add Brer Rabbit, Brer Bear and Brer Fox to make it work. So we added 10 new figures to the 75 existing figures from *America Sings*. We had a show of 85 figures for the cost of ten. So we did it, and *Splash Mountain* was one of the first projects that Michael Eisner approved, and it opened in 1989. It took a while to build, because it is a fairly complicated show.

A little background on the background: Tony was referencing America Sings at Disneyland. This attraction was at Disneyland's Tomorrowland from June 1974 to April 1988. The show used a revolving-theater format similar to the Carousel of Progress. Instead of watching a family evolve over the years, you watched and listened as characters performed a twenty-four-minute musical medley of patriotic American music.

As Tony said, before this attraction closed, they salvaged many of the audio-animatronics to use at Disneyland's version of Splash Mountain. What we find in Walt Disney World are obviously reproductions of Disneyland's version of the ride.

It's an interesting story about how the attraction came to be, but it doesn't really explain why an attraction based in the old South is featured in Frontierland, which is based on the old West. But hey, this is Disney, after all. It's all just fantasy, right? Not everything has to be logical!

Despite (or because of) the probability of getting wet, the ride is great. It lasts about eleven minutes, and as you progress through the attraction and see the story unfold before you, you'll notice each drop during the attraction increases with severity, until you take the really big plunge!

As you crest the top of the final plunge, if your eyes are open, take a look around. For a split second, it gives a great view of the park. But don't forget to smile, as plunging down a mountain makes for a great photo opportunity!

Adventureland

Welcome to Adventureland, home to pillaging pirates, talking birds, an exotic river cruise, and a tasty treat known as Dole Whip.

But it be too late to alter course, mateys—and there be plunderin' pirates lurkin' in every cove. They pillage, plunder, rifle, and loot, so let's go pay our respects to Captain Jack Sparrow, as dead men tell no tales!

Pirates of the Caribbean is located in the Caribbean Plaza section of Adventureland. The area features Spanish and English architectural styles based on the West Indies of the eighteenth century.

The attraction's origins date back to Disneyland in 1967. The Disneyland attraction was originally conceived by Walt Disney as a wax museum and walk-through exhibit, but it changed to a boat ride as technology within the company advanced. Believe it or not, Pirates of the Caribbean almost didn't come to fruition at Walt Disney World.

In a 2009 news release by Disney in their *Walt Disney World Newsletter*, the company explains:

Pirates of the Caribbean wasn't included in the original

plans for Magic Kingdom at Walt Disney World Resort—the Disney Imagineers thought that since Florida sits in the middle of the real Caribbean there would be little interest in a pirates-themed adventure. Soon after opening in the fall of 1971, Walt Disney World Resort was inundated with guest comments expressing disappointment that the renowned Disneyland attraction was nowhere to be found in Magic Kingdom. By fall of 1972 Pirates of the Caribbean was under construction in Florida. Pirates of the Caribbean opened in Florida's Magic Kingdom on Dec. 15, 1973. It was one of the first major additions to the park following its grand opening in 1971.

Wow, it's hard to think of a Magic Kingdom experience without a trip aboard Pirates of the Caribbean. It's one of the most beloved attractions at any theme park around the world and was even the catalyst for the highly successful film franchise of the same name.

The nine-minute gentle boat ride aboard a flat-bottom boat uses 155,000 gallons of water (there is one fourteen-foot plunge in the dark) to take visitors through a seaport of swashbuckling scoundrels who sing and besiege a port in the Caribbean. There are 125 audio-animatronic figures: 65 pirates and villagers and 60 animals and birds.

As mentioned above, the attraction didn't debut when the park opened in 1971; it came two years later. But the Walt Disney World Railroad, which chugs along around the perimeter of the park, had existing train tracks where Disney needed to put the building for the pirate attraction.

So, Disney's imagineers went to work and devised a way for the attraction to operate without disrupting the train route. The boats would pass below the tracks from one show building into another. Guests would enter the attraction from one building and descend down this drop below the tracks into another building containing the rest of the attraction.

Here are a few highlights and secrets to observe. As you enter

Castillo del Morro, the Spanish fortress housing the attraction, there's lots to check out as you work your way through the queue.

It appears as though the castle is under attack. Check out the walls; there's damage from cannonballs, and in a few spots, you'll notice a few still lodged in the wall.

If you can spot a jail cell window with bars in the Fastpass line, take a peek in. You'll find two intellectual skeletons in a chess battle. This little detail was originally set to have them deadlocked, pun intended, as the game board shows a tie between the players, which Imagineers created with accuracy.

However, from time to time, the chess pieces have been skewed inadvertently, and they don't always make their way back to the proper position of being at a stalemate.

Once you board your boat, get ready to experience the full legend and lore of pirates, visiting the Pirates Grotto, the Fort, the Town Square, the Burning City, and, of course, the Dungeon. There's so much to see and appreciate from all angles here, in addition to trying to spot some hidden magic.

As the ride is coming to an end and you sail up to the scene with Captain Jack, glance at the lock on the cell. It looks a lot like a hidden Mickey.

Oh, and a little spoiler alert: don't be too alarmed about the fire effect throughout the attraction. The illusion is a combination of cloth, fans, and lights, but when you're just glancing at it, there is a very realistic effect to it.

Pirates of the Caribbean is a very popular and high-capacity ride, moving guests through quite efficiently. The queue is pretty long, and it can be hard to tell how long the wait really is. If you can, Fastpass this, as it's a must-see attraction!

In keeping with the water-based adventure attractions, hang a right out of the Castillo Del Morro and walk to the **Jungle Cruise**, another legendary Disney attraction with its origins at Disneyland.

The catalyst for this attraction was Disney's award-winning True-Life Adventure films. Walt originally hoped to feature live animals on this ride but quickly realized that wouldn't be the best idea, because of the high unpredictability of animals. The film *The African Queen,* starring Humphrey Bogart and Katharine Hepburn, helped influence aspects of this attraction as well.

When the attraction debuted at Disneyland in 1955, there was a more serious, educational tone to it. However, by the early 1960s, the story line evolved and became a bit more lighthearted and humorous, as guests encounter hippos, elephants, and maybe even a headhunter or two during their boat tour of the rivers across Asia,

Africa, and South America.

As you enter the queue, listen to the music and banter over the public-address system for the ride. There are a few cheesy announcements and songs being played overhead.

At any point during your trip on the Jungle Cruise, take a look down at the river. You won't find a hidden Mickey in the murky water, but the water does have some secrets to tell. On your way out, check the message board for the list of missing persons and missing boats—there's a good play on words here!

Throughout the park, where there's outdoor water, such as the Jungle Cruise, the water is dyed to give the illusion that the water is deeper than it actually is and to not reveal components of the ride. Tom Morris elaborated on the topic for me:

> The water is circulated throughout the park to other bodies of water, of varying depths, so it's mostly to camouflage the bottom and any apparatus there may be like tracks and pipes, etc., but it's also to create a more natural look. Because water chemistry is different in each geographical location around the world, the recipe is different at each resort and it usually takes a year to fine-tune it.

Who knew? Disney even finagles the water! Actually, they've been finagling it in Florida since 1965!

Walt Disney loved waterways. He once remarked to Admiral Joe Fowler, who helped oversee construction of Walt Disney World, that water is one of Florida's greatest attractions and he wanted to take advantage of it to the fullest extent.

Admiral Fowler was in charge of the construction of the recreational waterways throughout the property. General Potter, we heard him mentioned earlier in the chapter, handled the creation of the canals and levees that provide irrigation and flood control throughout Walt Disney World. In all, forty-eight miles of canals, twelve miles of levees, and twenty-four water control structures were established. One of Fowler's major tasks was getting Bay

Lake, a natural waterway near Magic Kingdom, ready for opening day and connecting it with a sister body of water, the Seven Seas Lagoon, that he created in the park.

In the mid-1960s, when Disney acquired the property, the water in Bay Lake was stained brown by tannins, chemicals released from the surrounding cypress groves. The solution to getting rid of the brown, stained water was to drain and clean the 400-acre lake and then fill it back up, adding an additional foot to the water level. This extra water caused a change in hydrodynamic pressure, resulting in a situation that would keep tannins and other pollutants out of the water, which was exactly what the Admiral ordered.

Workers dredged Bay Lake, pumping out the three-and-a-half-billion gallons of water and removing an eight-and-a-half-foot-deep layer of muck from the bottom. To the workers' surprise, beneath the mud and muck was pristine white sand. They used this sand to line the shores of both Bay Lake and the Disney-made Seven Seas Lagoon.

Disney created the Seven Seas Lagoon by excavating over eight million yards of dirt, which took over three years to accomplish. This landfill wasn't wasted; it was used to raise the construction site of Magic Kingdom over twelve feet, allowing for the utilidors to be built. Without this landfill, the underground area of the park would not have been able to be built since Florida's water table is extremely high.

Leaving the Jungle Cruise, let's head out across the walkway to **Walt Disney's Enchanted Tiki Room.**

I've been throwing around the term *audio-animatronic*, or *animatronic*, quite freely throughout the book and haven't defined or fully described it. More than likely, you're familiar with the term, which describes the electronic actors at Walt Disney World who never flub their lines, don't need a coffee break, and never ask for a pay raise.

Since we're about to check out the Enchanted Tiki Room, the

attraction where animatronics debuted at Disneyland in 1963, now would be a good time for a little storytelling and scratch just below the surface of these mechanical creations.

The official Disney fan club, D23, published a great article about the origins of these characters, "The Birds, Beasts, and Beauty of Disney's Audio-Animatronic Characters." Here are a few lines from the story:

> When Walt Disney found an antique mechanical singing bird in a shop while on vacation in New Orleans, he was intrigued. He reasoned that he and his staff had been doing animation on film for years, but it would be fun to try some three-dimensional animation.
>
> Walt had Wathel Rogers and other studio technicians take the bird apart to see how it worked. Then work was started to come up with a prototype figure. Charles Cristadoro, a sculptor, modeled some human heads, utilizing actor Buddy Ebsen and staff members around the Studio as models, and experiments were made with cams, hydraulics, and other methods of enabling the figures to move realistically.
>
> One early concept was for a figure of Confucius, who would interact with guests in a Chinese restaurant at Disneyland. The Chinese restaurant was never built, so the technicians turned instead to the nation's sixteenth president, Abraham Lincoln.
>
> When Robert Moses, in charge of the 1964–1965 New York World's Fair, saw the figure being tested at the Disney Studio, he knew that he had to have it for the Fair. Walt agreed to speed up development of Lincoln, and the state of Illinois came forward to act as sponsor. The exhibit opened in April 1964, to great acclaim. But, *Audio-Animatronics* had actually been used in a show that had opened at Disneyland the previous year.
>
> Less sophisticated figures of birds, flowers, and tiki gods

populated the *Walt Disney's Enchanted Tiki Room*. From then on, *Audio-Animatronics* would be an accepted part of many of the attractions at the Disney parks.

An even more interesting story comes from Walt himself, in the *Desert Sun* newspaper, on May 13, 1963, before the attraction at Disneyland debuted. Here's what Walt had to say:

> "I always want to try something that's never been done before. When our government began the missile program it built exactly the kind of equipment I needed for this audio-animatronic display." As matter of fact, he confided "The same machine we use to trigger our mechanism is used in the program of the Polaris missile. If the government hadn't done all the research it would have cost us a fortune to develop the system."

So, Cold War missile technology was the catalyst to bring you the entertaining bears, cars, dinosaurs, Olafs, and Ursulas. But let's get back to the birds!

Obviously, the Enchanted Tiki Room at Disneyland was a success, seeing as the attraction has been a mainstay at Walt Disney World since 1971.

The show you see today is a tribute to the original Disneyland presentation Walt created, though it has been enhanced with a state-of-the-art show-control system, remastered audio, and a more versatile and energy-efficient lighting system.

As the lights dim, four colorful macaws quickly spring to life and begin the show. Over the next ten minutes, the cast of over 225 choreographed audio-animatronic performers sing and entertain with a South Seas Polynesian flair.

Before or after the show, take a gander at the bird perches. Just below the birds, off to the right if you're facing the birds head on, you may find a classic hidden Mickey.

When we visit Disney's Animal Kingdom in a few chapters, you will really be able to appreciate and see how far this technology has come, as Disney's most advanced animatronic is the focal point of an attraction in Pandora.

Sure, the whole missile story and tie-in to animatronics is a cool part of history, but I would be less than honest if I didn't tell you part of my motivation to come over to the Tiki Room was for something else—a little thing called Dole Whip, which is a delicious treat with a cult following. (Check out tiki.dole.com; it's pretty entertaining!)

Go ahead, leave the Tiki Room, walk next door to Aloha Isle, and treat yourself to a Dole Whip. You've done a lot of walking today, and you deserve one!

So, with Dole Whip in hand, keep walking past the **Magic Carpets of Aladdin** and follow the walkway past the **Swiss Family Tree House**, and I'm sad to say our trip through Adventureland is just about over.

As you wander out of Adventureland, feel free to branch off to the pathway on the right and walk across the bridge leading to the Crystal Palace rather than go directly to the hub.

As you pass the Crystal Palace, you'll also pass the park's **First Aid Station** and then Casey's Corner. (If you're coming from the entrance of the park and walking up Main Street, note the red-and-white umbrellas in front of Casey's Corner, which are a great landmark to find First Aid.)

You can head down Main Street, USA, and take in the sights again, or if you prefer to avoid the hustle and bustle of the street, you can enter Casey's Corner and walk through the stores that link together for the full block. You will exit into Town Square and can proceed out of the park.

Chapter Two

Epcot

> *We have always tried to be guided by the basic idea that, in the discovery of knowledge, there is great entertainment—as, conversely, in all good entertainment, there is always some grain of wisdom, humanity or enlightenment to be gained.*
>
> **—Walt Disney**

You've just walked out of the Magic Kingdom and back into reality, so to speak. When you pass through the exit, head to the right and make your way to the monorail station. Take a quick ride on the highway in the sky to the Ticket and Transportation Center. You're going to switch monorail lines and head over to Epcot.

As the monorail pulls out of the Ticket and Transportation Center and heads toward Epcot, running parallel with the highway, World Drive, try to look to the left. You should be able to sneak a peek at the Lake Buena Vista STOLport, or Walt Disney World airport.

For a brief time after WDW opened in 1971, Disney operated a STOLport (short takeoff and landing), and small planes were actually able to land at the two-thousand-foot landing strip.

Shawnee Airlines was one of the two airlines operating at the STOLport. As one of their advertisements stated, you could fly from McCoy Jetport (which is now MCO, Orlando International Airport) directly into WDW for just seven dollars! When you deplane, you're only three minutes to the Magic Kingdom.

Flying directly into WDW was short-lived, and by December 1971, Executive Airlines ceased their operations into Walt Disney World. Shawnee Airlines met the same fate by December 1972.

Planes are cool, but, some may argue, monorails are even cooler. Before you pull into Epcot, here are a few interesting tidbits about the Walt Disney World Resort Monorail. The system, in operation since 1971, was expanded in 1982 with a four-mile extension to Epcot.

Shawnee Airlines...
your magic
carpet into

Walt Disney World

Now Shawnee has nine daily shuttle flights from McCoy Jetport, Orlando to the Vacation Kingdom of the World. When you deplane from your STOL flight, you are within three minutes of the Walt Disney World hotels, Magic Kingdom theme park, and the Golf Resort.

Only $7.00 per person — for more information, ask your travel agent or Eastern Airlines representative.

STOL... Short Take Off and Landing Aircraft

SHAWNEE AIRLINES
The Convenient Commuter

Each of the six-car trains (identified by a unique color stripe) is 203 feet long and has an overall height of 10 feet, 5½ inches. The monorail travels on a 26-inch-wide concrete beam supported by tapered concrete columns approximately 110 feet apart. The beams and columns are constructed in sets of six and post-tensioned together to form a single six-hundred-foot structure. As trains move along the beamway, they pick up electrical power from a metallic buss bar.

In total, the Walt Disney World monorail system consists of 14.7 miles of elevated beamway that services stations between Epcot, Magic Kingdom, and three resorts:

Disney's Contemporary Resort, Disney's Grand Floridian Resort, and Disney's Polynesian Village Resort. On a typical day, more than 150,000 guests use monorail transportation, with nearly 7,000 guests per direction, per hour, riding along the highway in the sky.

By now, the monorail should have completed its loop through Future World, and you're ready to enter the park, which makes this a good time to talk a bit about what you're about to experience. As mentioned earlier in the book, Epcot was supposed to be Walt's community of the future, an all-encompassing revolutionary city where folks will live, work, and play. If you think back to your time on the Tomorrowland Transit Authority's PeopleMover, you saw the ambitious model of Progress City, Walt's dream.

As we know, this dream never came to fruition. It can be fascinating to think about what could have been. But this isn't a road we are going down.

Instead, let's try to appreciate what is here today: a 305-acre park that debuted on October 1, 1982. In theory, this theme park is inspired by Walt's philosophies and passions. The two regions of the park seek to celebrate innovation, human achievement, and cutting-edge technology, in addition to an appreciation for Mother Earth and her culturally diverse inhabitants.

These celebrations of our world can be experienced in the neighborhoods called World Celebration, World Nature, World Discovery, and World Showcase. The two distinct areas of Epcot are separated by the forty-acre **World Showcase Lagoon.**

Let's start the walk in and make our way to the iconic centerpiece of the park: Spaceship Earth.

At 180 feet tall, the geodesic sphere was inspired by the geodesic domes created by architect R. Buckminster Fuller during the 1940s. Fuller was never able to achieve a geodesic sphere as large as the one seen at Epcot, but he did leave an indelible mark on the park. Fuller was the one to coin the term Spaceship Earth, which came from this quote during the 1960s: "I've often heard people say: 'I wonder what it would feel like to be on board a spaceship,' and the answer is very simple. What does it feel like? That's all we have ever experienced. We are all astronauts on a little spaceship called Earth."

WALT DISNEY WORLD
MONORAIL SYSTEM

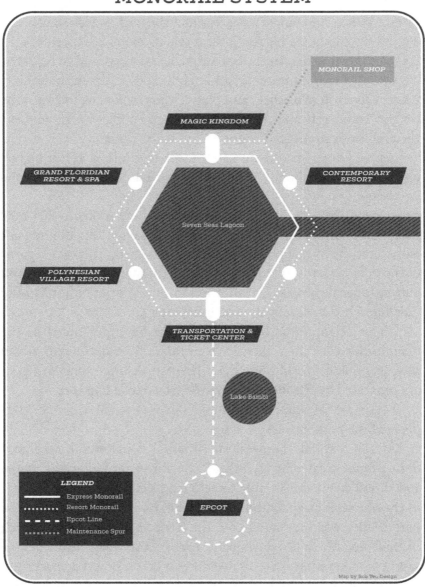

So, how did Disney's iconic geodesic sphere come to be? Legendary Imagineer John Hench explains in his book *Designing Disney*:

> At our first design meeting, the engineers showed a drawing that pictured a dome sitting directly on the ground. We needed a sphere, however; I asked if the dome could instead rest on a round platform with legs underneath to hold it up, which would allow us to suspend the bottom quarter of a sphere from the underside of the platform, completing the sphere.
>
> After several days, the engineers concluded that yes, my idea would work, but that it would be expensive. The geosphere we built was 164 feet in diameter, standing 18 feet off the ground on three sets of double legs [buried from 120 to 180 feet deep] with more than 2 million cubic feet of interior space. It so far has withstood winds of up to 200 miles an hour. It wasn't complicated at all, really. I was simply able to visualize how the self-supporting dome could be built as a perfect sphere seeming to float on its legs.

As John explained in an interview with the *Orlando Sentinel* on October 24, 1982:

> The columns of Spaceship Earth are constructed to reach out like beckoning arms. "I defy anyone who is depressed to still be depressed when they walk through here," Hench says. Nothing is happenstance, and Hench knows the reason behind each detail.

All in all, the sphere weighs in at sixteen million pounds and actually consists of two spheres. The inner sphere has a thick, protective rubber membrane, and over top of the membrane is the outer sphere, made up of 11,324 aluminum alloy panels. The sphere has a sophisticated gutter system to collect rainwater and send it back to the World Showcase lagoon.

Let's hop aboard the spaceship and watch as audio-animatronics show us the evolution of communication, from the Stone Age to the Computer Age.

This sixteen-minute history lesson, which was created by renowned author Ray Bradbury.

Many of the original scenes written by Bradbury from the 1980s are still true to his vision today.

As you travel back in time, the transitions between time and place are smooth and seamless, and there are plenty of hidden Mickeys and other tidbits to observe during your voyage. I'll point out a few for you. Also, don't forget to see if you can spot John from the Carousel of Progress.

The second scene you will see, the first with audio-animatronics, begins when you enter the cave. There is a man speaking, with antlers on his head and cave paintings behind him. On the thirty-fifth anniversary of the opening of Epcot, on October 1, 2017, Disney revealed what the caveman is saying and the English translation.

> Mahree mooteer…
> Bahl skeetom. Madostee eelgar
> Olk. Eem bahlo…Erksma erkeems
> Erkweendahl felahges oomuhday
> Heedo eelahges merk freer eelgahr.

> Feer madostee olk om feero
> Esto eelsteh orombo kail Madostee
> Oombahday madostee oombady
> Oombady ahee recondorall.

> Many moon times ago…in the bleak skytime
> (just before dawn), a great mastodon came to this valley…
> He destroyed the trees, the bushes, and the small animals with his
> wild strength.

> We all ran away from him in terror. Then we made a great fire.
> We surrounded him with our torches of fire and then the mastodon became afraid and he ran from us. Then, in our valley—we were no longer afraid.

The next notable scene has more to do with smell than sight. As you approach the scene portraying the fall of Rome, the scent of burning wood is very prominent—great use of the smellitizer here!

Just after this scene, where Jewish and Islamic scholars are seated on the floor, look at the second bookshelf from the bottom. You should see a hidden Mickey in the form of three scrolls stacked together.

As you progress through the ride, keep an eye out for the scene featuring a radio studio. The man in the booth is talking into a microphone with the letters "WDI," which happen to be the initials for Walt Disney Imagineering.

After this scene, the attraction takes you into a typical family's living room during the moon landing. Check to the left of the television; it appears there's an album from *The Wizard of Oz*.

As an interesting side note, in the October 17, 1933, issue of the Hollywood trade paper *Variety,* there is a quick blurb about a little film about to go into production with a *Disney* influence:

> Favorable public reaction to Disney's color cartoon the *Silly Symphonies* has prompted Sam Goldwyn to plan production of *Wizard of Oz* in Technicolor.

When you exit Spaceship Earth and enter into the neighborhoods seen today, you're experiencing a much different Epcot than what was around during the first thirty years of the park's existence. When the park opened in 1982, it was considered more of an adult or sophisticated park.

Mickey Mouse and crew weren't roaming the park to greet guests, and Disney planned it this way. Imagineer Rolly Crump, whose creative fingerprints are all over Disney theme parks, recounts a story in his book, *It's Kind of a Cute Story*:

> We realized there wasn't much there for young kids to do. Scott Hennesy came up with this pavilion called EPTOT, which would have been for little kids. We made a model of our idea to show to Management.

Each section of the model represented a little kid version of all the pavilions located in EPCOT. There was one for The Living Seas, one for The Land, and so on. It was basically a mini play area based on all the big pavilions. We thought it would be a great little addition, but Marty Sklar and John Hench shot us down. They thought EPCOT was strictly for adults, and not for children.

There you have it: Epcot Center (In December 1993, the "Center" was dropped from the name, and it became just Epcot) was all about adults, the future of science and technology. There were exhibits and pavilions about energy—which featured solar panels on the roof that helped to operate the ride cars—health, transportation, and future technology.

In the early 1980s, many visitors to Epcot Center had their first interactions with not only computers, but two-way videoconferencing (think yesterday's version of FaceTime) and touchscreen computers, things we interact frequently in our daily lives today but were cutting edge and very much futuristic for the time.

Leaving Spaceship Earth, stop at the **Electric Umbrella**, where you can grab a burger, a flatbread, or, for you vegetarians out there, a very tasty Veggie Naan-wich.

Rolly Crump came up with the name for the restaurant and explained how this name came to be:

> I also did the design for the Electric Umbrella restaurant, too. It was originally called Stargate Restaurant, but that entire area was going through a re-design in the mid-1990s. The name came about one day in a meeting, when some guy asked if we would be interested in electric umbrellas to sell in EPCOT.
>
> They literally were electric umbrellas, because they had some lights on the top of them. Well, the design of them stunk, but I absolutely loved the name, and thought it would be a great title for the new restaurant.

In fact, when we pitched the idea to Michael Eisner, he liked the name so much that he wanted to name the whole damn building the Electric Umbrella! Obviously, that idea got squashed, and it turned out to be called Innoventions.

OK, so you won't find an actual electric umbrella at the Electric Umbrella, but what you will find is an electric trash can, one that talks to you. Walt Disney World takes its trash very seriously. Throughout the parks, you'll find a trash can just about every thirty feet or so; many of the cans are themed to fit into their locale within the parks. Look for the entertaining trash can near the restrooms at the Electric Umbrella. It's a bit of a trash talker!

Up next is **Mission: Space** and **Test Track**. Heading over to Mission: Space, you're go for launch! Disney partnered with NASA to create this very realistic (some will say very intense) trip into space.

If you're an adventurous, thrill-seeking person, this is an amazing, must-see, and must-Fastpass ride.

As you're queuing for the attraction, check out the **Simulation Lab**, which houses a thirty-five-foot-tall gravity wheel similar to what NASA uses to simulate gravity in deep space. Disney's involvement with the gravity wheel on display here at Mission: Space transcends theme park entertainment.

Beginning in 1955, the *Disneyland* television program aired three shows discussing the realistic possibility of space travel, "Man in Space," "Man and the Moon," and "Mars and Beyond."

These programs, while containing animation and humor, were very much scientific and factual, and they were an overwhelming success. Disney collaborated with Dr. Werner von Braun, both on-screen and off, to develop this anthology—as his official NASA biography states, "Werner was one of the most important rocket developers and champions of space exploration in the twentieth century."

During the episodes "Man and the Moon" and "Mars and Beyond," von Braun illustrated and explained the possibilities for using a gravity wheel concept in space. His concept happened to

be 250 feet wide, would move at three revolutions per minute, and would provide artificial gravity in space.

Many folks from government and within the aeronautical community acknowledge that Disney's involvement in promoting the notion of space travel during the 1950s helped the space and rocketry program gain momentum and come to fruition.

Mission: Space has two flavors, so to speak, **Green (Earth Mission)** and **Orange (Mars Mission)**. The Orange Mission uses centrifuge technology similar to what NASA uses to simulate the physical experiences astronauts would encounter during spaceflight.

A trip on Orange spins and tilts to simulate the speed and G-forces of a spacecraft launch and reentry. A trip here provides you with a slingshot around the moon and then a tough landing on Mars. Disney even reached out to NASA to replicate what a landing on the Martian planet would look and feel like. When creating the ride, more than 650 Imagineers spent over 350,000 hours (the equivalent of roughly forty years!) to develop the attraction.

New for fall 2017 is a revised trip aboard Green. This experience is less intense and provides a realistic orbit around the Earth, where you can see the Hawaiian Islands and the Northern Lights.

These views are realistic and authentic, as they were captured by astronauts and cosmonauts during their stay on the International Space Station, which is also viewed during this ride.

The Green experience doesn't use a centrifuge and opts for a simulated spaceflight via a motion simulator. If you're a bit claustrophobic, you may not be a big fan of either Orange or Green, as the compartments you ride in are a bit cramped.

Fans of the show *Firefly* may recognize Gina Torres as your mission guide. As you leave the attraction, notice the patterned asteroid concrete. There's even a hidden Mickey or two hiding in the pattern.

Now that you're back on Earth, get ready to reach peak land speeds of nearly sixty-five miles per hour as you whip around **Test Track, Presented by Chevrolet.**

General Motors has had a presence within Epcot since opening day, when the company sponsored the now-extinct attraction World of Motion, which Test Track replaced.

As you approach the attraction, you'll notice the building is circular, resembling a wheel. Inside you will find a world of automotive design, as you're able to create your own virtual concept car and then board a "SimCar" ride vehicle to race through a thrilling series of performance tests during your journey.

This ride is unique, interactive, and very fast, along with being extremely high tech. As described in the *Imagineering Field Guide to Epcot*:

> The technology employed in Test Track rivals that of any theme park attraction ever produced. Each car carries on board more than enough processing power to run the Space Shuttle.
>
> It's a very complex effort to manage each car through its paces, at vastly varying speeds (including a complete stop), all the while maintaining the proper intervals between vehicles. Each vehicle is equipped with onboard audio-visual systems. This vehicle, combined with many complicated

special effects and show elements made Test Track one of WDI's most challenging achievements.

The chassis of each vehicle is made entirely of composite materials, meaning there is no steel between the front and rear wheels. Each vehicle carries three on-board computers and generates 250 horsepower of power.

If you emptied the body of water from the pavilion of **The Seas with Nemo & Friends** into one-gallon milk containers and laid them side by side, they would stretch for 540 miles.

At 5.7 million gallons, this pavilion is home to one of the largest man-made ocean environments in the world. When the $90 million pavilion debuted in 1986, it was the world's largest aquarium.

To celebrate the grand opening of the pavilion, Mickey Mouse put on scuba gear, as did Frank Wells, who was at the time president of Walt Disney Productions. Both man and mouse jumped into the aquarium and performed an underwater ribbon-cutting ceremony for Epcot's newest pavilion.

While it isn't the world's largest aquarium today, it is still home to over three thousand creatures across two hundred different species. Rays, sharks, turtles, fish, and coral can all be found at The Seas with Nemo & Friends, along with a few really smart dolphins.

Since the early 1990s, researchers working at The Seas have been conducting cognitive research with the dolphins on-site.

The March 1992 issue of *Popular Science* goes into detail about a giant "dolphin typewriter," roughly the size of a minivan, which was developed at Epcot. Bottlenose dolphins would poke their snouts into the "keyboard" in an effort to communicate with their trainers.

The research program into dolphin communication and cognition is still going strong at Epcot. If you're interested, head over to Google and search for the article "Cognitive Research with Dolphins (*Tursiops truncatus*) at Disney's The Seas: A Program for Enrichment, Science, Education, and Conservation" from the *International Journal of Comparative Psychology*. It provides an excellent overview of the research being conducted.

But it's not all science and research at the pavilion. You can go talk to a turtle at **Turtle Talk with Crush,** or board a "clamobile" and go under the sea to try track down Nemo from the Pixar movie *Finding Nemo.* Don't worry; you won't get wet, as this ride is on land.

You're technically looking for Nemo on land, as the only water you're experiencing is through the visual effects. However, the pavilion adjacent to The Seas with Nemo & Friends is the **Land Pavilion,** which takes you on a boat ride, on actual water! I think Disney may have confused the modes of transportation for these two rides.

The Land Pavilion has much more to offer than merely a boat ride. It's dedicated to telling the story of our interaction with Earth, with a strong emphasis on agriculture, which is seen throughout the boat ride, **Living with the Land.** Here are a few interesting tidbits and things to look out for, should you take the fourteen-minute boat ride.

The attraction offers a great perspective and appreciation for how our food is grown. Throughout the four greenhouses, witness how chocolate, coffee, vanilla, tomatoes, and rice, many of the common things we eat every day, are cultivated.

What the pavilion really demonstrates well are the nontraditional techniques on display, such as the nutrient film technique and hydroponics; both occur without the use of soil to grow plants.

These techniques can yield some pretty impressive fruits and vegetables, such as a nine-pound lemon and a one-of-a-kind "tomato tree," which has produced thirty-two thousand tomatoes from a single vine. These tomatoes, along with the more than thirty tons of fruits and vegetables grown at the Land Pavilion, are served in Walt Disney World restaurants.

When you board your boat, look at the colorful mural on the wall; there are a few hidden Mickeys throughout. As you cruise along through the scenes of the attraction, note the number on the mailbox of the farmhouse; it's 82, the year Epcot opened.

If you notice above the house, you can see the **Garden Grill.**

This restaurant offers a unique dining experience, as it rotates ever so slightly, affording you great views of the rain forest, farmhouse, and prairie scenes of Living with Land.

If you do have a meal at the Garden Gill, when the farmhouse comes around, you get to check out the second floor and the fully furnished bedroom of the home, which you're unable to see during the boat ride.

A little side note: breakfast is a great meal to have here. It's an all-you-can-eat character breakfast featuring Chip and Dale, and if you get an early reservation, it's a great opportunity to hop on Soarin' with little to no wait if you're able to finish breakfast just as Soarin' opens.

Much like The Seas with Nemo & Friends, the Land Pavilion is also conducting its fair share of research. Depending on the day and time of your trip on Living with the Land, you may just see Disney's scientists working in the lab. These aren't audio-animatronics or folks working with props; these are real scientists doing actual work!

The lab first opened to public view in 1988, as covered by the *Orlando Sentinel* on October 8 of that year:

> "It's a real laboratory but also an exhibit to stimulate interest among young people, maybe even stimulate some scientific vocations," Lyng said.
>
> Visitors can view the 500-square-foot lab at the end of a boat ride through The Land pavilion, where the story of agriculture is told through animation and exhibits of various crops.
>
> Plants such as pineapples, strawberries, bananas and peanuts developed through tissue culture propagation in the laboratory are used to replenish the living exhibits as well as provide some of the fresh fruit and produce for the attraction's restaurants, Epcot officials said. The lab has been in operation since the attraction opened in 1982 but only now is being opened for public viewing.
>
> The laboratory is a joint effort of Disney, the US Department of Agriculture and Kraft Inc., corporate sponsor of

The Land. "Our major goal is to communicate the excitement of agriculture…and the fact that it is high technology," said Henry Robitaille, manager of The Land and director of biotechnology research for the lab.

He said an estimated 10 million visitors a year will see the exhibit. Research at the lab also will help advance understanding of plant genetics and development of crops with improved characteristics such as drought resistance and improved nutrition.

Over the years, the lab has accomplished some very noteworthy science. During the 1990s, Epcot's scientists worked on genetically altered peanuts to create a more nutritious peanut oil.

Next, they worked with genetically altered peach trees to create peaches that stay firm longer. In the early to mid-2000s, the lab worked to molecularly alter the design for the pear tree.

Scientists worked to create a new rootstock for pear trees that would stunt the growth of the trees, making them shorter and easier to grow and harvest. This would make the trees more attractive for industry, as they would be more productive. None of the genetically altered or engineered plants the lab works with ever makes its way onto your plate at Walt Disney World.

If you care to learn more about the science and agriculture at the Land Pavilion, there is a "Behind the Seeds Tour." Information about the tour can be found at the desk located near Soarin', which is our next stop.

Now boarding all passengers for an exhilarating adventure! Get ready for a true wonder of Walt Disney World as you prepare to hang glide around the globe with **Soarin'.**

The Imagineers pulled out all the stops when they created this attraction. As you're raised forty feet in the air (approximately one million pounds of steel provide the structure for the ride, and thirty-seven tons are hoisted each time a flight leaves), you're immersed in a 180-degree, eighty-foot IMAX projection dome; your entire field of vision is captivated by panoramic scenes of the world. The attraction is visually stunning, and the sense of flight is realistic.

Soarin' offers a bird's-eye view of many of the wonders of the world, and the smellitizer pumps out smells of the grasses of Africa, the ocean breeze over the South Pacific, and roses over India. All the while, the London Studio Orchestra delights with the attraction's musical score. This is a *definite* Fastpass attraction.

As you're waiting for your flight, if the chief flight attendant, Patrick, sounds and looks familiar, that's Patrick Warburton, known for his work on *Seinfeld*, *Family Guy*, and *Rules of Engagement.*

As you walk out of the Land Pavilion, it's hard not to notice the beautiful mosaics that cover both walls of the building. The mosaic is supposed to represent a slice through the Earth, portraying the different layers of the crust and the mantle.

The mosaic was done by the father and daughter-in-law team of Hanns and Monika Scharff. This dynamic duo was also the team that created the mosaics in Cinderella Castle.

The mosaic at the Land Pavilion is composed of polished and unpolished marble and granite, slices of brick, Venetian glass, Byzantine glass, ceramic tile, and Venetian mirrored glass, as well as smooth and rippled gold leaf.

I had the pleasure of speaking with Claudius Scharff, Hanns's son and Monika's husband. He shared this story with me:

> My dad and wife were given the commission for the mural. They asked Disney for the exact measurements of the mural, which Disney could not provide because the walls were still under construction. Disney flew my wife and dad to Orlando (first class) to measure the wall themselves. They couldn't do it because of the ongoing construction. Disney decided to give the go-ahead based on the drawing because of the lead time involved with doing the mural.
>
> It turned out that that the drawing and subsequent mosaic were three feet greater than the finished wall. My dad and

wife and the Disney artist were devastated and were at a complete loss of what to do.

I suggested they ask Disney to let the mural flow into the floor. Disney agreed, and thus is the mural on the wall and into the floor, and no one is the wiser.

Claudius tapped into his imagination to problem solve at the Land Pavilion. And what do you know—the building next to the Land Pavilion is bursting with imagination!

Everyone needs a lovable purple dragon in their lives, so let's go meet the one residing at Epcot. **Journey into Imagination with Figment** is located next to The Land Pavilion. Before you walk in to meet the little guy, look at the water fountain out front; the water is flowing up as opposed to down.

Over the years, Figment has become a beloved member of the Disney family, holding a special spot in the hearts of many visitors to Epcot. Today, he's a host and guide through the Imagination Institute.

When you enter the attraction, witty references to Disney movies are immediate. Walking through the hallway leading to the attraction, notice the names on the doors of the institute. You'll see Dean Finder; this is a reference to DreamFinder, the original host of the attraction; Figment was his sidekick. (Losing DreamFinder and the original concept and show behind this pavilion is a bit of a sore subject for diehard members of the Disney community.)

The name Professor Wayne Szalinski may look familiar here as well. Professor Wayne is a character from the movie *Honey, I Shrunk the Kids.*

Next up, Professor Phillip Brainard is a reference to a character in *The Absent-Minded Professor* and in a reincarnation of the story via the movie *Flubber*, starring Robin Williams.

As you approach Dr. Nigel Channing's office (Channing is played by renowned actor Eric Idle), have a listen. It sounds a bit chaotic in there!

During your trip through Imagination, you may notice a red-and-white letterman jacket with the letter *M*. This is for Medfield College, the fictional college from the film *The Absent-Minded Professor.*

There are a few other things to look out for during your tour through the Sensory Labs. When you go through the Sight Room, see if you can spot the Mickey Mouse head on the whiteboard.

When you enter the upside-down room, check out the table with food; you'll find onion rings assembled to resemble a hidden Mickey.

In the final scene, Figment is using a piece of sheet music as a hang glider. The sheet has a few bars of the attraction's legendary theme song, "One Little Spark."

One last story involving Figment may be the most entertaining yet: how he got his name. It comes again from an interview with Imagineer Tony Baxter:

> Yes, I came up with the name and the idea. Steve Kirk, Andy Gaskill, and X. Atencio gave him form. I was watching *Magnum, P.I.* with Tom Selleck on TV. He was in the garden,

and the butler Higgins had all these plants, and they were all uprooted. It was a mess. Magnum had been hiding a goat out there, and the goat had eaten the plants.

Higgins said, "Magnum! Magnum! Come out here! Look at this! Something has been eating all the plants in the garden," and Magnum says, "Oh, it is just a figment of your imagination." And Higgins says, "Figments don't eat grass."

I thought, there is this name, the word "figment" that in English means a sprightly little character. But no one has ever visualized it, no one had ever drawn what a figment is.

So, here is great word that already has a great meaning to people, but no one has ever seen what one looks like. So we had a name that was just waiting for us to design the shape for it.

I came to work and said, "I have the answer for our show; it is going to be Figment." We had come out with "Dream-Finder" earlier. That was easy; he was a Santa Claus type who is wise and older and knows all the great things, a great thinker. But we needed a childlike character that had like a one-second attention span and was a little crazy.

Another strong part in that show was the presence of the Sherman Brothers, Richard and Robert, the songwriting team from *Mary Poppins* and *It's a Small World*. Once again, they were like idols to me. With my role as director, I had the ability to go after top talent, so I said, "I would like to have the Sherman Brothers come in." And they said, "OK, fine." And I thought, Wow! because they were so important to me.

They are wonderful; they are such nice guys. What I found right away is that when the Sherman Brothers believe in a show, and when they understand an idea fully, they write better music. When they do not feel that good about it, the music has an absence of wonder, since they were not able to sense any magic to build the themes on.

It was a fun time and a real challenge because we had to figure out what imagination is. It took us six months to come up with a simple thing: "You gather, you store, and you recombine." Right now, Didier, you are gathering information from me and you are storing it and you are going to recombine it with things you already know and create a new product, which is what you will write.

Whether you are a writer or a scientist or an artist or a teacher or someone making a cake, it is the same thing: "gather, store, and recombine." So we gave those words to the Sherman Brothers, and they wrote "One Little Spark" based on that premise.

That last story just about wraps up Journey into Imagination with Figment. But before we tackle the second half of Epcot and the World Showcase, there is one more secret I forgot to mention.

Each pavilion or attraction actually has hidden or secret VIP lounges, accessible to the employees of the company that sponsors the attraction.

Let me backtrack a bit here. The Walt Disney Company has traditionally relied on corporate sponsors for both Disneyland and Walt Disney World, to defray the costs and maintenance of the attractions they develop.

This business of sponsorship was leveraged heavily for the construction of Epcot, both throughout Future World and the World Showcase. An article in the *Orlando Sentinel* from October 24, 1982, sheds a bit of light on Disney's innovative way to finance their park:

> They have already made sales pitches from Russia to Japan, but Walt Disney World's globe trotting sales team is on the road again in search of additional participants for Epcot Center.
>
> The search is the continuation of one that began seven years ago and netted more than 20 participants for the billion-dollar

project. The Disney company has relied on sponsors for its theme parks to supply funds since Walt Disney had to muster enough money to pay for his first theme park in the 1950s.

In return, the sponsors harvest a promotional bonanza for their products. Now about 35 companies sponsor attractions and exhibits in Disneyland and Disney World's Magic Kingdom. At Disney World alone, participants chipped in about $8 million in 1981.

Epcot's participants will contribute more heavily. They are reported to be paying Disney between $10 million and $50 million apiece over a 10 year period, for a total of $300 million.

Some of the cash is in, but Disney is footing most of the start-up costs for Epcot, said Jack Lindquist, senior vice president of advertising, publicity, promotion and public relations for Walt Disney Productions.

Lindquist said the search began in 1975 for Epcot World Showcase participants. The sales team tried working through government channels. They found interest and enthusiasm, but no money. So within a year, the Disney team began approaching private industry, Lindquist said. "When we started out we were very naïve and ignorant," he said. "The company had not been involved in the international market before. It was 'a long learning process," he said.

Lindquist said other Disney representatives found that foreign officials didn't understand the Disney theme parks. So they began bringing government and industry officials to Disney World to show them firsthand what the theme park is all about.

As the Epcot concept expanded to include Future World, the company turned to US corporations to participate in the project. Disney officials used a variety of selling points as they wooed perspective participants. They said the participants' names and products would be exposed to millions of visitors expected to pass through Epcot.

Sponsors are allowed to use the Disney name in promotions and publicity. In addition, Lindquist said the company assigned a marketing representative to each participant to help develop promotions. Most participants also will have an office and lounge for corporate use in the pavilions.

Although sponsor names will be apparent to visitors, Disney officials have maintained creative control over the shows to keep them from becoming too commercial. Lindquist said the company also relied on advisory boards to keep the shows accurate as well as entertaining. But sponsors will have some areas in which their products will be on display.

Kodak sponsors the Journey Into Imagination pavilion. It will feature a ride exploring the imagination process with two Audio animatronic figures, Dreamfinder and Figment, as hosts.

The ride will not open until December. The attraction also features an area for visitors to tinker with electronic devices producing light, sound and three-dimensional film.

Michael Donnelly, coordinator of promotional activities for Kodak, said it will be difficult to measure the impact of this type of program. But he said the company's intent "is not to promote sales per se." He said the company hopes visitors will leave with a good feeling about Kodak.

Kraft's sponsorship of The Land pavilion was a natural because most of the products the company markets come from the land, said Dick Courtice, vice president and director of The Land pavilion. Courtice said it will take visitors about an hour to tour the pavilion. It will be hard to measure impact, he said.

Courtice said he didn't think exposure would prompt the homemaker to go out and buy two more boxes of Kraft cheese. But he said that if a shopper is in the store examining a couple of products, pleasant memories of The Land might tip the scales in Kraft's favor.

Is the sponsorship a high price to pay for promotion? Courtice said assuming the cost of sponsoring the pavilion was $50 million, the price would be 50 cents a head if 10 million people pass through the attraction. "I can't send them a brochure and a long story for that price," he said. He declined to say what Kraft was paying for its sponsorship.

Disney officials will continue recruiting even though Epcot has opened. Lindquist said the company still is looking for sponsors for the Living Seas and the Health pavilions. He said the company also is working with the governments of Spain and Morocco on pavilions for the World Showcase area.

Other pavilions in the design stage include one for Israel and one for Equatorial Africa. There are about nine more spaces available in the World Showcase, he said. The selling is never easy but, Lindquist said the job will be easier now that Epcot has opened and people have seen it.

That's a pretty good overview of the marketing and sponsorship opportunities when Epcot first opened.

Most of the original sponsorships and a few original pavilions have gone by the wayside, and many of the VIP lounges have been abandoned. But if you know where to look, you can still see a lingering reminder of what used to be.

Spaceship Earth: Siemens sponsored the attraction until October 2017. The lounge is located above "Project Tomorrow: Inventing the Wonders of the Future." You can see the windows for it if you're looking at the back side of Spaceship Earth from the center of Innovations plaza.

Mission: Space: Hewlett-Packard sponsored this lounge until 2013. There is an entrance down a corridor to the left of Mission: Space's entrance.

Test Track: This lounge is sponsored by General Motors, current as of 2017. To the right of the main entrance to the attraction, there is a GM plaque on the wall that leads the way.

The Seas with Nemo and Friends: The lounge was sponsored by United Technologies until 1998. The entrance is to the left of the entrance to the Coral Reef restaurant.

The Land: Nestle sponsored this until 2009. Chiquita currently sponsors only the attraction Living with the Land. When in the lobby and facing the restaurant, the Garden Grill, you can see the windows of the lounge above the restaurant.

Journey into Imagination with Figment: Kodak was the sponsor until 2010. This lounge is actually accessible if you're a Disney Vacation Club member. Flash your DVC membership card, and you will have access to the second-floor lounge. You can gain access from the ImageWorks merchandise location within the Imagination Pavilion.

Obviously, these areas are restricted unless you're an employee or have permission to venture inside. As stated, most of the lounges aren't currently operating but may be rented for an event.

As the article from the *Sentinel* states, another area of Epcot where Disney used the sponsorship program was the World Showcase, a kaleidoscope of nations featuring architecturally authentic buildings and backdrops of culture, arts, and entertainment from eleven nations and an African-themed outpost. So leave your passport at home and get ready to stroll around the world in roughly 1.3 miles.

Since our last destination was Journey into Imagination with Figment, let's proceed into the World Showcase from the entrance closest to Figment, which would bring us first to the United States' neighbor to the north, Canada. (If we started around the World Showcase from the other end, our trip would start with Mexico, the neighbor to the south.)

O Canada! Where do we begin? Let's start with the architecture and theme. The **Canada Pavilion** is a combination of Native Indian villages, an ornate French-inspired chateau, and the maritime areas such as Prince Edward Island and Nova Scotia, topped off with the ruggedness of the Canadian Rockies.

The geographic and cultural diversity of Canada's regions are symbolized and represented with accuracy. There are thirty-foot totem poles that mark the Native Indian villages, where a log cabin and its trading post carry out the north woods theme.

In January 2017, two new totem poles were introduced to the pavilion. Carved by Tsimshian artisan David Boxley, the two poles each tell a unique story. The Eagle Totem Pole tells a cultural tale in which a boy finds an eagle caught in a net on a beach and frees it. Years later, when hunger strikes the boy's tribe, he walks on the same beach, only to find the eagle there waiting for him with food—paying him back for his kindness years ago.

The bottom of this totem pole also tells the story of how a family of beavers taught a human family the importance of treating all creatures—human and animal—with respect.

The Whale Totem Pole depicts the tale of the first potlatch, a ceremonial feast celebrated by the Nagunaks and creatures of the undersea world.

After the totem poles were installed, the Git- Hoan Dancers (People of the Salmon) performed a dedication ceremony. Based in Washington State, Git-Hoan members can trace their ancestral roots to some of the main tribes of southeast Alaska, the Tsimshian, the Haida, and the Tlingit.

Another distinctive landmark of the pavilion that will attract your eye is the Hotel du Canada, featuring its nineteenth-century limestone chateau architecture. Before you reach the building, note the beautiful flower gardens inspired by Victoria's Butchart Gardens, and behind the building are the scenic Rocky Mountains—forced perspective is in full effect here—and a flowing waterfall.

Tucked inside the boulders of the mountain is a theater featuring a film about the country. If you decide to stay for the movie, as you exit the theater and walk up the path, you will pass Canada's restaurant, **Le Cellier Steakhouse**. It's a great meal (try the cheddar cheese soup), but you will most likely have a difficult time walking in and grabbing a table.

Definitely make reservations to dine here for lunch or dinner—and when you're checking in for your reservation, look behind the check-in desk. See if you can spot the three wine bottles arranged to form a hidden Mickey!

As we will see during our trip through the World Showcase, each pavilion features the culture, cuisine, architecture, and friendly faces of that country.

Disney staffs the World Showcase (and, to an extent, some other areas of Walt Disney World) via their Cultural Representative Program. Acceptance into the program allows young folks from the countries represented in the World Showcase to come live in America for one year or so and work at the park.

Disney touts the program to prospective applicants as a way to not only earn money but experience working and living the Disney way. Those accepted into the Cultural Representative Program will not only work in Epcot but will live in Disney housing with others from the program.

As its website says, "Whether you're assigned to a one, two, three or four-bedroom apartment, you'll share a bedroom with one or two Disney International Programs participants. Often times, your roommate(s) will be from another country, allowing you to learn about other cultures as you share your own.

"In addition, you'll improve your communication skills by being immersed in an English-speaking environment. You'll also learn about guest services directly from the company that's showing the world how it's done."

Leaving Canada, you'll find that Tudor cottages, cobblestone streets, and architecture spanning Elizabethan to Regency await you in the **United Kingdom**.

Approaching the UK, you'll notice the buildings' facades change throughout the area. The architectural style is representative of different styles from the 1500s to the 1800s and the locale of merry old England.

From London Victorian to Yorkshire Manor, Tudor to Georgian, Hyde Park and Regency to a Shakespearean cottage, Imagineers spent three years researching historic sites throughout England, Scotland, and Wales.

Signs, chimneys, lampposts, and even a bright-red English telephone booth lend themselves to the charm of a jolly holiday in London.

One of the beautiful parts of Epcot's United Kingdom is Britannia Square, which emulates Hyde Park and features a gazebo and a hedge maze modeled on the one at Somerleyton Hall.

The facades of the buildings overlooking this area were taken from the set drawings from *Mary Poppins*. This would be a perfect setting for a wedding—and if your wallet can afford it, Disney can make that happen for you and your forty-eight closest friends and family members.

Another remarkable detail can be seen at the Sportsman's Shoppe, which is modeled after King Henry VIII's Hampton Court Palace. The four regions of the United Kingdom, England, Scotland, Northern Ireland, and Wales, are all represented via crests on the windows.

Across from the Sportsman's Shoppe is the **Rose and Crown Pub**. As you're walking across to the pub, turn back around and look at the sign for the Sportsman's Shoppe. The soccer ball, tennis racket, and rugby ball form the shape of a hidden Mickey.

The sign for the Rose and Crown Pub has a witty phrase on it. In Latin, it's *Otium cum Dignitate,* which translates to Leisure with Dignity, the motto of the Rose and Crown.

A few weeks before the pub was scheduled to open, a battle was brewing. According to the employee newsletter, *Epcot Center News Brief,* from September 19, 1982,

> Forty-three degrees cold. It's a enough to send a shiver to the soul of a countryman. "Drinking it that cold, it has no flavor, you see," says Bill Windsor, the 27 year old Scotsman who is assistant supervisor of the Rose & Crown. Bill says the ales, lager beers and stout are at their flavorful best at about 52 degrees Fahrenheit.

> At the temperature preferred by American "beer" drinkers (as low as 38–40 degrees), Bill says the brews are merely "wet and cold."

> Randy Hiatt, Manager of Research and Food Development for the Food Division, acknowledges that at 52 degrees the drinks are "smoother, and they have good flavor." Yet, from the perspective of an American, they are also "warm…it's like drinking Coke with no ice; it's not refreshing." Drinks

are being poured at 43 degrees out of deference to the large number of Americans visiting the pub.

It appears the American tastes won out. For several years after the opening of Epcot, the pub did use a specially designed ale warmer to maintain your Guinness at a proper fifty-two degrees, but today, it's typically cold beer at the Rose and Crown. Apparently, Americans love authenticity, except when it comes to beer!

Beer-drinking accuracy aside, the Rose and Crown accurately portrays the four different styles of pubs found throughout the United Kingdom.

As the *Imagineering Field Guide to Epcot* states:

> The city or "street" pub dating from the 1890s Victorian city center—features brick and wood paneling on the facade and gives us our elegant mahogany bar, the etched glass, and the molded plastic ceiling.

> Dickensian pub, after the Cheshire Cheese pub in London— offers a brick walled flagstone terrace with covered tables, a slate roof and half timbered, Elizabethan-styled exterior.

> Waterfront, or "river" pub, on the canal lock—a facade with a modest stone building, a clay tile roof and decorative doorways, stone terrace with an iron fence lining the homey village-inn-styled dining room.

> Country, "provincial" pub from the suburbs of the 17th and 18th centuries—a slate roof, plaster exterior with stone-quoined corners.

Working our way around the forty-acre World Showcase Lagoon, our next visit is to France. Here at Epcot, we're not taking the Chunnel (the short name often used for the Channel Tunnel, running from Folkestone in the south of England to Calais in northern France), and we aren't flying. We're walking; but there is an interesting story involving airplanes, the UK pavilion, and the France pavilion at Epcot.

On October 18, 1982 to celebrate the opening of the World Showcase at Epcot, for the first time in history, two supersonic airplanes known as the Concorde touched down within a split second of each other.

One plane was from British Airways and the other from Air France; both companies were early sponsors of pavilions at Epcot's World Showcase. The two planes typically only flew into New York or Washington, DC, but due to their involvement at Epcot, Disney arranged for both planes to touch down simultaneously in Orlando. More than thirty-five thousand people witnessed this live.

As you leave the United Kingdom (on foot), just before you cross the bridge leading to Paree, you have the opportunity to exit Epcot via the International Gateway—this is also the spot to have a smoke or two.

Exiting here, you can walk to the Boardwalk, the Beach Club, the Yacht Club, and the Dolphin and Swan Resorts. If you're really interested in adding some steps to your Fitbit, you can even follow the signs for the walkway to Disney's Hollywood Studios.

If you're not that adventurous, just catch one of the Friendship boats, which make stops at the above-mentioned hotels and then offer continuing boat service to Disney's Hollywood Studios. But we aren't leaving just yet; it's time for Disney's version of "the City of Lights."

As you cross the bridge into **France** from the UK, you're walking on a replica of the Pont des Arts, a pedestrian bridge in Paris that crosses the River Seine and links the Institut de France and the central square of the Palais du Louvre.

One of the first things to catch your eye is the replica Eiffel Tower, created from the original blueprints drawn by Gustave Eiffel. Epcot's version is roughly one-tenth the size, standing about 103 feet tall.

Much like the experience in the United Kingdom, the Parisian cityscape Disney crafted here is the Paris of yesterday, specifically between 1850 and 1900. This is evident as you stroll along and approach the Palais du Cinéma, which is inspired by Chateau de Fontainebleau, one of the largest French royal châteaux.

This medieval castle and subsequent palace served as a residence for the French monarchs from Louis VII to Napoleon III.

Ornate and *elegant* are two great words to describe Epcot's Palais, and the appreciation for all things French is only heightened when you watch *Impressions de France*, the eighteen-minute film shown at the theater.

Much like the experience at the Canada pavilion, this film showcasing France's grandeur and charm—with a truly amazing musical score from the French composers Debussy, Saint-Saens, and Ravel—runs throughout the day in a 350-seat theater with a panoramic two-hundred-degree view. It's similar to the Circle Vision view in Canada, but here in France, you're seated.

If films about France aren't your thing, don't worry; the food and drinks here are spectacular. If you've always dreamed of a classic French meal but never had the opportunity, **Monsieur Paul** just may be what you're looking for.

"Monsieur Paul restaurant introduces the culture and the authentic taste of French cuisine that Chef Paul Bocuse has been preaching to the world," says Jerome Bocuse, son of the famous French chef and president and owner of the company that runs Monsieur Paul in the France pavilion at Epcot World Showcase.

The decor captures classic French architecture, with bright colors and a touch of modernism. "The restaurant inherits the air of hospitality of my father's restaurant as each staff member goes above and beyond to offer the warmest, most inviting service possible," says Jerome.

Monsieur Paul is decorated with mementoes of Chef Paul Bocuse's extraordinary culinary honors. He was awarded three Michelin stars for forty-eight straight years at his famous Lyon restaurant, Auberge du Pont de Collognes.

The Bocuse family has an important place in the culinary world, most recently with Paul Bocuse being named Chef of the Century by the Culinary Institute of America. "Monsieur Paul" was the name cooks used in the 1950s to address a young Paul Bocuse in the kitchen, to differentiate him from his father, George Bocuse, also an established chef—and the nickname has stuck throughout Paul's life.

"My father, Paul Bocuse, first opened Les Chefs de France here at Epcot in 1982 with Chefs Gaston Lenôtre and Roger Vergé—it was the first and only Bocuse-affiliated restaurant in America," says Bocuse. "Things have now come full circle, with me having the opportunity to open a restaurant here bearing my father's name. I've seen the dining scene change, and we are evolving with it."

The aim is not to replicate the dishes from the Lyon restaurant but to serve both classics and interpretations of them in a setting that's more contemporary. "We want guests to experience authentic French cuisine—but they don't have to dress up and spend a lot of time," says Jerome. "We've thoughtfully adapted Monsieur Paul to our guests' vacation experience."

If five-star French cuisine is not what you're looking for, or if you need something on the faster, sweeter side of things, grab a pastry from the **Patisserie**, or kick off your drinking tour of the world with an Orange Slush made with Grand Marnier, orange juice, and other libations. There are definitely more than a few things to enjoy at the France pavilion.

A relative newcomer to the World Showcase is **Morocco**, having debuted in 1984, rather than when Epcot opened in 1982. To ensure an authentic portrayal of the country, King Hassan II sent some of his craftsman to Epcot to collaborate with the Imagineers on the design and construction of the pavilion. From the *Orlando Sentinel* on September 14, 1984:

> The Morocco pavilion is the first to be constructed using government money from the sponsoring nation. Steve Baker, director of participant affairs at Epcot says most World Showcase exhibits are paid for by private investors and Walt Disney World.
>
> Although he won't release exact figures, Baker says the

Moroccan government paid a little more than half the cost of building the Morocco Showcase. Walt Disney World paid the rest.

Since construction began in July 1983, a similar spirit of cooperation has prevailed between the American tradespeople working on the project and the 19 Moroccan artisans who decorated it. (The artisans usually spoke French, the language of commerce in Morocco.)

"You can imagine the kinds of difficulties you might have," says project manager Jeff Burton, "but beyond a few communications problems there were zero problems."

The result of the artisans' four months of work is an exhibit that overflows with colors and repeating designs and characteristic of Morocco's Islamic art. Ceramic tile, brass lamps, carved plaster and cedar decorate the courtyard at the pavilion entrance. Ceilings, walls and floors of the Gallery of Arts and History and the tourism information building, which flank the entrance, are similarly ornate and colorful.

Through the courtyard's ogee, or wishbone-shaped arch, are reproductions of the Koutoubia and Chellah minarets (found in the cities of Marrakesh and Chellah, respectively), a façade of a traditional Moroccan home and a copy of the Nejjarine Fountain, found in the city of Fez.

In all of these, ornate Moroccan handiwork is dominant. (Absent from these decorations, however are depictions of living things. Such depictions are forbidden by Islamic law.)

Less ornate and formal is the retail market, or medina, typical of the older parts of a Moroccan city. As in most medinas, the displays of leather goods, ceramics, carpets and brass goods at the Morocco Showcase spill into the street. In keeping with Epcot standards, however, the market is otherwise immaculate, and the shopkeepers are uniformly costumed.

Another interesting story from the *Sentinel* from May 27, 1984, elaborated on the work of the Moroccan craftsmen:

> Altogether, 19 Moroccan artisans arrived in Orlando in late January, eight to carve intricate designs in plaster and eleven to assemble the tile panels along walls and columns, most of them working on the site of the pavilion itself.
>
> The tile artists, who came from the same cooperative workshop in Morocco with their master, first spent three months deciding on the colors and designs that they would later assemble and mount on blank walls at Epcot.
>
> They prepared the tiles in Morocco, cutting countless non-representational shapes and packing nine tons of them in nearly 400 crates for shipment to Lake Buena Vista.
>
> "Precutting and sending tiles was an economy move," Burton says. "That way all they had to do was reassemble them in panel form and install them."
>
> Nonetheless, assembling the lacy patterns that cover most of the space set aside for them wasn't always a cut and  dried process. The only rule in Islamic art—North Africans are among the most devout, following the ancient laws to the letter—is that geometric designs not portraying living things; only Allah can create life. But hundreds of individual designs can be combined in countless patterns.
>
> When the spirit moves them artisans are free to make up new patterns. On mounds

outside of the work area, near small wooden crates still partly filled with neatly cut stars, bars, crescents and ovals as tiny as sunflower seeds, are striking combinations that the master tile maker, Kandri Hassani Abdelali, laid out before he returned to Morocco.

The artisans work quickly and easily, laying chip after chip along penciled-in boundaries in patterns that they can see only in their minds' eyes.

Apprenticed around the age of 7, and skilled in every step of the trade, typical artisans like those at Epcot, just look at the design and know how to do it. They've done the same time-honored patterns thousands of times.

Once a pattern is complete, workers sprinkle its terra-cotta-colored back with cement powder and wet it down. That sets up the bond and prepares the panels for grouting. Then completing the job is a matter of carefully breaking the large panels into smaller pieces to make them more manageable,

installing them against walls or columns and cleaning their colorful surfaces.

On your way out of the Morocco pavilion and into Japan, look on the open door of **Souk-al-Magreb**; this translates into "Gifts of Morocco." Three brass plates will form a hidden Mickey.

Kon'nichiwa, and welcome to **Japan**! The Walt Disney Company has a very long history with the country. In 1962, when Japanese businessman Chiharu Kawasaki visited Disneyland, he told Roy O.

Disney that he wanted to bring Disneyland back to Japan. About twenty years later, in April 1983, Tokyo Disneyland, the first Disney theme park not on American soil, debuted.

Even Japanese emperor Hirohito was a huge fan of Mickey Mouse. When he passed away in February 1989, he was buried with many of his most treasured mementos: a microscope, a list of his favorite sumo wrestlers, and the Mickey Mouse watch he was presented during his visit to Disneyland in the early 1970s. So it should really be no surprise that the Land of the Rising Sun has a presence in Epcot's World Showcase.

As seen in the other pavilions, Disney's attention to detail and replication of centuries-old culture is remarkable. This is first noticed when you approach the red torii standing just at the edge of the World Showcase Lagoon, in front of Japan.

If you look toward the bottom of the torii, you'll notice what look to be barnacles around each *nemaki,* or bottom part of the pillars.

These barnacles are fake, created to give the illusion the torii has been in place there for a very long time.

Toriis have a special place in Japanese society. According to the official tourism website for the Hiroshima Prefecture in Japan, "the great Torii is the boundary between the spirit and the human worlds." The one residing at Epcot is based on the torii at Itsukushima, a small island in Hiroshima Bay.

In the pavilion, Disney tried to achieve a sense of balance, simplicity, and serenity with the strategic arrangements of waterfalls, rocks, flowers, lanterns, and pebbles throughout the area.

In fact, some of the original designs for Japan were deemed chronologically inaccurate by Disney's Japanese advisors. The designs Disney originally created portrayed a time when there was more of a Chinese influence in the design, which was not something Disney was trying to achieve and replicate, so changes were made.

The other iconic feature at the pavilion is the blue-roofed, five-story Goju-no-to pagoda (eighty-three feet tall), inspired by a shrine built at Nara in AD 700.

Topping it is a bronze, nine-ringed *sorin*, or spire, with gold wind chimes and a water flame. According to the *Imagineering Field Guide to Epcot*, "Each story represents one of the five elements of the Buddhist universe, in ascending order—Earth, Water, Fire, Wind and Heaven."

If you have the opportunity, find out what time the Matsuriza are playing. They are a group of Japanese drummers who perform at the base of the pagoda. The drumming is rhythmic, impressive, and almost hypnotic.

If you're facing the pagoda with your back to the lagoon, to the right of it stands the Shishinden, inspired by the ceremonial and coronation hall found in the Imperial Palace grounds at Kyoto.

Inside the Shishinden, guests can browse through the world-famous Mitsukoshi Department Store—one of the oldest department stores in the world, founded in 1673.

Still facing the pavilion with your back to the lagoon and the Shishinden on your right, you'll notice a castle at the rear of the pavilion.

It's based upon Shirasagi-Jo, a seventeenth-century castle in Hemeji, a city located in Hyōgo Prefecture in the Kansai region of Japan. Shirasagi-Jo is one of the best-preserved castles in Japan.

In front of the castle is the Katsura Grill. Check out the pond and see if you can spot the hidden Mickey drain cover.

As you leave Japan and start walking toward

the host pavilion, America, you'll notice a little quick-serve kiosk selling drinks and a delicious shaved ice treat called Kakigōri. Pick the flavor of your choice; be sure to order it with the condensed milk.

Welcome to the **American Adventure**. The pavilion is located at the center of the World Showcase and features prominently in your line of sight as you enter the showcase from Future World. This was not originally the plan for the host pavilion. In fact, some at Disney wondered if America should even be represented here.

From the book *Since the World Began: Walt Disney World, the First Twenty Five Years*:

> The question of how to present the spirit of America daunted the Imagineers. The United States was not one of the original World Showcase pavilion concepts; it was to be a sleek two-level structure on stilts in a transitional area near Future World.
>
> As the host country, the United States was to have a walk under facility, with an attraction above—a gateway to World Showcase. There was concern that placing the United States in the Showcase itself might appear arrogant, but that setting it apart might appear aloof.
>
> Finally, the Imagineers decided to celebrate the very spirit that could produce a project like EPCOT Center. The United States pavilion with its spectacular show, The American Adventure, would become the central focus of World Showcase.

With the location of the pavilion determined—there was even a time when Disney considered having the World Showcase as a stand-alone park located adjacent to Magic Kingdom—it was time to once again secure a corporate sponsor. This time, Disney secured two symbols of America in their own right: American Express and Coca Cola. Nothing screams *America* like credit-card debt and soda! Each sponsor contributed thirty million dollars for the pavilion.

The façade of the American Adventure Pavilion is made of

110,000 bricks, handmade from Georgia red clay, aged for an authentic look and feel. Its central rotunda is approximately thirty-five feet high, with its dome adding another ten feet.

The 108,000-square-foot building we see today is reminiscent of a colonial American manor, indicative of the late 1700s.

Places such as Colonial Williamsburg, Independence Hall in Philadelphia, Thomas Jefferson's Monticello, and the Old State House in Boston were the inspiration.

The original design for the building was more along the lines of the Hirshhorn Museum in Washington, DC, but the Imagineers decided to steer clear of having a building look like a government facility or museum. Instead, what we see today is the "people's mansion," containing a theater where a thirty-minute show, *The American Adventure*, plays continuously throughout the day.

Depending upon what time you walk into the building, you may be hearing the **Voices of Liberty** singing in the rotunda underneath an acoustically perfect dome, which amplifies and purifies the sound.

Costumed in garb from the 1800s, Voices of Liberty is a choir of a cappella singers that performs in the pavilion rotunda throughout the day.

This eight-member group runs through a fifteen-minute set list of some of America's most beloved and patriotic music: "America the Beautiful," "This Land Is Your Land," "This Is My Country," "You Raise Me Up," "The Battle Hymn of the Republic," "Yankee Doodle Dandy," and, of course, "Let It Go."

Now it's time to head into the theater and view the American Adventure. Benjamin Franklin and Mark Twain are your guides on this journey through American history.

The 1,024-seat theater features elegant Corinthian-style chandeliers, archways, and columns. Twelve faux marble carvings, six on either side of the seventy-two-foot screen, embody the American ideals of individualism, innovation, independence, and self-reliance.

As you watch America's story unfold on a stage measuring 130 by 50 feet (about half the size of a football field), scenes of American history featuring thirty-five audio-animatronic figures appear and disappear seamlessly throughout the show, which unto itself is a performance of American ingenuity at work.

The choreographer of this computer-controlled show is a moveable device under the stage dubbed the "war wagon." Ten different sets are stored there and are moved forward or backward on cue.

The silent 175-ton scene changer is housed under the electronic wiring; electrical connections; and air, hydraulic fluid, and water lines that give lifelike movement to the figures and help create special effects such as rain.

The scene changer—a steel framework measuring sixty-five by thirty-five by fourteen feet—is as long as a boxcar and twice as wide. Operated by computer, the scene changer moves the sets into place horizontally.

The sets then rise into audience view on telescoping hydraulic supports. There are also seven lifts that bring sets into view from either side and above. More than two dozen computers control the entire operation.

Once the button is pushed, audio-animatronic actors move and speak, music plays, lights brighten and dim, curtains open, sets rise, and motion-picture projectors roll.

The production, five years in development, involves some of the most technically demanding staging techniques ever used.

Behind the thirteen three-dimensional settings and performers, the rear-projection screen adds dimension to the settings and transition between decade-spanning scenes.

The rear projection screen is 28 feet high by 155 feet long, and the background film uses more than three thousand feet of 70mm film.

If you follow along closely, any situation or scene portrayed before the invention of the camera or film is shown via artwork or with an animatronic. This was done to maintain the integrity of the story line.

That's a lot to digest, so I will leave you with only a few more tidbits before we head back out to the World Showcase. Listen to the voice of Ben Franklin; his voice should sound somewhat familiar if you rode Big Thunder Mountain at Magic Kingdom. Will Rogers Jr. recorded the voice of the audio-animatronic of his father, Will Rogers.

During the scene for the Civil War, the story line involves two brothers who fight against each other. You'll also hear the song "Two Brothers." Pay attention to the photo portraying the family and the two brothers. Looks authentic, right?

The two brothers are actually Imagineers John Olson and Jeff Burke, portraying the dueling family members. The man portraying the father is Bob McCarthy, the patent holder for the smellitizer!

The pavilion has a good number of hidden Mickeys scattered among the paintings hanging in the rotunda. See if you can find them in the following paintings: *Building a Future Together, Defending Freedom, Election Day, Reaching for the Stars,* and *Seeds of Hope.* The patriotism even lends itself to the plants outside, as the flowers are often planted around the area in a grouping of red, white, and blue.

We're now heading over to the **Italy Pavilion**. The pavilion was designed to capture the spirit and aesthetics of Venice—more of a Venetian influence rather than total replication.

As you approach, you'll notice gondolas are docked and tied to the striped moorings in the lagoon, definitely reminiscent of Venice.

Front and center are a couple of re-creations of Venetian landmarks, Doge's Palace and St. Mark's campanile. Doge's Palace, or the Palazzo Ducale, was the seat of the government of Venice for centuries. As well as being the home of the doge (the elected ruler of Venice) it was the venue for its law courts, its civil administration, and its bureaucracy.

St. Mark's campanile is the bell tower of St. Mark's Basilica in Venice. The real tower is 323 feet tall; Epcot's version measures in at 83 feet tall. Both of these iconic Italian landmarks are found in Venice's St. Mark's Square.

If you've ever been to Venice to see Doge's Palace and St. Mark's campanile, you may notice something a bit different about Epcot's portrayal; don't worry, if you've never been there, check out the photo.

The buildings here at the World Showcase are reversed. Imagineer Bill Martin didn't want the replication to be an exact copy; he wanted Epcot's Italy to have its own identity and therefore switched the positioning of the buildings.

Leaving the influence of Venice and resuming with the influence of Rome, Epcot's version of the Trevi Fountain, featuring a statue of Neptune, makes for a great photo opportunity.

Italy Pavilion at Epcot

The Italy Pavilion doesn't have a ride or a movie or a stage show, but that doesn't really matter. Because what they do have is some excellent food! So let's get down to business.

The options are great. There's the **Tutto Gusto Wine Cellar**, which, as the name says, has the rustic look and feel of an Italian wine cellar. They carry over two hundred bottles of Italian wines—plus beer and a small-plates menu of meats, cheeses, panini, pasta, and desserts.

If you're interested in a more traditional Italian meal, **Tutto Italia Ristorante** serves lunch and dinner, offering chicken, fish, handmade pasta, and lasagna dishes. Authentic Italian dishes come from a menu created by award-winning chef and California restaurateur Joachim Splichal. The dining room features an Old World ambience with murals of ancient Rome throughout.

Those two dining experiences are great, but if you're visiting the Italy pavilion with me, we're going straight to **Via Napoli**. Seriously, the pizza is really good here—not just good for Walt Disney World, but good in general. Specifically the wood-fired Margherita pizza.

The Neapolitan pizzas served here use real Caputo flour imported from Southern Italy, and the water used to make the dough has a similar profile to the water used in Italy's Campania region.

The pizzas are baked in wood-fired ovens, which are a focal point of the restaurant. They are named after the three active volcanoes in Italy: Mount Etna, Mount Vesuvius, and Stromboli. The ovens reach temperatures up to nine hundred degrees and cook a pizza in roughly two minutes.

As good as the food is here, so is the ambiance and decor. There are a few things to look out for when you enter the restaurant. As you approach the building, look on the exterior for a tile with the number twenty-eight on it. The number represents the year Mickey Mouse made his debut, 1928.

Once you're in the restaurant, look up and you'll see a beautiful glass chandelier with twelve hundred pieces of glass fruit.

Much of the decor seen throughout the restaurant has been imported from Italy, and so has the wait staff! (You can't miss the enormous table that seems as if it stretches on forever. If you have the opportunity, look for the hand-painted tiles featuring all the monuments found in Italy.) The management of the restaurant go to Italy four times a year to recruit employees to work at the restaurant, truly giving it an authentic feel.

On your way out of Italy, stop in at **Enoteca Castello**, Italy's wine shop. See if you can spot the hidden Mickey in the woodwork on the front wine counter.

Moving right along, on October 3, 1978, the *Orlando Sentinel* published an article describing Disney's plans for Future World and the World Showcase: "The World Showcase pavilions will feature the cultures, traditions, and accomplishments of sponsoring countries, including: The Federal Republic of Germany—with traditional buildings, themed shops and a German rivers ride."

As the article stated, the original plan for Epcot's **Germany Pavilion** included a Rhine river ride, which would feature a cruise down Germany's most famous rivers; there was even a building built for it, but the ride never came to fruition.

While there's no show or movie at the pavilion, there is still much to see and appreciate here, most notably the design and architecture.

The pavilion isn't based upon one specific region of the country but borrows from several cities and timeframes. The pavilion features designs from the thirteenth to the seventeenth centuries.

The *platz*, or plaza, here in Germany almost has a whimsical feel of an Alpine village, replete with castle designs from yesterday—check the stair-step roof line, steeples, and turrets.

The castle walls at the rear of the pavilion are an amalgamation of the Eltz Castle, located between the cities of Koblenz and Trier, and Stahleck Castle, located in the Upper Middle Rhine Valley. Both of these castles date back to the twelfth century, with the Eltz Castle still owned by the same family, thirty-three generations later.

If you're facing the pavilion and the World Showcase lagoon is behind you, look to the right; you will see Das Kaufhaus. It's hard to miss the green awning for Bier (beer).

This building is based on the Kaufhaus found in Freiburg, Germany, built during the 1500s. The version in Epcot has three figures adorning the building.

Philip I, Charles V, and Ferdinand I were members of the royal family that ruled Austria-Hungary from 1273 to 1918. The actual building in Germany has four emperors on the outside, the three included here at Epcot plus Maximilian I. The scale of the building in Florida wouldn't permit for all four to be included. Sorry, Max; you didn't make the cut!

Germany Pavilion at Epcot

A trip to Germany wouldn't be complete unless you spent a little time at a biergarten. Epcot's version, the facade at least, is based on a biergarten in Rothenburg ob der Tauber, which is a town in the region of Bavaria known for its well-preserved medieval town.

Here's a statistic you might not come across every day: The Biergarten Restaurant at Epcot serves up roughly 26.2 miles of bratwurst every sixty days—the length of a marathon.

Just in front of the Biergarten is a statue of St. George slaying a dragon. According to the *Imagineering Field Guide to Epcot*:

> St. George is the patron saint of soldiers. German legends say that St. George killed a dragon to which a king's daughter was being sacrificed—slaying it with his magical sword, Ascalon. Almost all German villages have a statue of St. George as a symbol of protection. Ours is modeled after the one in Rothenburg.

Leaving Germany, we pass the Outpost. It's not much of a traditional pavilion per se, but you can pick up a few hand-carved crafts or grab a quick drink or snack.

Continuing around the World Showcase, you'll notice you're actually crossing a bridge to get to the **China Pavilion**. What you may not realize is this is a fully functioning drawbridge that is in use each and every day.

If you happen to be in the World Showcase between four and five o'clock in the afternoon, you'll see the drawbridge go up and a large structure on a barge float on through to the World Showcase Lagoon.

This is Disney making preparations for Epcot's evening entertainment.

As we approach the **China Pavilion**, there's an interesting story within the story of the pavilion. Back on February 2, 1978, the headline of the front page of the *Sentinel Star* newspaper (which eventually merged with the *Orlando Sentinel*) read "Taiwanese Reveal Epcot Plans." Here's what the article had to say:

> A delegation of Taiwanese trade representatives Wednesday told Florida officials in Tallahassee they plan to invest $10 million in Walt Disney World's EPCOT.

> Jack Lindquist, Disney marketing vice president in charge of the EPCOT project said, "We're surprised and delighted to hear about the announcement." Lindquist said Disney officials had been negotiating with Taiwan for some time, but added the company had not yet received an official announcement that the country had decided to participate.

> He said Disney had hoped to identify all the participating countries at one time, but added he was not unhappy the visiting Taiwanese's announced Taiwan's participation, if true.

Another interesting quote from the story:

> "It caught us by surprise—we never announce anything like this," said Walt Disney vice president C. Langhorne Washburn, who runs Disney's Washington D.C. World Showcase office.

> "It's true that the ambassador (of Taiwan) informed me the government has decided in principle to be a participant," he said. An agreement in principle is an expression of intent to go ahead with a deal. It is not binding, but is intended to lead to a binding commitment, or definitive agreement.

> Now, Washburn said, "we will enter a preliminary design stage" which will take another "six to nine months. Only after completing that design will we be able to give the size, shape and concept for the Taiwanese pavilion we will present to the world. We don't like to announce any agreements in principle. We like to announce fait accompli."

It sounds a bit as if Taiwan blindsided Disney with the announcement, and, as Mr. Washburn indicated, despite Taiwan's announcement, the agreement wasn't binding, and a lot can happen in the planning stages, which is exactly what took place.

Taiwan and China, and then by default the United States of America, have had a complicated relationship over the decades. Here's a little background from the Council on Foreign Relations (https://www.cfr.org/backgrounder/china-taiwan-relations):

> Taiwan, home to twenty-three million people, is an island off the southern coast of China that has been governed independently from mainland China since 1949.

> The People's Republic of China (PRC) views the island as a province, while in Taiwan—a territory with its own democratically elected government—leading political voices have differing views on the island's status and relations with the mainland.

> Some observe the principle that there is "one China" comprising the island and the mainland, but in their eyes this is the Republic of China (ROC) based in Taipei; others advocate for a de jure independent Taiwan.

> China and Taiwan maintain a fragile relationship, Beijing and Taipei sharply disagree on the island's status. The PRC asserts that there is only "one China" and that Taiwan is an inalienable part of it.

> In 1979, the United States established formal diplomatic relations with Beijing by concluding a joint communiqué stating that "the United States of America acknowledges the Chinese position that there is but one China and Taiwan is part of China." At that time, US President Jimmy Carter terminated diplomatic relations with the ROC government in Taiwan.

What does this have to do with Epcot? If you think back to Taiwan's Epcot announcement, that was in February 1978; months later, in 1979, President Carter ended diplomatic relations with the government of Taiwan, in essence putting an end to a Taiwan pavilion in the World Showcase.

Fast forward to January 25, 1980. Card Walker, then president of Walt Disney Productions, told the Dow Jones News Service, "I've been in contact with top Chinese officials, and I'm optimistic that we will have China in a later phase of our project."

As we see today, the **China Pavilion** is represented at Epcot and was an opening-day member of the World Showcase. But Taiwan had a little bit more to say on their Disney debacle.

In 1983 Taiwan tried to work their way into the showcase again in a rather creative fashion. Apparently, the city of Orlando and the city of Tainan, in Taiwan, are sister cities. And what do sister cities do for each other? Exchange gifts.

Quoting from the May 12, 1983, edition of the *Orlando Sentinel*:

> Walt Disney World won't display the mammoth, 25,000 pound hunk of marble sent to Orlando by its sister city in Taiwan three weeks ago, as the donors had requested.
>
> "The rock was meant as a gift to the city of Orlando," Disney spokesman Bob Mervine said, Wednesday. "We're not the city of Orlando. We don't feel it is appropriate to display it at all at Walt Disney World."
>
> Local observers and international experts had suggested that accepting the 12½ ton stone from Tainan, Taiwan, would present Disney with a heavyweight problem of international protocol.
>
> The World Showcase at Disney's Epcot Center is already home to an exhibit sanctioned by Taiwan's bitter rival, the People's Republic of China. But Mervine denied that political considerations played any part in the decision, which was made by corporate vice presidents on the Walt Disney World Operating Committee.

"We do try to stay away from the political thing at the World Showcase, where exhibits on the culture and heritage of nine countries are displayed," Mervine said. But in this case, politics "had nothing to do with it."

Orlando officials at first believe Disney would heed the request, which is inscribed in a gold lettered black marble plaque accompanying the stone. It asks the stone be placed "at a permanent location in your great Walt Disney World."

The rock, which resembles a gnarled tree trunk, is adorned with two gold symbols representing love of country and love of family. The stone was taken from a 5,000 foot high mountaintop in eastern Taiwan, and measures 19½ feet long, 5 feet wide and nearly 4 feet high, and weighs roughly 25,000 pounds.

Although he did not know about the gift in advance, T.H. Lin of Taiwan's Coordinated Council for North American Affairs said he guessed that the stone was designed to give Taiwan a presence at Epcot, which is visited by about 10,000 Taiwanese a year.

Ultimately Disney tried to avoid an international political incident here by not only refusing the gift from Taiwan but not including the country in the World Showcase.

Little did Disney know at the time, having a China pavilion in Epcot was catching the attention of the US government, specifically the FBI.

The Tampa bureau of the Federal Bureau of Investigation was worried about the communist influence and possible terrorism or spies lurking at the pavilion being staffed by Chinese nationals.

The documents pertaining to the FBI's concern were requested and released via the Freedom of Information Act and posted on the website Muckrock, www.muckrock.com.

Real-world politics intersects the fantasy world of a theme park; you can't make this stuff up!

Despite the covert FBI program, political turmoil, unauthorized announcements, and backdoor gifts, the path to the China Pavilion is still going strong at Epcot, and it's one of the most beautiful pavilions in the World Showcase, which is fitting for one of the world's oldest civilizations.

Entering the pavilion, guests walk under the Zhao Yang Men, which translates into "Gate of the Golden Sun." This gate was modeled after the main gate at the emperor's Beijing summer palace.

Just past the gate and at the back of the pavilion is the Temple of Heaven, which is based upon the Hall of Prayer for Good Harvest in the Temple of Heaven, constructed in China during the early 1400s. As the name suggests, the emperor would pray here for a bountiful harvest.

The building's intricate design and architecture are highly immersive. Imagineers spent countless hours screen printing detailed patterns onto every tile you see on the exterior of the building, in an effort to clone the intricate patterns on the original building in China.

Inside the hall, there are four columns in the center that represent the four seasons. The twelve outer columns are indicative of the twelve months of the year. As the *Imagineering Field Guide to Epcot* explains:

In Chinese design, circles define the heavens and squares stand in for the earth—used together they form the universe. This motif repeats itself throughout the building. The red and yellow that are found all around represent happiness and the emperor, respectively.

The medallion inset into the top of the prayer hall is an important symbol for the building and is representative of the

Chinese culture.

The dragon and the phoenix each carry meaning—the dragon is indicative of power (and if it has five claws, it specifically refers to the power of the emperor) and the phoenix represents peace and prosperity. Together they signify a marriage.

The years before and after Epcot opened, rumors flew, announcements were made, and even signs went up welcoming new countries to Epcot. Spain, Russia, Israel, Costa Rica, and Venezuela were all mentioned; even today, the rumors and chatter still persist.

But in the summer of 1985, the parliament of Norway and a handful of private corporations from the country came together and signed a deal with Disney to bring a Norway pavilion to the World Showcase.

The **Norway Pavilion** debuted in the summer of 1988 and features the ambiance of a Norwegian village, showcasing a medieval castle named Askershus.

The design for the castle comes from a fourteenth-century Norwegian castle with the same name in Oslo. Epcot's Askershus offers storybook dining and the opportunity to feast with Snow White, Cinderella, Belle, Princess Aurora, and Ariel. (Breakfast, lunch, and dinner are offered. Definitely make reservations if you plan to dine with these ladies!)

The other landmark in the fifty-eight-thousand-square-foot pavilion is the stave church, or *Stavkirke*. According to the official tourism board of Norway:

> Stave churches are considered to be among the most important examples of wooden Medieval architecture in Europe. In the Middle Ages, there were probably more than 1,000 stave churches in Norway. Today, only 28 remain.
>
> A stave church is made of wood, and the construction is made out of poles ("staver" in Norwegian), hence the name.
>
> Most of the remaining stave churches in Norway were built

between 1150 and 1350. In the middle ages there were similar types of churches all over North-Western Europe.

In Norway there was a tradition for using wood in artwork as well as in constructions, and this lead to the development of a unique technique that the stave churches are a perfect example of. The decoration features a unique mix of both Christian and Viking symbolism.

So clearly, the stave church is on the endangered-species list of culturally significant and historical buildings. Lucky for us, we have a great replica here in central Florida.

Disney's Imagineers traveled extensively through Norway to research architecture and decor, and what they brought back were the characteristics and styles of the towns Bergen, Alesund, Oslo, and Setesdal.

The big attraction in the Norway Pavilion is the boat ride, **Frozen Ever After.** Go ahead, put the book down and go make your Fastpass reservation for the ride. More often than not, you will be facing a long line if you plan to ride via standby.

When the Norway Pavilion debuted, it featured a ten-minute boat ride called Maelstrom, but with the runaway success of the movie *Frozen,* Maelstrom and its trolls were bumped for Anna and Elsa in June 2016.

The boat journey through Arendelle uses a similar track layout to Maelstrom, but that's about all that resembles the Norway boat ride of yesterday.

Today, this family-friendly adventure in the Norway Pavilion picks up after the events of the movie left off. The attraction celebrates a "summer snow day," as you see the kingdom of Arendelle and visit with Queen Elsa, Princess Anna, Kristoff, and Olaf. All the actors who voiced the characters in the hit movie recorded dialogue and songs for the attraction.

After disembarking, guests can top off their *Frozen* experience by meeting the royal sisters in their new Royal Sommerhus greeting location. Inspired by a Norwegian countryside cabin, Anna and Elsa have opened their summer home for visitors.

Again, Walt Disney Imagineers traveled to Norway for architecture and design research, specifically visiting the Detli House in Sverresborg and the Open Air Museum of Cultural History in Trondheim to perfect their piece of Norway in Florida.

Only the magic of Disney can bring you the country of Mexico next to the country of Norway! Our last country in the World Showcase is the United States' neighbor to the south.

Throughout the eighty-five-thousand-square-foot pavilion, the pre-Columbian culture and architecture of Mesoamerica is showcased, with different aspects of the Toltec, Mayan, and Aztec civilizations being well represented here. At one point during the early design phase of the pavilion, Disney consulted with the ambassador to Mexico, who pointed out that their designs might be leaning too much toward a Spanish colonial influence, so they changed the design to what you see here today.

Disney really captured the spirit of the Mexican culture from yesterday with not one but two pyramids. The thirty-six-foot-tall pyramid outside is an amalgamation of Mesoamerican motifs, concentrating heavily on Aztec design, with its five-tiered sloping walls fifty steps high. There's even a spot at the top of the pyramid that helps coordinate components of IllumiNations each night.

Inside the pavilion, it's perpetually nighttime as you stroll the Plaza de los Amigos. A second pyramid, a bit weathered looking, looms over the plaza and the **San Angel Inn**.

This restaurant replicates the popular Mexico City restaurant of the same name and ownership, which has played host to such famous Mexican figures as General Santa Ana and Pancho Villa and was built in 1692.

The major attraction at the Mexico Pavilion is the "**Gran Fiesta Tour Starring the Three Caballeros**," an eight-and-a-half-minute boat trip showcasing the people, history, culture, and arts of Mexico.

During the experience, guests catch a glimpse of some of Mexico's favorite locales and are amused by both live-action footage around Mexico and the animated adventures of Panchito, the

Mexican charro rooster; José Carioca, the Brazilian parrot; and Donald Duck. The attraction is inspired by the 1944 Disney film *The Three Caballeros*.

The animated sequences for the ride were done by Eric Goldberg, who animated Genie in the film *Aladdin*.

There are quite a few hidden Mickeys lurking throughout the Gran Fiesta Tour. As you're cruising along and come across the scene where Donald Duck is parasailing, look for a dark tree in front of the buildings along the shoreline; you will see a dark hidden Mickey all the way off to the right.

About halfway through the ride, if you look to your left, you'll see that Donald takes a dip in the lagoon, and an octopus pops up, as do a variety of bubbles. Spot the bubbles above the octopus and to the left that are shaped like a traditional Mickey head.

Toward the end of the ride, there's a room with fiber-optic fireworks on the ceiling. Some of these form a classic hidden Mickey. As you enter this room, there's a barge on the left side that has the words "VIVA DONALD." In the right corner are three drums that form a hidden Mickey.

That last hidden Mickey brings us to the end of the Mexico Pavilion and wraps up the World Showcase and Epcot. As you walk out of the pavilion, make a right and start walking to the Mexico Pavilion boat launch, just before the Disney Traders building.

We need to get back across to the other side of the World Showcase, and rather than walk it, we will take this boat to the other side of the lagoon. When the park originally opened, you could actually hop aboard a double-decker bus and be carted around the countries, but for now, if you don't feel like walking, it will have to be a boat.

The boat won't actually save you a ton of time, but it's scenic and can get you off your feet. Once you're across to the other side of the lagoon, walk over toward France, cross the bridge, and make a left to the International Gateway.

Just after you exit the park, on the left is another boat dock.

Here, another Friendship boat will take you to Disney's Hollywood Studios, our next destination. As mentioned earlier in the chapter, you can also walk there if you're so inclined.

Chapter Three

DISNEY'S
HOLLYWOOD
STUDIOS

> *Fantasy, if it's really convincing, can't become*
> *dated, for the simple reason that it represents a*
> *flight into a dimension that lies beyond the reach*
> *of time.*
>
> **—Walt Disney**

Throughout the Disney theme parks, thousands of different colors are omnipresent. During the design phase, the Imagineers pay close attention to the various shades of each color and the relationships between them.

As John Hench is quoted in his book *Designing Disney*:

> Like music, color is one of the great joys of life, mysterious and wonderful. We know that color is a direct experience: people see color, and they feel color's emotional effects. Color brings the Disney parks alive with drama, romance and playfulness. Well-chosen color draws guests in; it catches the eye, and directs and focuses attention.

We've talked a lot about John. If you're interested, the appendix of the book has his bio.

Colors may also be used to avert your attention or camouflage certain things. In these situations, Disney is an expert here too.

As you stroll through any of the Disney parks, there are plenty of things within the park that are necessary components of the Disney experience, but Disney hopes you don't notice them—items such as administrative offices, back or side portions of show buildings, fences, handrails, Dumpsters, light posts, things under construction; the list could go on and on.

Many of these items are painted a specific color in an effort to make them blend in with the landscaping or to help disguise them in plain sight. This color—or actually colors, as there are many different shades of it—is known throughout the Disney company as "no-see green" or "no see 'em green" or "go-away green."

It's a neutral shade that your eyes seem to just glance right over. As former Imagineer Tom Morris informed me, "My impression is that John Hench spec'd the Disney version of the color (and there are variants of it) starting around the same time that the show buildings for Pirates and Small World were going up at DL." ("Pirates" meaning Pirates of the Caribbean and "DL" meaning Disneyland.)

So why all this talk of color? Well, up until late 2019, Hollywood Studios had numerous coats and shades of "no-see green" throughout the park. As the park's attractions became a bit stale, a much-needed update came from two new additions: Toy Story Land and Star War's Galaxy's Edge.

Before we tackle what is featured in the park today, perhaps we should go over what was once here.

On July 8,1985, Michael Eisner, then president of Disney, and Florida governor Bob Graham held a press conference in Tallahassee announcing the plans for Disney-MGM Studios. At the time, Eisner had been at the helm of Disney for roughly a year.

When he joined the company in 1984, one of his early thoughts was to add on to Epcot Center. Eisner envisioned an entertainment-themed pavilion for Epcot's Future World; keep in mind, Epcot was only about two years old then.

But as thoughts and ideas started to come together, and more minds got involved, the pavilion seemed to grow and become a bit more ambitious. The notion of a pavilion evolved into an entire theme park experience.

In actuality, this whole concept of an interactive Disney studio for guests to visit actually dates back even further than Michael Eisner and started with Walt.

Going back decades, folks have been able tour Universal Studios in Hollywood, California, and Walt knew fans wanted to see his operation as well.

During the heyday of Disney animation, the studio was inundated with letters asking for tours and details about the comings and goings of the studio. There's even a cute Disney movie from

1941, *The Reluctant Dragon*, which is essentially a tour of the Disney Studios.

Walt first considered a park on his own back lot. Land issues combined with potential traffic problems caused him to look elsewhere—namely, Anaheim. As is often the case with dreams and plans, things grew and evolved into what we know today as Disneyland.

If we fast forward a few decades, everything came full circle for Disney in Florida. With plenty of land to work with, the company combined production facilities with theme-park attractions to give Disney guests a behind-the-scenes Hollywood experience.

As Michael Eisner declared on opening day of the park, May 1, 1989, Disney-MGM studios was "the Hollywood that never was and always will be."

The park was designed to provide guests a little taste of Hollywood in central Florida, immersing visitors into the glitz and glamour of show business.

The park would feature the usual Disney theme park attractions and shows, but visitors would also have the opportunity to see actual television and film production on-site.

Early on in the life of Disney-MGM Studios, television and movie production actually happened. *Ed McMahon's Star Search, Wheel of Fortune, Honey I Blew Up the Kid, Quick Change, Passenger 57, The Mickey Mouse Club,* and a few other movies and television programs were filmed there.

Through the mid- to late 1990s and early 2000s, things started to change at the park. The experience was less and less about the actual filming or production of big-screen or small-screen entertainment, and its identity started to differ from opening day.

In fact, in 2008, the park went through a name change. The MGM was dropped. When Disney first opened the park, they were interested in the content and licensing of MGM Studios, so the two studios partnered up in Florida.

The rebirth of Disney's Hollywood Studios commenced with

the debut of Galaxy's Edge in the summer of 2019 and Toy Story Land in the summer of 2018. We will take a stroll through that area of the park a little later in the chapter.

So let's enter the park.

If you're a native of Los Angeles and over the age of thirty-five, the facade of Disney's Hollywood Studios may look familiar to you (and no, it's not because you can find a similar facade at Disney's California Adventure Park). The entry is based on the Pan Pacific Auditorium, which was a landmark location in Los Angeles from 1935 to 1989.

The Pan Pacific Auditorium featured an architectural style called streamline modern. This style didn't last very long but was prominent during the late 1930s and the 1940s.

During its heyday, the auditorium hosted sporting events, car shows, the circus, concerts—in October 1957, the King of Rock and Roll, Elvis, played a marathon set featuring nineteen songs—and political events.

In late May 1989, the Pan Pacific Auditorium burned down; it was built out of wood. In an odd coincidence, the fire happened just a few weeks after Disney's Hollywood Studios debuted. Since the auditorium is now gone, Disney has preserved a sliver of the unique design and history of yesterday's Los Angeles.

Another landmark not too far from where the Pan Pacific Auditorium stood is the Crossroads of the World. Built a year after the auditorium, in 1936, this iconic piece was a focal point of what has been called America's first outdoor shopping mall. Today it primarily houses offices.

While the actual Crossroads of the World is located at 6671 Sunset Boulevard, here at Disney, the re-creation welcomes you onto Hollywood Boulevard.

Hooray for Hollywood! Disney's version of Hollywood Boulevard is similar to Main Street in the Magic Kingdom; it greets guests and transports them to another time and place. In this case, it's Tinsel Town during its golden age.

The first building on the left side, just past the Crossroads of the World, is Mickey's of Hollywood. You may notice an adjacent sign that says **Pluto's Toy Palace**. This facade and sign were inspired by a former veterinarian's office, the Dog & Cat Hospital, 940 N. Highland Avenue in Hollywood.

  Across the street from Pluto's Toy Palace is **Adrian & Edith's Head to Toe.** This facade is based on the Chapman Park Market Building on Sixth Street in Los Angeles. The names Adrian and Edith are a reference to two very accomplished costume designers —one of whom, Edith Head, received eight Academy Awards for her work in costuming. Both women could dress you from "head to toe." According to the Los Angeles Conservatory website:

> Opened in 1929, the drive-in Chapman Park Market was one of the first markets in the western US designed for the automobile. The market presented a fortress-like facade, with thick concrete walls worked to resemble sandstone and ornate, Churrigueresque towers on the corners.
>
> A large rooftop sign invited motorists off Wilshire. Patrons drove in through a Spanish Revival archway to find an inner courtyard surrounded by various grocers.

Adrian & Edith's brings us toward the end of the block. Making a right turn will take you down **Sunset Boulevard**. This area of the park didn't exist when Hollywood Studios debuted and was added in 1994.

Chapman Park Market

As you turn right down Sunset Boulevard, gear up for some excitement, because at the moment, about half of the park's rides are right here, the **Twilight Zone Tower of Terror** and **Rock 'N' Roller Coaster Starring Aerosmith.**

Before we get there, let's slow down a bit and take in a few sights. As you stroll along the sidewalks, look for a concrete stamp around Hollywood and Sunset. "MORTIMER & CO. CONTRACTORS 1928." Mortimer is a reference to the original proposed name for Mickey Mouse.

The first shop on the right side of the block is **Legends of Hollywood**. The exterior architecture features the streamline moderne  style, as seen at the entrance to the park. The building itself is inspired by the 1938 Academy Theater in Inglewood, California.

The next block down on the same side of the street is the store **Sunset Club Couture**. Check out the upper-level windows, which feature the dog from the 2008 movie *Bolt*. Another window says "Director's best friend," a wink and a nod to the Disney movie.

At the end of this block and a store down from Sunset Club Couture is the shop **Once Upon a Time**. This building is a replica of the Spanish Revival–style Carthay Circle Theater in Beverly

Hills. The theater was built in 1926 (and demolished in 1969) at 6316 San Vicente Boulevard.

For those familiar with Disney movie history, the Carthay Circle was the location of the world premiere of *Snow White* in 1937. If you go in and check out the store, there's a photo from the big night back on December 21, 1937. If you listen closely, you'll hear a radio broadcast of the premiere.

Across from Once Upon a Time is the **Sunset Ranch Market**, which is inspired by the still-standing 1934 Farmers Market on the corner of Third Avenue and Fairfax in LA.

Just next to the Sunset Ranch Market is **Rosie's All-American Cafe**. The Rosie inspiring the name of the cafe is the cultural icon Rosie the Riveter. Rosie was representative of the hardworking women who worked tirelessly in factories and shipyards during World War II. (*We Can Do It!* 1942 poster by J. Howard Miller).

Now it's time for thrills and chills. At the end of Sunset Boulevard are the two big-name attractions featured at the park. First up, the **Twilight Zone Tower of Terror.**

The Twilight Zone Tower of Terror is based on the popular television series, which originally aired from 1959 to 1964. Created, hosted, and written by Rod Serling, the award-winning show was

wildly successful in its day and still lives on today as a classic television series. Disney adapted and tweaked the premise of the series into a thrill ride.

From the Walt Disney World website:

> Classic stars of the silver screen sought rest and relaxation at the Hollywood Tower Hotel during the Golden Age of Hollywood.
>
> In 1939, during a gloomy Halloween night, 5 unfortunate hotel patrons were riding in the elevator when a violent storm struck the building…and they were never seen again.
>
> Whatever became of them and wherever they may have gone has remained a mystery to this day. The hotel closed down that night and has remained abandoned ever since.
>
> You're invited to take a tour of the Hollywood Tower Hotel—and experience an unforgettable ride—on a stormy night very similar to the evening when the unexplained event occurred. Be welcomed by Rod Serling as you journey to the 5th Dimension.

Well, the funny thing about this attraction is, not only have the "5 unfortunate hotel patrons" been lost, but so has that episode of the television show.

As Michael Sprout, a show writer, is quoted in *Walt Disney Imagineering,* "A lot of people have told me they don't remember a *Twilight Zone* episode about an elevator. And they're right. This is the 'lost episode' no one has ever seen."

In preparation for writing the story line, Imagineers watched 156 episodes of *The Twilight Zone* for inspiration, so I'm pretty sure they would know if one of the episodes is "missing."

However, in typical Disney fashion, the research and development for the attraction went above and beyond merely watching television and dreaming up an ordinary free-fall ride.

Originally, Michael Eisner envisioned the concept for this ride to take place in an actual hotel, with the ride dropping into the middle of a working hotel lobby. Eisner claims this idea was abandoned for reasons of cost and practicality.

With the working hotel concept put to rest, Disney visited with Otis Elevator—in 1852 Elisha Otis invented the safety elevator, which automatically comes to a halt if the hoisting rope breaks—to research their idea of a runaway elevator. What they experienced during this meeting was not what they expected.

> Otis invited the team to visit a high-rise building in Los Angeles where they had just completed installation of their fastest generation elevator. The team was anxious to give it a try since, above all, the ride had to be fast.
>
> Dropping from the fiftieth floor, even after Otis had adjusted the elevator to "full speed," the team found themselves quickly at ground level without feeling a thing.
>
> "So what did you think?" asked an Otis executive. "It's fast, all right," responded a concept team member, "but we were really looking for gut-wrenching, hair-raising, free-falling thrill!" To that, the surprised executive responded, "What? And undo everything we've been trying to perfect for more than a century?
>
> "Our success comes when you feel like you're not moving at

all!" It was then the team realized how incredibly different this new elevator would have to be—and that it would be up to Imagineering to take it to a whole new level.

With that, Disney created one of the world's largest ride system motors to power the attraction.

> Twelve feet tall, 7 feet wide, 35 feet long, and weighing in at 132,000 pounds, the two massive motors had to be hoisted atop the towers framework—specially constructed to support their weight—via giant cranes. The motors are capable of accelerating ten tons at a rate of fifteen times the speed of a normal elevator, while generating torque equal to that of a combined 275 Corvette engines.

The Tower of Terror opened on July 22, 1994. The design and architecture were inspired by several Southern California landmarks, most notably the Mission Inn and Biltmore Hotel, and the landscape and grounds around the attraction have hints of Griffith and Elysian Park. The building housing the attraction stands 199 feet tall and features more than twenty-seven thousand roof tiles.

Changed from its original format, the Twilight Zone Tower of Terror at Disney's Hollywood Studios multiplies the thrills inside the thirteen-story haunted hotel with a recent technology upgrade that actually places the attraction in control of each ride experience.

It's the first Disney attraction in the world to offer random experiences and the first where the attraction actually determines the ride sequence. All the ride sequences are unique and random.

These random ride and drop sequences make the attraction faster and more entertaining. In addition, visual, audio, and olfactory special effects make the Tower of Terror one of the most advanced multisensory attractions anywhere in the world. Ghostly apparitions, rocketing ascents, more "air time," and cannon blasts of chilling air are just a few of the surprises in store for you as you check in to the hotel. Here's a bit more from one of the attraction's show producers:

"Tower of Terror affects every one of the senses, leaving you feeling as if you have really been in your own episode of *The Twilight Zone*," says Theron Skees, show producer for Walt Disney Imagineering.

"A team of Walt Disney Imagineers worked very hard to break the barrier and truly immerse guests in the experience. Adding sound technology, scent, and visual effects is only part of the way we achieved this. We wanted the guest to feel completely out of control—not knowing what to expect next, and giving the die-hard fans a lot more to talk about."

The ride's fright-filled ascent begins when visitors board a decrepit hotel freight elevator that passes through mysterious hotel passageways where ghostly images of lost guests seem to appear and disappear at will. As the journey progresses, the elevator-cage hurtles through the "fifth dimension" in a pitch-black shaft, as guests embark on a not-to-be-forgotten journey.

A trip on this elevator could definitely become problematic for some younger riders; it's dark and has sudden drops. Put on your best screaming face, as your pic will be taken. Fastpass+ this bad boy, especially since there aren't a whole lot of other things to do at this park.

Disney's Hollywood, or real Hollywood, a trip down Sunset Boulevard, wouldn't be a proper trip unless you experienced some rock and roll.

Legendary venues along the real Sunset Boulevard, such as the Whiskey A-Go-Go and the Roxy Theater, have been rocking music lovers for decades, so, of course, Disney Hollywood Studios' rock-and-roll-centric roller coaster would be found on their own Sunset Boulevard.

Are you ready to rock? I hope so, because 3,403 feet of twists, turns, loops, corkscrews, hills, and dips await you at **Rock 'n' Roller**

Coaster Starring Aerosmith, just next to the Tower of Terror.

The attraction begins with a tour of a fictional record company, where you'll encounter Aerosmith finishing up a studio recording session. The band, formed in the early 1970s, actually recorded a few special tracks for their namesake ride. Their hit "Love in an Elevator" can be heard as "Love in a Roller Coaster," and "What Kind of Love Are You On?" became "What Kind of Ride Are You On?"

After being invited by the band to see them in concert, guests climb aboard a twenty-four-passenger "super-stretch limo" (inspired by early 1960s Cadillacs) and begin their journey into the darkness, which is fueled by speed and music.

The ride features two rollover loops and one corkscrew—Disney's first coaster in the United States to feature inversions—and starts with a high-speed launch that catapults each Limotrain to approximately 60 mph in 2.8 seconds. Have you ever wondered what it felt like to take off in a supersonic jet from an aircraft carrier? Well, the beginning of this ride has a similar feel.

In addition to the speed and excitement of the ride, each Limotrain has a total of 120 speakers, and each guest seat on the attraction has two high-frequency tweeters, two midrange speakers, and one subwoofer mounted under it. All in all, the entire attraction boasts nine hundred speakers and puts out more than thirty-two thousand watts of audio.

Here are a couple things to look out for as you enter the attraction and work your way through to the actual ride.

Note the name of the fictional record company: G-Force Records. According to dictionary.com, a g-force is a force acting on a body as a result of acceleration or gravity, informally described in units of acceleration equal to one g.

For example, a twelve-pound object undergoing a g-force of two g's experiences twenty-four pounds of force. As you enter the first inversion of this ride, you'll feel roughly four to five g's.

As you exit the attraction, check out the forty-foot-tall electric guitar neck that morphs into a roller coaster track and extends out 320 feet toward the entrance arc. Definitely Fastpass+ this ride too. The height restriction here is forty-eight inches.

Let's walk back down the street and go toward Hollywood Boulevard. When you're at the corner of Sunset and Hollywood, make a right, walk a few feet, and you'll see the **Hollywood Brown Derby**.

This restaurant has a lot of Hollywood and culinary history attached to it. As the *Imagineering Field Guide to Hollywood Studios* explains on page 32:

> Opened in 1926, its novelty form, that of a brown derby hat, was reportedly inspired by the hat worn by 1928 Democratic presidential nominee Al Smith. This location was such a success that plans were made to open a second restaurant nearby.
>
> Just up the street near the corner of Hollywood and Vine, the Spanish Colonial-style Hollywood Brown Derby opened in 1929 and immediately became a hub for the social activity of the movie crowd from the growing film industry. Celebrities and studio executives frequented the place, which quickly became known for covering its walls with caricatures depicting all the famous faces that came to the restaurant.
>
> The Brown Derby is known for several signature dishes, which are always offered on the menu at our restaurant. The Cobb salad, according to legend, was invented one night when Brown Derby owner Robert Cobb went into the kitchen to pull together a late-night snack for Chinese Theater owner Sid Grauman, who was supposedly suffering from some dental work done earlier in that day.
>
> The finely chopped mix hit the spot to such a degree that Mr. Grauman and others began requesting it. And another legend—sometimes debated—holds that the Shirley Temple beverage was created at the Brown Derby so that the underage starlet would have her own special drink.

Since we're still near the Hollywood Brown Derby, let's walk toward the Echo Lake area of the park. You won't be able to miss the lake in front of you.

This lake is inspired by a man-made lake in Los Angeles, Echo Lake Park. In the early days of Hollywood, many silent films were shot there, most notably a few flicks starring Charlie Chaplin and Laurel and Hardy.

You'll see **Min and Bill's Dockside Diner**, a boat docked at the lake. The Min and Bill referenced here are characters from the 1930 movie with the same name. Marie Dressler and Wallace Beery were the stars of the movie; Dressler won an Oscar for her role.

Behind Min and Bill's boat, just across the lake, is **Gertie the Dinosaur**. Gertie is a character from the 1914 animated cartoon *Gertie the Dinosaur.*

Gertie was created by animator Winsor McCay. As you wander around this area, be on the lookout for a few of Gertie's footprints!

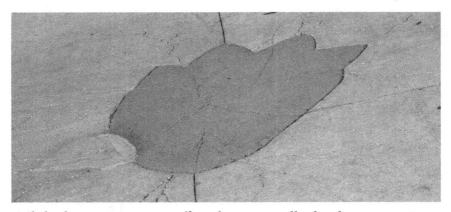

While this area may not offer a lot to actually do, there are quite a few places to eat. The restaurant **Hollywood & Vine** offers a buffet-style meal with some of your favorite Disney characters.

If you look at the exterior of the restaurant, there are a few references to the movie *Who Framed Roger Rabbit?* One window has the outline of Roger Rabbit, and another makes reference to Eddie Valiant, the private detective from the movie.

Again, as we've seen throughout Walt Disney World, there's a

1928 for the building's address, which is numerically symbolic for Mickey Mouse.

Inside the restaurant, check out the painting on the far-left wall. You should be able to spot a rough sketch of Mickey Mouse, and if you look really carefully, find the groupings of trees in the same mural. The trees make up a traditional hidden Mickey shape.

If you like your meals with a side of sauciness, then look no further than the **'50s Prime Time Cafe**, which is next to **Hollywood & Vine**.

Here you can enjoy comfort food from the 1950s, but be sure to keep your elbows off the table, or you may get scolded! The food here comes with a heaping side of sarcasm and humor. If you're seated near one of the black-and-white televisions, look at the brand name; it's not a Sony but a Disney!

Hopefully, you're not too full from all the food at Hollywood & Vine or the '50s Prime Time Cafe, because it's time for two big helpings of George Lucas. The next two attractions we are going to cover are based upon Lucas's blockbuster movie franchise Star Wars.

When Disney decided to utilize Lucas's work in their theme parks, it was a big shift for the company, as **Star Tours** would be the first attraction at a Disney theme park where the story or movie being featured didn't come from an exclusively Disney or Disney-adapted story line.

As then head of the Walt Disney Company Michael Eisner wrote in his book, *Work in Progress*:

> Disneyland and Walt Disney World remained immensely popular and successful long after Walt's and Roy's deaths.
>
> Unlike movies and television, which needed to be virtually re-launched from scratch, when Frank and I arrived, all the parks required was updating, expansion, and renewed excitement.
>
> We turned our attention first to Disneyland, where it seemed possible to make a difference most quickly and easily. One of the first calls I made was to George Lucas.
>
> No moviemaker had a more original blend of storytelling skills and technological imagination. Our idea was to recruit George Lucas to help us produce new attractions, building them around the immensely popular characters from movies such as *Star Wars* and *Raiders of the Lost Ark*.
>
> George was instantly enthusiastic, partly because this was a way to reintroduce the movie characters he'd created to young audiences, but mostly because it would give him the chance to experiment with new forms of three-dimensional storytelling.
>
> He quickly set his sights on an Imagineering project based

on NASA-developed flight simulation technology. Using *Star Wars* characters, the ride was designed to create the feeling of a wild trip through the universe. George had the idea that the spaceship ought to be flown by a psychologically unbalanced rookie pilot named Rex—making it plausible for a series of disasters to occur in the course of the flight.

Frank and I arrived at Imagineering one day to see an early version of the ride, which we were calling *Star Tours*. We were dressed in business suits but ready for thrills. At this stage, the outside of the ride was little more than a giant box on stilts.

I was completely intimidated by its long legs and shaky ladder we'd have to climb to get into the box. Frank led the way. I followed reluctantly, along with two or three Imagineers I hoped could double as paramedics.

When the ride began we rocked to *Star Wars* music. We rolled to a comedy soundtrack. We tossed and we turned. When we emerged, I felt elated. I had just experienced a genuinely new kind of ride. Frank had turned a pale shade of green and looked as if he was about to faint.

Based partly on this experience, we modified the ride so that not even queasy or nervous riders would get flight sickness.

The "Frank" Michael was referencing in this passage was Frank Wells, who was Disney's president until he tragically died in a helicopter crash. Check out his window on Main Street; it pays homage to his love for adventure and mountain climbing.

The magic of Lucas and Disney came together and brought the Star Wars galaxy to life in Star Tours at Disneyland in 1987.

On December 15, 1989, Star Tours blasted off to Endor at Walt Disney World Resort. The original version of Star Tours was in operation until 2010.

In 2011, the version we see operating today, **Star Tours—The Adventures Continue** debuted, featuring an improved ride-simulator attraction with advanced 3D technology, unique branching story lines, and an expanded universe of scenarios and characters based on the entire Star Wars saga.

With multiple story combinations, Star Tours—The Adventures Continue offers a unique experience and trip almost every time, as more than fifty random story combinations are used.

The many different twists, turns, and destinations include the underwater realms on Naboo, the bustling city-planet of Coruscant, the dreaded Death Star, and encounters with C-3PO, R2-D2, Darth Vader, Boba Fett, and Admiral Ackbar—or any combination of the above.

At the moment, Disney's Hollywood Studios is very Star Wars–centric.

Since Disney purchased Lucasfilm in 2012 for $4 billion, the company has continued to expand the Star Wars franchise and universe. In 2019 Disney's Hollywood Studios became home to a Star Wars-inspired land where guests are able to see the Star Wars stories come to life.

Star Wars: Galaxy's Edge takes visitors to the 14-acre Black Spire Outpost of Batuu, which is a newly created planet in the *Star Wars* story, and not a planet or locale previously used in the movies.

Disney's decision to create an entirely new setting and not use an established locale, such as a place like Tatooine, had a few motivations, but it primarily came from the need for the land to appeal to both diehard *Star Wars* fans and casual fans. If you've never watched a *Star Wars* movie, you can walk right into Batuu and be immersed into the story without having to know much about the *Star Wars* franchise.

As Scott Trowbridge, creative director for Walt Disney Imagineering said, "Why not make a place that is very familiar from the classic *Star Wars* films . . . ? The answer really is we know those places, we know those stories that happen there, and we know that we're not in them . . . Black Spire, outpost is an opportunity. It's designed from the very get-go to be a place that invites exploration and discovery, a place that invites us to become a character in the world of Star Wars, and, to the extent that we want to, participate in the stories of Star Wars."

With that being said, people, places, and things happening in Galaxy's Edge take place at some point during the blockbuster movies we've grown to love on the big screen. For example, around the land you'll see Kylo Ren and Stormtrooper droids, along with Rey and friends.

Disney's Imagineers and creative minds from Lucasfilm deliberated for over a year, going through hundreds of possible names, before they settled on Batuu and Black Spire Outpost.

As you walk through the planet, the namesake black spires are featured prominently throughout—with the tallest spire coming in at over 130 feet tall. What were once giant trees on the planet have now become petrified rock and broken chunks, which create the background and setting. If you pay attention, in the center of the village, there is one specific spire that is darker and more prominent than the rest.

While the storyline all leads back to *Star Wars*, the physical representation we see throughout the land takes much of its inspiration from the ancient markets of Morocco, Turkey, and places throughout Europe and Northern Africa, which Disney's design team visited for inspiration during their creative process.

In addition to the geography of earth-inspired Batuu, the LucasFilm archive was an incredible resource in nailing the accuracy of the land. Like so many of the lands throughout Walt Disney World, the ground you're walking on helps sell the immersive story.

As you roam the outpost, look down at the ground from time to time and you will be able to spot some droid tracks in the "dirt." As Paul Bailey, Show Systems Engineer at Disney's Imagineering, explained, "Our world, where guests are this close to something, it's got to be that next level. A good example of that is, droids move through our land. That's part of the story that we're trying to tell. We got access to one of the original Kenny Baker, New Hope, 1976–1977 era droids. We took rubbings of the bottoms of the droid feet. We turned that into a set of three files, which then, we turned into a set of 3D wheels." Bailey's team then "built a little droid trolley" that was pulled through the hardscape concrete, leaving "a little trail of droid tracks."

This same attention to detail can also be seen throughout the land in the tens of thousands of props, which were created specifically for Black Spire. Many of these props were created with materials available pre-1980 to keep with the authenticity of the original *Star Wars* trilogy.

As Eric Baker, Creative Director at Imagineering explains, "To start out, my first day on the job, I was put on a plane to go to England to visit the film set and work with the Star Wars film crew ... One of the philosophies that they told me is they said, 'We don't use anything that you couldn't buy before 1980 because the original films were made pre-1980.' . . . A lot of the stuff we build is built on recycled goods. For example, Xerox machines were filled with thousands of parts that we used to build stuff. We would always try to find some of those pre-1980."

Baker and his staff even stripped parts from the same jumbo jets that the film team utilized, so the look and feel around Batuu is as close to the films' as possible.

Authenticity and attention to detail throughout Galaxy's Edge clearly isn't a first for Disney; it's often what makes Disney "Disney." But for those working in Batuu, for the first time in the history of a Disney theme park, cast members are able to develop their own unique personalities and allegiances to the Resistance or the First Order, along with choosing their own outfits and accessories. With consideration for the hot and humid environment of central Florida, many of the costumes are actually lightweight, and while they may seem layered and heavy, the clothing is often made of a single garment pieced together to look that way.

Batuu's landscape wouldn't be a truly immersive Disney experience without food, drink, and merchandise! The land has nine different retail locations with over 700 unique items for sale. You can even build your own droid or try some of the infamous *Star*

Wars blue or green milk—it isn't actually milk but a plant-based dairy creation.

And oh yeah, see if you can spot some relevant numerology relating to the original film trilogy above Docking Bay 7 Food and Cargo. There is also a mural on the wall of Dok-Ondar's Den of Antiquities depicting a battle between the light side and the dark side of the Force. The original bas-relief of this mural was seen in Chancellor Palpatine's office in *Star Wars: Episode III – Revenge of the Sith*.

But enough about the background, setting, and shopping—it's time to get to the attractions. The two rides featured here are *Star Wars*: Rise of the Resistance and *Millennium Falcon*: Smugglers Run.

Rise of the Resistance is extremely immersive. With larger than life scenes and settings married and modified to some not-so-run-of-the-mill IMAX-like technology, the attraction simulates space and makes your experience and secret mission truly memorable. Disney sprinkles in some groundbreaking technology, projection mapping, numerous animatronics, and trackless ride vehicles to complete this one-of-a-kind experience for guests. The Rise of the Resistance is an exciting experience, but for so many diehard fans of *Star Wars*, it's all about the Millennium Falcon.

For the first time anywhere, *Star Wars* fans can see and board the meticulously detailed 110-foot, life-sized Millennium Falcon, as the fastest hunk of junk in the galaxy is the focal point of the Smugglers Run attraction.

This attraction is very much like a next generation simulator ride, similar to something like Star Tours but extremely evolved and more interactive. Now, just like Rise of the Resistance, I'm not going to give too much away about the storyline or your mission, but I do want to talk about one of the amazing Audio-Animatronics in the attraction: Hondo Ohnaka.

Mr. Ohnaka is a Weequay pirate from the Clone Wars, and he is the second-most advanced Audio-Animatronic you will encounter at Walt Disney World—the most advanced can be found over at Disney's Animal Kingdom, which we will cover in the next chapter.

The animatronic Hondo is roughly seven feet tall, and he has over fifty total functions. His skin is made from lifelike silicon, and he features a speaker in his chest, which provides directional sound. Hondo is even able to bend his knee, which makes it seem like he is able to walk about.

This animatronic is truly a sight to be seen, as is all of Galaxy's Edge. Even if you're not a fan of *Star Wars*, the land is highly immersive, highly detailed, and definitely worth your time. And oh yeah, move over Hidden Mickeys: there's a tiny hidden Millennium Falcon on the Millennium Falcon—see if you can spot it under the cockpit, near a set of pipes.

We are leaving one major Disney acquisition and heading over to another, this one from the opposite end of the entertainment spectrum—or, shall we say, universe. Just a quick stroll down the walkway from Star Tours is **Muppet Vision 3D.**

Despite having different owners (or parents), Kermit the Frog and friends and Mickey Mouse and his pals almost seem to be kissing cousins. Therefore, the entertainment world wasn't too shocked back on May 16, 1991, when the Muppets set up shop at Hollywood Studios.

This date was exactly one year and a day after Jim Henson, creator of the Muppets, passed away. Disney codeveloped and coproduced this attraction with Jim Henson Productions, and it was the last major project Jim personally worked on.

During the time of production, Disney was in talks with Henson to acquire Kermit and his crew, but Jim's sudden death derailed the acquisition.

In 2004 Disney finally sealed the deal, and according to Jim Henson's daughter, her father would be pleased:

> Commenting on the sale to Disney in a press release, Lisa Henson said: "In the months before his death in 1990, my father Jim Henson pursued extensive discussions with The Walt Disney Company based on his strong belief that Disney would be a perfect home for the Muppets.
>
> "As such, the deal we announced today is the realization of my father's dream, and ensures that the Muppet characters will live, flourish and continue to delight audiences everywhere, forever."

The twelve-minute 3D film, with a smattering of live action in the actual theater, is inspired by the classic television program *The Muppet Show*, which aired from 1976 to 1981. Even the 584-seat theater is inspired and designed to resemble the theater the Muppets would frequent on their show.

During the film, get ready for a few 4D pranks, and if you have a sharp eye, you will be able to notice the hidden Mickeys toward the end of the film.

Watch as the fireworks are ignited. When one of them explodes, you'll see it form a hidden Mickey. This one may be a bit tough to see, but you'll have another opportunity to catch a little

Mickey eye candy.

In the last scene of the film, Kermit the Frog is on a fire truck; don't fixate too much on Kermit. People in the background are wearing Mickey Mouse ears and carrying Mickey-shaped balloons.

One last story about the Muppets, which also has a minor tie-in to *Star Wars*. Legendary actor, director, producer, puppeteer, and all-around great guy Frank Oz—who voiced such notable critters as Yoda, Miss Piggy, and Cookie Monster, among countless others—worked alongside Jim Henson for decades.

As stated, Muppet*Vision 3D was the last project Jim worked on before he died. In fact, Jim passed away before the project could be completed. Frank stepped in and completed the project according to Jim's plans.

When former Disney President Michael Eisner called to discuss payment for Frank's work, Eisner offered him $50,000. Frank would not hear of it and declined the amount. When asked what he wanted, he informed Disney that he didn't want money; he was finishing Muppet*Vision 3D for Jim. He did, however, mention that he was running low on socks. After Frank completed his work, Disney sent him a basket full of socks!

As you exit the film, head back up the walkway toward Star Tours and make a left and head into the **Sci-Fi Dine-In Restaurant**. The setting here is a '50s-style drive-in theater, where you're served a big helping of kitschy '50s sci-fi clips and cartoons during your meal—think burgers and fried pickles—which happens to take place in a retro car.

The scene is set as the stars twinkle in the nighttime sky in this "outdoor" drive-in, set within the Hollywood Hills. Disney designed and handcrafted thirty-four car-shaped booths for your dining experience.

As recounted in the book *Walt Disney Imagineering*:

> Bill Casey's early concept design combined the styling of a classic 50s convertible with restaurant tables, thus creating the world's first and only "conver-table."

For the auto upholstery selection, they actually tracked down a source in Detroit that carried "New Old Stock," an auto restorer's term for goods that are vintage, but brand new in condition (the fabrics actually came with certificates of authenticity).

As you're dining and relaxing on some of that "new old stock," check out the license plates on the backs of the cars. The letters and numbers are the initials and birth dates of some of the Imagineers who worked on the restaurant.

Walking out of the Sci-Fi, make a left and walk toward the **ABC Commissary**.

We're going to continue all the way down Commissary Lane, head back toward the center of the park, and make a quick stop at the **Animation Courtyard**.

Feel free to pop in and go under the sea, at the **Voyage of the Little Mermaid**. The seventeen-minute show runs throughout the day and features live puppetry based on *The Little Mermaid*. As you walk past the building, look at the large mural and see if you can spot the hidden Mickeys represented in bubbles near Ursula.

Walt Disney once famously remarked, "I hope we never lose sight of one thing—that it was all started by a mouse." That was a very humble statement by him, but, as we all know, it was all started by Walt.

So when you leave the Voyage of the Little Mermaid, take a few minutes to appreciate the genius and legacy of your host, Walt Disney, at the multimedia presentation and self-guided gallery tour of **Walt Disney Presents**.

The presentation of Walt's life was originally created to commemorate the one hundredth anniversary of Walt's birth. Walt

Disney Presents gives you the chance to discover the man behind the mouse, his many achievements, and his ongoing legacy—from Mickey Mouse to Magic Kingdoms…and beyond.

The next stop at Disney's Hollywood Studios is **Toy Story Land**.

Just like the Muppets and Lucasfilm, Disney had a relationship with Pixar Animation Studios—albeit, this relationship at times was complicated and turbulent—but the fate of Pixar's Woody and Buzz ended up just like Kermit's and Darth's, in an acquisition.

The blockbuster movies created at Pixar became another jewel in the crown of the kingdom of Disney when Pixar was acquired for $7.4 billion in 2006. Believe it or not, Steve Jobs became a billionaire due to his ownership of Pixar, not his financial interests in Apple.

So, after the Pixar acquisition, it only seemed natural that another Toy Story presence should happen at the Disney theme parks.

Remember, Buzz Lightyear is in Tomorrowland at the Magic Kingdom, and in 2008, Disney took the concept of an interactive, shooting-type game with Pixar characters to the next level, with Toy Story Mania.

The theming and design are terrific and immediate. Even before you enter the attraction, you may notice the scale of things are a bit off.

As you step inside the building, you're actually stepping into Andy's room. You'll notice enormous board-game boxes as the walls and board games on the ceiling. Guests are meant to experience life at the size of a toy, so in Andy's room, a five-foot-six-inch person will feel about fourteen inches tall. The murals located in the load area are the largest murals painted since Epcot was built. With 3-D glasses in hand, you climb aboard a twentieth-century-inspired carnival ride tram, complete with a spring-action shooter. This allows you to take aim at a variety of targets during the five unique virtual carnival games. Sharpshooters can hit targets that trigger special 4-D effects.

It has been estimated that each day guests may break more than one million virtual plates using the spring-action shooters during this interactive game.

In order to create a show that responds not only to every pull of the guests' spring-action shooters but also every move the midway tram makes, there are more than 150 computers communicating over multiple networks throughout the attraction.

So how did this supersuccessful attraction come to be? Disney gave the *New York Times* an in-depth look at the backstory and creation of Toy Story Mania in the article "Will Disney Keep Us Amused?" from February 8, 2008.

The introduction of a ride called Toy Story Mania, more than three years in the making, and estimated to cost about $80 million, the attraction essentially puts guests inside a video game.

Riders, wearing 3-D glasses, board vehicles that careen through an old-fashioned carnival midway, operated by characters from the popular "Toy Story" film franchise. Vehicles stop at game booths—56 giant screens programmed with 3-D animation from Pixar—and riders play virtual-reality versions of classic carnival games.

Work on Toy Story Mania got under way on a stiflingly hot September day in 2005, when a team of Disney creative developers went to the Los Angeles County Fair. The goal was to research how carnival games operate.

Two developers, Kevin Rafferty and Robert Coltrin, had devised an idea for a new California Adventure ride that would juxtapose the old-fashioned romance of a carnival midway with high-tech video game elements. They had a hunch that "Toy Story" and "Toy Story 2," the Pixar films about toys coming to life, would provide a good theme. But they didn't know much about carnival games.

"We looked at each other and said, 'Are the games we remember from our childhoods even relevant anymore?'" Mr. Coltrin said.

At the fair, the two were thrilled as they walked through rows of game booths—wooden structures that carnival operators call "stick joints"—to find crowds enjoying classic games like the ring toss and water guns. "We were like, 'Score!' and gave each other a high-five," Mr. Coltrin recalled.

Using digital cameras, members of the development team documented details, from the colors of the canvas covering each booth—red and yellow—to how far apart the games were spaced.

They quickly ruled out some games as options for the ride. "Toss a coin in a cup didn't really do it for us," said Chrissie Allen, a senior show producer. But other games, like one in which customers threw darts at balloons, piqued their interest. "We thought, 'This just might work,'" Ms. Allen said.

Reassembling at Disney's offices in Glendale, Calif., the team worked on the concept that would become Toy Story Mania. Because carnivals sell commotion, there would be lots of flashing lights, barkers trying to capture riders' attention, buzzers and bells.

Mr. Rafferty and Mr. Coltrin dreamed up a fanciful story: The classic toys in "Toy Story" had come to life and staged a carnival under their owner's bed while he was away at dinner.

To give birth to Toy Story Mania, Mr. Rafferty and Mr. Coltrin went to work turning drawings of the ride into foam models, toiling in the same 1950s-era building in suburban Los Angeles where Walt Disney himself once tinkered.

Upstairs, designers entered blueprints for the ride into a computer program. This would allow them to start building and refining the entire project, which is made up of 150 computers, with 90 of them moving around on the ride vehicles and communicating with one another via a secured wireless network.

With a click of a mouse, developers could jump to any spot inside the vehicles for a virtual dip into how the experience might look to someone on the ride.

"We don't want anybody to be able to see multiple versions of Woody at the same time, and seconds make a difference," said Mark Mine, the technical concept designer. "Every part of the ride has to be magical."

Across the street, in a cold, unmarked garage,
more than 400 people of all ages—all had signed strict nondis-
closure agreements—sat on a plywood vehicle set up in front of a
projection screen and played various versions of the games. Disney
workers studied their reactions and interviewed them afterward.

"We were looking to see if some effects were too scary," Ms.
Allen said, "or if there wasn't enough laughing happening
during certain sequences."

Among the discoveries: People wanted to be able to compare
scores after they were finished playing, while some children
had a hard time reaching the cannonlike firing controller,
christened by Disney as a "spring action shooter."

Engineers added a computer screen to vehicles to display
scores and installed the controls on movable lap bars.

"We were trying to find out things we didn't even know to
ask about," said Sue Bryan, a senior show producer.

The ride's psychological components started to take shape
during this phase. Disney decided that riders were happi-
er when they got a bigger visual payoff. (One of Little Bo
Peep's balloons now pops with greater force when hit with
a virtual dart and a blast of air shoots into a rider's face.) A
game involving shooting at a paper target was dropped. ("It
was hard to make paper interesting," Ms. Bryan said.) And
developers decided that the last game before the exit needed
to be the easiest, so riders would feel that they were coming
out as winners, even if they weren't very good.

After Disney closed the Pixar deal, in January 2006, Toy
Story Mania became more elaborate. Mr. Iger wanted Pixar—and particularly one of its co-founders, John Lasseter,
who had worked as a skipper on the Jungle Cruise ride at
Disneyland after college—to contribute to creative advances
in the parks.

One of Mr. Lasseter's major concerns about Toy Story Mania centered on the animation. Disney had hired an outside contractor to handle it, but Mr. Lasseter insisted that Pixar staff members who were involved in creating the films should also work on the ride.

The Disney team had also decided to leave out Buzz Lightyear, the modern spaceman toy in the films, because he was already showcased in an older ride called Astro Blasters. But Pixar felt that the character was essential to the "Toy Story" franchise. Buzz will now be a host of a game, and he shares top billing on the ride's marquee.

Well, nearly a decade after the ride debuted, I think it's safe to answer the *NYT*'s headline question, will Disney keep us amused? Just by watching the standby lines for this attraction when you're at the park, the answer is a resounding yes!

After roughly a decade of incredible success as a stand-alone attraction tucked in the back of the park, Disney announced in August of 2015 that they would expand Toy Story's presence at Hollywood Studios.

In preparation for this new land, Toy Story Mania received a new entrance. As you approach the attraction, you'll notice that the entrance is actually the box Andy's Toy Story Mania! game came in, as Andy laid out this game as a play set in his room. In addition to the new façade and updated queue, the attraction also expanded its footprint, receiving an additional third ride track to boost capacity.

Speaking of footprints, don't forget to look down on the ground as you traverse the area. Visitors to Toy Story Land are supposed to feel as though they have been shrunk to the size of a toy. This is quite evident when you see the ginormous footprints on the ground. These prints are 25 feet long or roughly a size 240.

Now, that footprint isn't just any old footprint; it's actually Andy's. Toy Story Land is themed to represent his backyard, a pretty large backyard at 11 acres, where Andy has set up a couple of his favorite toys for us to play with.

Our first attraction is **Slinky Dog Dash**, an attraction Disney calls a family-friendly coaster which bends and twists around curves, over hills, and down drops—it's a fun attraction to ride at night.

Here's the backstory for the ride, Andy assembled his Dash and Dodge Mega Coaster Kit, but instead of using the roller coaster vehicle that came with the kit, Andy has put his Slinky Dog—a spinoff of Slinky, a classic 1940s American toy—a floppy-eared dachshund with a stretching coil body on the track.

Each 18-passenger coaster train zips riders around and above Toy Story Land, catching great views of the land. In a first for a Disney coaster, Slinky Dog Dash features a second launch at its midpoint as riders experience cool sound effects and spinning lights, darting through a series of rings on their way to the attraction's finale featuring Wheezy, the squeaky penguin from the *Toy Story* films.

As you make your way through the queue for this attraction, keep your eyes out for a few interesting things. If you're riding via the standby entrance, as you pass the sign that provides the wait time, check the shape, it sort of looks like a dog's tag. In fact, it is a dog tag; it's Andy's dog Buster's tag. When you pass the sign look back, you'll see Buster's information.

Next, just before you approach the load platform to board the ride, you may notice a wall of giant stickers. One of the stickers, says "Triple R Ranch." This reference goes back to *The Mickey Mouse Club* television show from the mid-1950s.

One of the serials featured on the television show was "Spin and Marty," also known as "The Adventures of Spin and Marty." These were television shorts set at the Triple R Ranch, a boys western-style summer camp.

One of the fans of Spin and Marty was Pixar's John Lasseter. Wanting to pay homage to one of his favorite childhood shows, he made sure Andy wore a Triple R Ranch t-shirt in the movie *Toy Story 2*, and now as a result the logo is featured in the queue for this ride.

Another interesting tidbit is the large mural along the wall as you load onto the ride itself. This mural is actually Andy's original blueprint for the ride. The mural features a few scenes which were initially planned for the ride but didn't come to fruition. However, what did come to fruition is a hidden Mickey. Take a look at the last mural on the right, find the green parachuting Army men, and look at the blue clouds, there's the hidden Mickey.

Lastly, as you pull out of the load station, you can't miss the large box Rex the toy dinosaur came in. The box is priced $19.95, from Al's Toy Barn, which features prominently in the film *Toy Story 2*. Above the $19.95 is an 11 and a 22. Put all of those numbers together and you have 11 22 1995, which symbolizes November 22, 1995, *Toy Story's* release date in theatres.

Fastpass+ is definitely suggested for this attraction, riders must be 38 inches tall, and oh yeah, be sure to smile, as you will have your picture taken!

Alien Swirling Saucers is the last attraction here in Toy Story Land. Again, we are immersed in Andy's imagination after he won a toy playset from the Pizza Planet restaurant featured in the *Toy Story* movies.

Basically, the little green Aliens from the *Toy Story* movies—you know the guys, the ones who love the "the claw," which you will see hanging overhead—will guide and spin you around different large circles, while you rock out to some music and coordinated lighting.

Check out this attraction at night. The ride itself is nothing spectacular and has a much more immersive and entertaining feel when you're able to appreciate the lighting which is synced with the music of the attraction.

If you're not a fan of spinning around, feel free to sit this one out, as there's a viewing area where you can take in the sights. Before boarding Alien Swirling Saucers, feel free to grab a photo with Buzz Lightyear who is standing more than 14 feet tall near the entrance to his Star Command Station Playset. Riders must be 32 inches tall, and **Fastpass+** is offered.

That basically brings Toy Story Land to an end for us. If you need a little bite to eat, just across from Alien Swirling Saucers is **Woody's Lunch Box**. As the saying goes, everything is better with bacon, so stop and grab Disney's version of a Pop Tart—it's a pastry filled with chocolate and hazelnut and coated in maple fondant and candied bacon.

Let's close out our trip to Disney's Hollywood Studios with a bang. As you leave Toy Story Mania, start heading toward the exit of the park.

Make a left onto Sunset Boulevard and walk down the street toward Tower of Terror. Enter the **Hollywood Hills Amphitheatre**, a 6,900-seat building (that can also accommodate 3,000 standing guests) designed specifically for the evening finale, **Fantasmic!**

Lights, lasers, fireworks, and water (lots of water; the moat around the stage holds 1.9 million gallons) play a crucial role in this nighttime outdoor musical.

Fantasmic! takes you into the colorful imagination of Mickey Mouse as forces of good and evil battle it out. The characters and spirit of *Beauty and the Beast, Sleeping Beauty, Peter Pan, The Little Mermaid, Cinderella, Aladdin,* and *The Lion King,* to name a few, all play a part in this spectacular of dancing and synchronized water and song from Disney classics.

The twenty-five-minute spectacular features about fifty performers, who use about eighty costumes per show. The dragon in the show is roughly fifty feet tall and has a wingspan of fifty feet, and the steamboat is eighty feet long and weighs about seventy thousand pounds—quite impressive and entertaining.

Fantasmic! is presented on select nights, with performance times varying based on park hours and weather.

There's even a Fantasmic! dining package you can reserve. Have dinner at Mama Melrose's Ristorante Italiano, Hollywood & Vine, or the Hollywood Brown Derby, and this allows you to secure guaranteed seating for the show after your dinner.

Fantasmic! closes out Disney's Hollywood Studios for us. We're now off to the final theme park at Walt Disney World, Disney's Animal Kingdom.

Chapter Four

ANIMAL KINGDOM

> *I have learned from the animal world, and what everyone will learn who studies it, is a renewed sense of kinship with earth and all its inhabitants.*
>
> **—Walt Disney**

First a rabbit (Oswald), then a mouse (Mickey). Add a few dogs (Pluto and Goofy), a grumpy duck (Donald), an elephant (Dumbo), a deer (Bambi); the list could go on and on. Disney is very animal-centric.

Walt Disney's love and appreciation for animals dates back to his childhood days on a farm in Marceline, Missouri. Today, it's hard not to acknowledge that much of the success of the entire company is rooted with animals.

As the company grew and thrived through the 1930s and 1940s, the interaction and utilization of these critters leaped from the cels of animation and into the realm of documentary with *True-Life Adventures,* an Oscar-winning nature series beginning in 1948. Disney basically created the concept of the nature documentary.

By 1955 Walt had his theme park, Disneyland, stocked with plenty of animals—mostly mechanical. As mentioned in the first chapter, Walt really wanted to use live animals at the Jungle Cruise, but it didn't come to fruition.

When speaking about Disneyland in 1956 to reporter Pete Martin, Walt remarked, "The park means a lot to me in that it's something that will never be finished. Something that I can keep developing, keep plussing and adding to—it's alive. It will be a live, breathing thing that will need changes."

About forty-two years after this interview, Walt's company opened a park that is alive, living, and breathing—literally. Disney's Animal Kingdom debuted on April 22, 1998 (Earth Day, no less) and features over two thousand animals, representing roughly three hundred species.

Every day, about four tons of food is consumed by the park's residents, including more than two thousand pounds of vegetation. Over forty thousand mealworms, wigglers, and nightcrawlers are consumed weekly, in addition to eighty thousand crickets per month. It's no wonder that since the park opened, Disney's lab technicians have analyzed more than forty thousand samples of animal poop!

Over on the flora side of things, there are more than four million trees, plants, shrubs, vines, epiphytes, grasses, and ferns (three thousand different species) from every continent on Earth except Antarctica.

Across the theme park's four hundred–plus acres, more than 770,000 shrubs were planted, with nearly seventy thousand trees being planted in Africa alone.

So, how did this cow pasture / tree farm / fireworks test site at Walt Disney World turn into Disney's fourth theme park?

It all started back in early 1990. Imagineer Joe Rohde had a meeting with Michael Eisner about an animal theme park. Rohde envisioned a park with three equal components: traditional theme park, Epcot-style pavilion, and nontraditional zoo.

He pitched the idea, and Eisner agreed on the basic framework. That initial meeting even decided the park's name when Eisner remarked, "You know we have the Magic Kingdom; we should have Disney's Animal Kingdom." The name stuck.

A consistent underlying vibe that loomed large over the project was how the park wouldn't be a zoo, per se, as research showed fiscally, a traditional, run-of-the-mill zoo wouldn't make sense or money for Disney.

Another doubt about the park was the notion of being able to give guests a feeling of shared space with wild animals. Is observing animals really that thrilling or exciting?

This concept was explored and elaborated upon in the book *The Making of Disney's the Animal Kingdom*:

> Eisner wondered, "Are guests going to feel that animals are exciting enough?" As the design team caucused in their

Spartan warehouse, their rallying cry was, "Proximity equals excitement!"

The plan that emerged was so audacious that the team dared not confide it even to Marty Sklar, Imagineering's creative leader.

Joe Rohde began the next meeting with corporate executives by squarely addressing the issues of animal encounters: "We know that there are concerns about whether animals are, in and of themselves, dramatic.

"The heart of the Animal Kingdom park is animals, and our guests encounters with them. We have gone to great lengths to make sure the animals will be displayed in a way that will bring them and people together as never before…"

The door to the room opened. A 400 pound female Bengal tiger, restrained by only a slender chain, stalked in. Rohde ignored the huge cat and kept talking as she prowled the room, coming within inches of Disney's key executives.

The effect on everyone present was palpable as the tiger, all rippling muscle and powerful claws, walked restlessly around the edges of the room. Disney president Frank Wells edged his chair closer to the table. Eisner stared. Sklar, kept in the dark by the team, gasped and looked at Rohde.

Twitching its whiskers, the tiger sat in the corner of the room, yawning, as Rohde continued, "Yes, there's an element of danger, but that's necessary for drama. Physical danger is an essential fact that animals deal with every day, and we want to drive that idea home."

The tiger sauntered behind Rohde and was led out of the room as he concluded: "So you can see our position: proximity to animals—the illusion that they are right next to you—is essential."

In a brief interview I had with Joe after referencing this story, I asked him if he had anything else he could share about that day.

He told me, "Honestly, the event is very well covered in the book. I think we made the point that we never told anybody or asked permission. One humorous note is that this event has been reported by various resources over the years with quite different versions of what the tiger did. Jumping up on a table. Growling at Michael Eisner. Letting me ride in on its back…lots of variations."

And with that, it was quite obvious that Disney's Animal Kingdom would be a different species of theme park. Disney's planning and research were kicked into high gear.

On the corporate level, an advisory board was created to guide the assembly of a humane, ecofriendly, conservation-minded park. The board would consist of consultants, members of animal and wildlife-protection groups, zoologists, and curators from zoos across the country. Even legendary primatologist Jane Goodall joined the team.

For the design and creative component of the park, executive Joe Rohde and a core team of seven Imagineers crisscrossed the globe to the tune of more than five hundred thousand miles (the equivalent of circling the world twenty times) to ensure the authenticity of the areas of the park they were seeking to replicate. As reported in the *Orlando Sentinel* on April 19,1998:

> "We've tried to be very thorough in inventing this place," said Joe Rohde, the park's chief designer. "We sent probably 30 people over five or six years to Africa, six or seven different trips, and took thousands and thousands and thousands of photographs."

While Disney's Animal Kingdom is accredited by the American Zoo and Aquarium Association, everyone associated with the park will tell you it's *not* a zoo! Yes, there are animals throughout the park, but they are involved in a story, a story that transcends the simplicity of a zoo.

While the animals are the stars of the show, the underlying story line and presentation is how we live and interact with animals and their environment and to recognize and value this man/animal/environmental dynamic through conservation.

Believe it or not, Disney's Animal Kingdom isn't the first live-animal-centric park with an eye toward conservation at Walt Disney World.

Before Joe Rohde and Michael Eisner had a spark of imagination about Disney's Animal Kingdom, Walt Disney himself, on one of his early flyovers of the land he purchased in Florida, became smitten with an eleven-acre piece of land residing in the middle of a lake.

This little island caught his eye and helped him to decide that this area of his property should be developed first.

That little island still stands today, in Bay Lake, just adjacent to Magic Kingdom. When Walt Disney World originally opened, the island was dubbed Blackbeard's Island, but it never opened as an attraction.

Three years later, in April 1974, it was renamed Treasure Island and debuted with a pirate-hideaway and lost-treasure theme, which was short lived.

On June 1, 1976, Discovery Island debuted, featuring an animal-centric theme. The island was home to many exotic birds, plants, American alligators, and Galapagos tortoise exhibits.

The island was created to educate guests on conservation efforts, breeding, and research. At its height of popularity, it was home to more than 130 species totaling roughly a thousand animals. Although the majority of the animals were birds, there were also small, exotic mammals, such as the Patagonian cavy, a kangaroolike rodent, and ring-tailed lemurs. In 1979 the island was accredited by the American Zoo and Aquarium Association.

Through the 1980s, Discovery Island worked to raise and breed many rare birds. Often, birds that were injured and wouldn't be able to survive in the wild would call the island home.

In 1987 a nonprofit organization that places trained monkeys in homes with disabled people forged an agreement with Disney to help oversee their breeding.

Helping Hands: Simian Aides for the Disabled placed their colony of fifty-three capuchin monkeys in a specially created colony on Discovery Island.

The monkeys were there to educate the public and share the ways they were being trained to help those suffering from paralysis.

By the late 1990s, declining attendance numbers and competition from Disney's Animal Kingdom spelled the demise of Discovery Island. The park closed in April 1999, a year after Animal Kingdom opened.

Discovery Island still lives on today. Obviously, the actual island can still be seen when you're near the Magic Kingdom, but the hub, right in the center of Disney's Animal Kingdom, which leads you to the different areas of the park, originates at Discovery Island, so let's go check it out.

As you stroll toward the entrance of the park, keep an eye out for a mythical-looking creature, or perhaps something a little beastly. You may see a unicorn or a dragon on a park bench or a symbol on a pole in the parking lot.

These are references to one of the original lands planned for the park, the Beastly Kingdom. The area would have had a theme centered around mythical creatures, but it never came to fruition. These little details are the lingering reminders of the some of the initial plans for the park.

As you pass through the entrance of the Animal Kingdom, the shady, lush, and very green **Oasis** awaits you. This peaceful pathway of streams, flora, and fauna fully embraces you—the giant anteater, exotic boar and wallabies are a couple of the animals residing in the Oasis. There are also a few observation areas to enjoy the scenery or snap a photo or two.

Walking deeper into the Oasis, you can almost feel the stage being set for something grand, perhaps larger animals and a greater adventure. The transfer to a different time and place has commenced.

The vibe here is similar to, yet different from, visiting the Magic Kingdom. You walk under the train station and onto Main Street. You walk a few steps and see Cinderella's Castle; the same feeling occurs as you leave the Oasis and walk toward the **Tree of Life**.

This iconic structure is surrounded by a village and situated on Discovery Island, which is the hub of the Animal Kingdom, the epicenter of the park. It leads to the lands of Pandora, Africa, Asia, and Dinoland, which surround the island.

As you look around **Discovery Island**, colors and cultures abound. The love of animals is clear throughout, with folk art and colorful architecture from the Caribbean, the South Pacific, and coastal Africa.

Much like Main Street, Discovery Island is rife with shops and restaurants. Rather than conveying the feel of "Anytown, USA," here the setting is a village, and many of the items you see throughout this area actually came from villages.

Fifteen hundred two- to three-foot-long hand-painted wooden folk-art animal carvings were crafted on the island of Bali by native craftsmen. Imagineers brought these items back from their research trips so they could adorn Discovery Island.

Another great example of authenticity in artifacts can be found at two of the restaurants on the island, **Pizzafari** and **Flame Tree Barbecue**. Page 96 of the book *The Making of Disney's Animal Kingdom Park* recounts an interesting story for Pizzafari:

Four hours up a dirt-and-boulder mountain road, in Oaxaca, Mexico, Imagineering's interiors team found Rojelio Blas and his family. Rojelio carves fantastically shaped animals, then his wife and kids paint them in bright colors and whimsical patterns. The Imagineers ordered 300 bats, 120 bugs and 150 butterflies to hang in Pizzafari.

The creativity and details that complement the story line are also seen within Pizzafari's murals and mosaics throughout the five themed rooms.

Quoting from the same book, page 97:

> For Pizzafari's five dining rooms, 34 stunning murals were painted by Imagineering veteran Frank Armitage and his artist daughter, Nicole.
>
> Oversized animals rendered in bright colors look down from the walls of one room, while animals that hide in their environments peek out in another. Creatures that carry their houses on their backs—turtles and snails and hermit crabs—creep along in a third room. Another theme is animals that come out at night. There is even a whole room based on animals that hang upside down.

Within all the detailed and elaborate themes, there's still a hidden Mickey or two within the murals on the walls. In the room with the various forms of sea life on the walls, spot the turtle and see if you can find the hidden Mickey on the lower-left portion of the shell. A similar hidden Mickey is depicted in the spots of a leopard in another mural.

As you leave Pizzafari, keep an eye out for the animal-shaped benches around Discovery Island, made entirely of recycled materials.

On the other end of the culinary spectrum and the island is **Flame Tree Barbecue**. It's not hard to figure out what's on the menu here. What may be a little more intriguing is the often-overlooked theme of the restaurant, the dynamic between predator and prey. Look for a few examples such as snakes and mice or ants and anteaters.

The prey are painted on the tables, and the predators are depicted in the chairs. Have a seat and become part of the food chain!

The atmosphere and architecture of the building are primarily that of a traditional Balinese water garden, but there are also influences from the American Southwest, Spain, Iran, and the Philippines.

Just across the way from the Flame Tree Barbecue is the entrance to the show **It's Tough to Be a Bug!**, which is housed inside the iconic symbol of the park, the Tree of Life. The original concept for this location was for it to be home to a restaurant, tentatively called the Roots, but as it turned out, a 3-D show featuring the stars of *A Bug's Life* was a better fit.

Another early concept for the Tree of Life was for folks to get a bird's-eye view of the park by taking a trip to the top of the tree and enjoying a bit of a scenic overlook; those plans too were eventually scrapped.

While those two plans didn't come to fruition, what did make it off the drawing board is still very remarkable, especially when you know that what you're actually looking at is a repurposed offshore oil-drilling platform!

During the initial planning phase of the tree, Disney was going to borrow a page from the Epcot playbook and build a geodesic dome. The branches and leaves would be attached to its surface to form the tree. However, one day, inspiration that brought about a design change struck at an odd time.

A member of the design team was watching a television program that talked about offshore drilling platforms. Eureka! It just so happens the shape, strength, and ability to withstand nature's elements would be a perfect fit for the park's iconic symbol.

With the details and design concept complete, Disney went to work creating the 145-foot-tall tree, spanning 50 feet at its base. According to the Imagineers' mythology, "the tree is supposed to have been the first thing here—the village came here to the Tree. It is the source of life and water for the village and Discovery Island, and presumably for the rest of the Animal Kingdom as well."

Ten artists and three Imagineers worked full time for more than eighteen months to create more than three hundred animal carvings, in no particular order, size, and scale. From a sea horse to an elephant, the full spectrum of animals is well represented. Sculptors had between six and ten hours to create each masterpiece before the plaster hardened and their work was immortalized.

While the exterior of the Tree of Life was coming to life, world-renowned primatologist (feel free to address her as Dame or Doctor, as she's the owner of both of those titles) Jane Goodall, who works closely with Disney, visited the park while it was under construction.

She inquired as to whether there was a chimp on the tree. Within a few weeks, Goodall's most famous subject, David Graybeard, was sculpted into the tree. As you enter It's Tough to Be a Bug!, feel free to give your regards to David, as he's featured prominently near the entrance.

The Tree of Life features 45 secondary branches that lead to 756 tertiary branches that taper to 7,891 end branches, which feature roughly 103,000 footlong leaves in five different shades of green that actually blow in the wind.

And to think, the final look of this massive tree was actually based on a bonsai tree the design team saw at Epcot's International Flower and Garden Festival, which they visited during the design and concept phase for the iconic structure.

If you want a closer, more detailed look at the carvings on the tree, wander around the Discovery Island Trails that meander around the tree and offer a peaceful, self-guided view of different angles of the tree. They also offer opportunities to spot any of the following animals along the way: white stork, Asian small-clawed otter, red kangaroo, West African crowned crane, African crested porcupine, Galapagos tortoise, lesser flamingo, macaw, ring-tailed lemur, saddle-billed stork—and who would want to miss the lappet-faced vultures?

By its very definition, Discovery Island is obviously surrounded by water—the Discovery River, to be exact. The river is composed of twenty-seven million gallons of water, which could fill about eighteen hundred average-sized backyard swimming pools, and while the river looks great for the aesthetics of the park, starting in early 2017, it became an integral part of the evening entertainment scene.

For much of its existence, the Animal Kingdom was primarily a day park, with very little in the way of evening offerings. All of that changed in 2017, when Discovery Island became the center of evening entertainment.

As day turns to night, the **Discovery Island Carnivale** ushers in an evening cavalcade of dancers, stilt walkers, and musicians for a nighttime dance party along the streets.

As the carnivale sets the mood for the evening, the majestic Tree of Life awakens from its daytime existence and comes alive with color and light every ten minutes.

Watch as flickering fireflies magically appear and stir to life the wondrous animal spirits carved into the tree's towering trunk.

Gaze upon a young doe embarking upon a thrilling journey. Behold love blossoming between a pair of hummingbirds. See a fox spreading gifts of love among the denizens of a wintry forest.

These two evening experiences take place somewhat informally as background experiences when you stroll the area, but the evening show **Rivers of Light** celebrates the beauty of all living things. It premiered along the Discovery River in February 2017.

Here's a bit more about the fifteen-minute outdoor show:

> Eastern festival traditions merge with innovative technology to make Rivers of Light come alive. Featuring evocative, never-before-seen footage from Disneynature, live performances and floating set pieces set to a soaring original musical score—this nighttime show employs a host of magical devices to create an immersive experience that's unique to anything else on the planet.
>
> The flickering ornamentation of fireflies illustrates the migration of light—a central motif of the production. As the story unfolds, original video projections and choreographed laser animation combine to create the appearance of glowing fireflies, illuminating moments of the celebration like living pixie dust.
>
> Mysteriously, the show's "storytellers" never utter a word. Instead, they communicate volumes through fascinating forms of authentic Asian dance, music, song and shadow puppetry. The lush lagoon setting is a central character itself—an ever-changing canvas for the unveiling of an unforgettable tale.

Discovery Island features some great evening entertainment, but for the real showstopper, walk across the Discovery Island bridge that leads into Pandora and check out all the world of *Avatar* has to offer.

As mentioned earlier in the chapter, the Beastly Kingdom didn't make it off the drawing board and into the park. But that's OK, because in 2017, another mystical place, **Pandora—The World of Avatar**, took a leap from the big screen and landed at Walt Disney World.

The largest addition to Disney's Animal Kingdom is based upon the 2009 record-breaking blockbuster movie *Avatar*. The addition of this land to the park stays consistent with Disney's theme for the Animal Kingdom. Sure, there's fun, adventure, and heaps of Disney magic, but the appreciation of nature and conservation is still at the forefront of both the movie and its theme park representation.

In May 2017, to celebrate the grand opening of Pandora—The World of Avatar at Disney's Animal Kingdom, Walt Disney Parks and Resorts and the Disney Conservation Fund announced "Connect to Protect," a commitment of up to $1 million to help protect and restore habitats critical to ten at-risk animals.

The contribution will be unlocked by guests who participate in conservation "missions" while exploring the immersive land of Pandora. For the first time ever, guests will get to choose which animal that donation will support.

If $1 million to help endangered animals sounds great, how does $65 million sound? This is the amount Disney has donated, since they launched their conservation efforts, to reverse the decline of at-risk wildlife and increase the time kids spend in nature.

Disney's Conservation Fund has helped to protect more than four hundred species, including elephants, butterflies, and coral reefs throughout more than 115 countries of the world.

The fund was created during the conception of the Animal Kingdom park. The members of Disney's Animal Kingdom advisory board implored the company to get involved with conservation efforts around the world, and this has been the backbone of the theme park ever since.

Naturally, it's only fitting that Disney and James Cameron came together to showcase Pandora, the setting for a film with a strong environmental and conservation message.

If you haven't had the opportunity to see the movie, don't worry; you'll still be able to appreciate this area of the park. As Joe Rohde explains:

It is the planet Pandora where you can come, you can visit, and have your own unique adventure. Rather than reliving the adventures of characters from the film, you're going to come to the planet where those things happened—and have your own set of adventures you can own.

We are taking our guests on a journey to this world in an experience that's as realistic and immersive as possible. In the movie, the world of Pandora is a setting for the action and characters whose story we follow. Here, guests are the primary characters immersed in an extremely vivid, authentic experience.

As you walk over the Discovery River and enter Pandora, you're no longer a visitor to Walt Disney World but an ecotourist, now part of Alpha Centauri Expeditions (ACE), who has traveled to an exoplanet located in the Alpha Centauri star system, 4.4 light-years from Earth. (One light-year is roughly six trillion miles!)

As you make your way into the Valley of Mo'ara, this area is undergoing a rebirth long after the destructive mining operation known as the Resources Development Administration ceased operation and the human conflict with the Na'vi—the indigenous blue people who call Pandora home—has ended.

As you walk through the valley, all of your senses should perk up (especially at night; the bioluminescence is remarkable) as out-of-this-world sights and sounds surround you. Na'vi drums, totems, and culture abound—along with some very bizarre animals and plants.

One of the first things to experience is the **Flaska Reclinata**, a very large plant on the right side of the walkway as you enter the land. There should be an ACE expert there to provide some information about the plant. Help the environment and touch the plant. See what happens when your touch helps to reseed the planet with the Flaska Reclinata.

As you continue your journey through Pandora, see if you can spot the **Dapophet** plant. It features a starburst bloom that resembles the live agave plant alongside it.

Other unique Pandoran plants to look out for are the puff-ball tree, vein pod, scorpion thistle, and episoth. Each one of the Pandoran plants was hand sculpted, and more than 250 varieties of Earth trees are intermingled within the Pandoran flora. Disney planted more than five hundred trees and ten thousand shrubs across the landscape in this area.

Many of the plants throughout the land are interactive and feature a glowing bioluminescence at night. This is a great complement to the paths and walkways around the land that also glow at night. The walkways that glow are charged by the sunlight during the day, and Disney uses a black light, among some other tricks, to complete this vibrant experience.

As you continue down the path and work your way deeper into Pandora, one of the first things your eyes are drawn to is the iconic floating mountains. There's a good chance you even noticed them when your vehicle pulled into the Animal Kingdom entrance. Well, now's your chance to get up close and personal with the twenty-two mountains that peak at about 130 feet above the valley floor.

A team of more than sixty artisans from across the globe (United States, Japan, Ireland, Portugal, and Peru) came together to create the out-of-this-world artistic mountain landscape.

If you look closely, you'll see a few Pandoran stingbats (with their lethal tail spines) in the mountains. You can get a better view of the mountains when you get in the queue for your chance to ride a beast on **Flight of Passage.**

I'll let Disney's website take over with the backstory for the attraction:

> The journey begins in the queue as guests begin an uphill trek around a massive root structure, over a land bridge above waterfalls to an authentic totem garden. Meandering passageways lead to a cave-like structure where the great-winged banshees, or Ikran as the Na'vis call them, are celebrated in paintings and majestic totems.
>
> Next, guests enter an old, once abandoned RDA facility with a laboratory partially restored. Here, there are scientific experiments in progress with references to habitat restoration, the ecosystem, water purification and the connection of all living things.
>
> Next stop is the genetic matching room where explorers are scanned and genetic material is sampled to connect them to personal avatars in preparation for a flight experience. Once matched, adventurers board link chairs, don flight visors and prepare for the flight.
>
> Next stop: a mystical world like no other. Flying on the back of a banshee represents an important rite of passage for the Na'vi and as visitors to the alien world, guests will have a chance to be tested and guided through the wondrous journey.
>
> After entering a state-of-the-art theater, each guest straddles

a single-seat simulator (like a motorcycle) that delivers a realistic sensation of riding a living creature. Guests will experience the swift and graceful movements of flight and even feel the banshee breathing beneath them. The multi-sensory experience uses cutting-edge technology and intricate special effects like never before.

This heart-pounding adventure transports explorers through the alien world of Pandora, offering lifelike encounters—splashing whale-like creatures, blowing wind, roaring banshees, and a threatening encounter with a flying predator. The exhilarating 4-minute flight through the sci-fi world of bioluminescence and floating mountains is orchestrated to a complex musical score recorded by the London Symphony Orchestra.

If that description doesn't make you get in line for the ride, here's what Joe Rohde, and then James Cameron, had to say about it. "In Flight of Passage, the sensation of flying is really visceral, really believable. Not only do you have the more obvious aspects of flying—the swooping and curving—but we've put in crosswind, air density, and banking."

"You know, riding the Ikran is a thrill. You're going to plunge. You're going to dive. You're going to swoop. It's like dreaming with your eyes open."

So there you have it—a full-on multisensory experience. Not only will you feel like you're flying, but you'll feel the banshee beneath you breathe as you soar through the air.

This is definitely a one-of-a-kind experience. Obviously, this is a must-**Fastpass+** attraction, and to be honest, if you have to wait in the long queue, it's worth it, as this experience is really unique and thrilling—and the queue is interesting in its own right.

Obviously, both Joe Rohde and James Cameron have their creative fingerprints all over Pandora. On your way out of the attraction, look for Cameron's and Rohde's literal handprints on the wall.

The technology used in Flight of Passage is really remarkable, but it isn't the only cutting-edge tech found in Pandora. Just across the way from the attraction is the **Na'vi River Journey**, a boat ride that culminates in an encounter with a lifelike ten-foot-tall Na'vi shaman.

This four-minute family-friendly expedition takes guests on a gentle river ride aboard an eight-person reed boat down a mysterious, sacred bioluminescent rain forest.

As you drift down the river, notice the animals and the Na'vi are moving in the same direction as you. Be sure to check out some of the plant leaves; you'll see a few critters scampering across.

Toward the end of the attraction, you'll meet the Na'vi Shaman of Songs, who is in the midst of a musical ceremony. She is deeply connected with Pandora's life force and sends positivity into the forest through her music.

The fluidity of her movement is extremely realistic and is Disney's most lifelike animatronic to date. Here's a quote about the shaman from Joe Rohde: "The shaman is even more extraordinary than we expected. Her facial expressions, little movements in the cheek, tiny movements in the eyelid—each one of these carries an emotion she's capable of conveying."

If you look across Walt Disney World, you can actually follow the evolution of their signature audio-animatronics. Think back to the Magic Kingdom and Walt Disney's Enchanted Tiki Room, featuring singing mechanical birds—which at the time seemed quite remarkable but now, after seeing the shaman, seem crude and unsophisticated.

Roger Broggie Jr., who helped pioneer the audio-animatronic technology, told a story about an early version of an animatronic bird used in the 1964 movie *Mary Poppins*, which is similar to what went into the Enchanted Tiki Room. "We ran the wiring for the *Mary Poppins* robin through its feet. The first one we made wasn't quite insulated enough, and there was a slight electrical current running from it right through Julie Andrews's finger. She was astonished. I can see her trying like crazy to shake it off."

Remember that quote after you experience the complexity and realism of the Shaman of Songs.

The experience along the Na'vi River Journey illustrates that music is a central component of Na'vi culture and is featured prominently in the Valley of Mo'ara.

Throughout the day, at the Swotu Waÿä (meaning "sacred place of song"), you can listen to the beats and rhythms of the Na'vi drum ceremony.

There are even a few ways for visitors to join in and interact with instruments of the Na'vi. The collection of instruments in this area (that anyone can play) are connected to Pandora's root system. If you hit one of the drums, a response to your drumming can be heard overhead.

Drumbeats aren't the only sounds you can hear throughout Pandora. You will hear critters moving through the landscape as you walk about.

Disney had to create the ambient background sounds for the land. Matt Beiler, a Disney show producer, comments on the Pandora soundtrack:

> For the land to feel like a real jungle from another planet, we don't have traditional background music in Pandora— we have a soundscape designed to make it feel as though it is an alien jungle. We hear vocalization patterns like mating calls and hunting moments, and this makes it feel real. When those moments happen, the lighting ties into that with waves of energy. It gives us a connectedness to nature.

The sights and sounds of Pandora are an experience in and of themselves, but if you have an interest in enjoying either of the two attractions found here, you know what to do—get yourself a Fastpass+!

To take your experience to the next level, visit at night as well, as the Pandoran experience is much more than the two rides.

Before we leave Pandora and head over to Africa, a few words about the food. Just like over at Epcot's World Showcase, you can experience the foods of a foreign land, and the same goes for Pandora.

Here's the backstory on the land's restaurant, from a Disney press release.

> Satu'li (Sa-too-lee) Canteen is the land's restaurant, with a design inspired by bases set up on Pandora by the Resources Development Administration (RDA) in the blockbuster "AVATAR" film.
>
> Once the main mess hall of the RDA base in the Valley of Mo'ara, the canteen is now owned and operated by the Alpha Centauri Expeditions (ACE) tour company and has been redesigned into a beautiful museum-like dining room open for lunch and dinner.
>
> The interior has been transformed with colorful Na'vi items filling the walls and hanging from the ceiling—hand-woven tapestries, natural Pandoran elements and cooking tools decorate the interior.
>
> Satu'li Canteen combines creativity and approachable flavors in a menu inspired by the healthful bounty on Pandora, with wholesome grains, fresh vegetables and hearty proteins.
>
> An on-stage grill is a prominent feature in the colorful dining room, "bringing all five senses into play," said Ed Wronski, director, culinary development for Walt Disney Parks & Resorts.
>
> Fast-casual Satu'li Canteen offers bowls that allow diners to customize their meal. Diners start with a base of quinoa and vegetable salad; red and sweet potato hash; mixed whole-grain and rice or romaine and kale salad. Next is either wood-grilled chicken, slow-roasted beef, sustainable fish or

chili-spiced fried tofu. And the bowl is finished with charred onion chimichurri, black bean vinaigrette or creamy herb dressing.

"This is one of our first fast-casual restaurants that gives guests the ability to customize their meal," said Wronski. "We played with the theme of Avatar, and ended up with the bowl concept that is healthful, lighter and with plant-based ingredients to tie back to the World of Avatar." The guiding principle, he said, was to "balance creativity with dishes that are approachable."

The menu also offers steamed "pods"—bao buns with either cheeseburger ingredients or vegetable curry served with root vegetable chips and crunchy vegetable slaw.

For little ones, there's an option of grilled chicken or beef, fish or tofu with greens or rice; a hot dog wrapped in Parker House dough; cheese quesadilla, or a steamed "pod" (cheeseburger bao bun).

Dessert is Blueberry Cheesecake with Passionfruit Curd or Chocolate Cake with a Crunchy Cookie Layer, Banana Cream and Goji Berries.

That blueberry cheesecake dessert just mentioned was created by Walt Disney executive pastry chef Stefan Riemer, who in July 2017 was named a top-ten pastry chef in America by *Dessert Professionals* magazine. Riemer also created the pineapple-cream cheese Pongu Lumpia, which is served at Pongu Pongu, also in Pandora.

Jambo! And welcome to **Harambe**, a little taste of **Africa** in central Florida. (*Jambo* means "hello" in Swahili, and *harambe* translates into "working together," also in Swahili.) Harambe is a fictitious place, in the sense that it allowed Disney to portray a village similar to many villages across Africa, one that wouldn't be tied to any political history of a region. As the *Imagineering Field Guide to Disney's Animal Kingdom* states:

There's a very specific reason that the choice was made to portray this particular version of African life—storytelling. In order to achieve dramatic impact with the stories we wanted to create, we have to focus on one story at a time. Here, it is that of Nature as a pristine thing with animals that must be protected from poaching.

Certainly, there are places in Nairobi or Lagos of Johannesburg in which one could mistake the setting for any large, modern city around the world. But to focus on that here would be to miss the point—this story is about animals, not humans.

Here in Harambe, we're in a place very much like many places in Africa where people really do live right on the edge of the wilderness, within close proximity of real wildlife.

Another reason we created a fictitious place is that it allowed us to avoid becoming linked to the political history of any specific country. We use the design of Harambe to imply its history.

Similarly, Swahili was chosen as the language of Harambe because it crosses geographic boundaries. It is important for this place to have a history, but equally important that it not get in the way of the animal story we're here to see and hear.

Even though the narrative has been created, that doesn't mean the scenery and setting in Harambe lacks authenticity. The designs of the buildings, along with their construction materials, are authentic.

Imagineers visited Lamu, an island off the coast of Kenya, and, inspired by the architecture, purchased pallets of bricks to send back to Florida. In Florida, the bricks were placed over steel frames and then coated in plaster, as is done in Lamu.

A beautiful example of this brick-and-plaster work is seen at the tower built to the left of **Tusker House Restaurant** as you walk into Harambe from Discovery Island. This tower is a replica of an actual tower Imagineers fell in love with during one of their research trips to Africa.

While you're at this location, roughly at the entrance to the village, you may notice a pattern of white bricks in the ground. These bricks portray what is left of the old city walls. As the story goes, Harambe was once walled off and had a brick perimeter, much like a fort; this is what's left of it.

Continue your tour of the village and check out the thatched roofs. A crew of thirteen craftsmen were brought in from Zululand, South Africa, to roof many of the buildings. The thatching was a family affair, as the Berg grass used on the roofs was harvested by the workers' wives, sisters, and mothers back home.

Once in Florida, the grass was tied in thick bundles with twine and hand-stitched utilizing tools called *tulu,* which are steel needles that are eighteen inches long and half an inch thick; this is the traditional Zulu way.

When in place as roofing, the thatch weighs in at seventy pounds per square yard and is four to six inches thick. Obviously, it's all natural and biodegradable but has an astonishing lifespan of thirty to forty years.

Since the design, building methods, and materials are authentic throughout Harambe, what's represented on the walls, interior, and exterior should be as well.

Disney's prop buyers purchased many tin signs to display in the area. Certain pieces of ephemera they weren't able to purchase, they had to reproduce stateside. *The Making of Disney's Animal Kingdom* shares some of the background on the process of how the names and verbiage seen around Harambe were created.

> On his many trips to Africa, Kevin Brown collected printed ephemera—stickers, signs, pamphlets, and newspapers— for use by Imagineering graphic designers. His research in East Africa helped him cast his prose in Kenyan English, with "tweaked" third-world Victorian phrasing like "Guests

here will receive the highest facilitation." "It was a little dangerous," confides Brown.

"The syntax can be intoxicating." With the help of a dictionary, Brown put any Swahili into roughly equivalent English, which was then vetted by a translator, Sara Mirza, who teaches at a Los Angeles university.

Brown mined the *Nairobi Times* obituaries for appropriate names. *The Daily Nation* inspired business ads like "The East African Seed Company—Always Sound and Reliable."

If you have the time, really soak up Harambe; it's quite an interesting experience. There are lots of details to see beyond the authentic and witty signage.

See if you can find a shout-out to a few Imagineers who worked on designing the Animal Kingdom—Joe Rohde, John Shields, and Ahmad Jafari. When you're done, it's time for the Kilimanjaro Safari.

Lions, tigers, and bears, oh my! Actually, no tigers and bears, but definitely lions and over thirty-four different species of exotic African wildlife await you on your safari tour in the Harambe Wildlife Reserve.

The **Kilimanjaro Safari** gives you an eighteen-minute, up-close-and-personal excursion in an open air-vehicle (**Fastpass** either a day or night safari), allowing for great views of black and white rhinos, cheetahs, elephants, giraffes, and hippopotamuses, to name a few—all in a natural habitat setting, as the animals roam free.

Where did all these animals come from? When Disney decided to create the Animal Kingdom, they vowed to stand by two principles. First, the animals would come from captive-bred populations whenever possible, and they would attempt to work at all times within the zoo profession's Species Survival Plans and Taxon Advisory Groups.

The Making of Disney's Animal Kingdom elaborates on animal acquisition:

> No animal will be acquired if it is to the detriment of the wild population of the species. Perhaps the park will take animals out of the wild one day, but only if they are doomed in the wild: if their habitat has been destroyed, or if they would be shot—for instance, when parks and refuges in Africa run out of room and need to "cull" their animals.
>
> For instance, Imagineers originally planned to have giant otters at the park but were told they would have to catch them in the wild. Instead, the park is now involved with giant otter conservation in the field.
>
> Ultimately, some of the creatures now residing at Disney's Animal Kingdom were purchased. Some were sent on loan, some were donated. The amount of money that changed hands was minimal. The cost of transporting the animals to the park was more than the cost of the animals in almost every case. For

animals on loan, the arrangement is often that Disney will donate half their offspring to the lending institution.

In 1996, two years before the park opened, Disney acquired their first two animals for the safari, Miles and Zari, a pair of young giraffes. Since then, the animals under Disney's care have thrived. The number of species that have reproduced since the park debuted is upward of 150—with the first birth at the kingdom being a kudu, a large African antelope.

Seventeen Micronesian kingfisher chicks were hatched there as well, raising the world population of these birds by 20 percent.

The two black rhino calves born at the kingdom made them two of only approximately two hundred worldwide. Impressively, Disney's Animal Kingdom is home to one of the largest groups of Nile and African elephants in North America. In late 2016, the Animal Kingdom welcomed a new female elephant calf, Stella. Her mom, Donna, has given birth to two other female calves, raising the number of elephants at the park to ten.

With the stars of the safari show acquired, Disney had to get to work creating the perfect setting and environment—an environment that was not only safe for both inhabitants and visitors but stimulating and entertaining for them as well.

The research was conducted via many African safaris, where Imagineers were most interested in the setting and scene, such as the plants, rockwork (there's over one million square feet of rockwork in the Animal Kingdom, which is twice the volume of rockwork at Mount Rushmore), dirt, pathways, and tire tracks, but not so much the wildlife. Disney did a great job capturing the essence of what they examined.

Obviously, with all the wildlife to take in during your safari, it's probably not the most entertaining thing to do (and you're more likely to feel it as you drive along). If you happen to glance down at the roadway, you'll see it was constructed of a reinforced concrete pathway. It's 7.5 inches deep, thick enough to withstand the daily abuse of loaded safari vehicles.

The ruts, potholes, hoofprints, and gravel were all placed deliberately; there are even strategically placed planters so grass will grow between the wheel tracks of the safari vehicles.

As mentioned in the beginning of the chapter, the land that is currently the Animal Kingdom was a cow pasture, as Joe Rohde explained to me. "There was a large fireworks testing ground approximately where the centerline of the northern park runs. Most of the site was a cow pasture. There were a few groves of native oak trees, which we preserved and now sit at the beginning of the Kilimanjaro Safari Savannah and behind Expedition Everest."

As you can see from this quote, Disney cleared most of the existing landscape for the safari; they even relocated groves of trees. The planting and replanting patterns of the trees and landscape were based on what designers thought the animals would do as they roamed the landscape.

Some of the real magic in design is how Disney manipulated the physical barriers to keep certain animals safe in their area. This was orchestrated with the creation of the landscaping and water to serve as barriers or fences when a particular animal needed to be kept at bay. Disney had a lot of work to do in order to get the site ready for an attraction of this magnitude.

Hoofed animals generally have fields of fifteen to twenty-five acres to roam about freely, with other animals generally confined to a specific space, where barriers are used to give them boundaries.

Most observers don't recognize or realize that while the proximity of the animals seems close, perhaps dangerously close, there are actually barriers camouflaged in plain sight to keep man and beast separated.

Fences, if used, are hidden behind rockwork or landscaping. A chain-link fence, which zoos use to mark the perimeter and enclose an area, aren't usually utilized here. Instead, Disney opts for a very steep slope at an angle the animals can't ascend. It is then covered in plants—you can see this often throughout the safari if you're looking for it.

More illusions and trickery are at work when it comes to keeping an animal like the hippos from getting too close to the safari vehicles. As explained in *The Making of Disney's Animal Kingdom*:

> The safari vehicle seems to plunge through the Hippo river with the two-ton critters threatening to swamp the jeep from both sides. Actually, concrete fins with a 45-degree angle—called hippo bumpers—turn the beasts back from their pools' walls on both sides of the road.

> The angle is so steep that the animals can't get their feet up on them; the length of the fins also keeps the hippos in the center of the rivers so that the guests can see them. Water pumped over the ride path creates the illusion that the two pools are connected and that the vehicle is fording the river.

While Disney tries to keep certain animals in specific locations with obstructions, they resort to other tricks to bring many animals to the forefront so folks get a chance to see the animals up close and personal.

Throughout the safari are strategically placed tree stumps, logs, rockwork, or termite mounds that provide shade (or scratching posts for the animals to leave their scent on), and often contain drinkers and feeders to encourage the animals to congregate in the area. All these things entice the animals to be more visible for the attraction.

Everyone's experience is different on the trek through the Harambe Wildlife Reserve. You could take one safari and immediately board another vehicle minutes later and have a unique and different experience; no two trips are ever the same.

Aside from the beautiful animals, there are a lot of little details and examples of ingenuity throughout the trip. It's hard to fathom that just about every tree and plant was deliberately placed where you see it. Many of the plants were specially grown in accelerators, so the variety of plant life, some more mature looking than others, was planted throughout.

Even with all the spectacular things to experience, Disney

couldn't help themselves with their hidden Mickeys. As you come upon the elephants, on the left side of the ride vehicle will be a little pond filled with flamingos. The center island in the pond is shaped like a hidden Mickey—as if seeing elephants weren't enough!

There are two more attractions to see here in Africa before we make our way over to Asia, and they are both adjacent to the Kilimanjaro Safaris.

First is the **Gorilla Falls Exploration Trail**, a self-exploration walking tour of tropical rain forest inhabited by native African wildlife such as gorillas, hippos, and a variety of exotic birds.

These shady trails lead to Pangani Forest (*Pangani* means "place of enrichment" in Swahili) and into the savannas, where you can see the animals in their natural habitats.

Disney used a bit of animal psychology throughout this trail (actually, wherever applicable throughout the park). The animal habitats were designed to keep the animals at eye level with us, the human visitors to their world.

Research into the psychology of gorillas and the big cats indicates they like to feel superior to us, and if we are looking down on them like many zoos around the world, this doesn't make them happy. So Disney specifically eradicated the human superiority complex by keeping us at least at eye level with our furry friends.

Our last stop in Africa is to **Rafiki's Planet Watch**. The only way to get to Rafiki's is via the **Wildlife Express**, a narrow-gauge railroad (3.3-foot rail width) that loops 1.2 miles round trip from Rafiki's Planet Watch and back to the train depot in Harambe.

The train depot for the Wildlife Express is modeled after the open-air stations built by the British in East Africa during the early 1900s. While the station may be modeled and inspired by something British, the three engines and two sets of cars that make up the train actually *are* British.

The engines and cars were built in 1997, only a few miles from William Shakespeare's cottage in Stratford-upon-Avon, by the model-railroad firm of Severn Lamb, Ltd., at Alchester, England.

Each five-car train seats 250 passengers on contoured benches facing sideways. The positioning of the seats allows travelers to view the behind-the-scenes facilities and nighttime shelters between Africa and Asia.

When the animals aren't out in the savanna or grasslands of the safari, the lions, elephants, warthogs, and antelope herds call this home.

Once the train pulls into the station at Rafiki's Planet Watch, a short walk brings you to Conservation Station, a facility that provides veterinary care to the animals in the park.

In addition to being an active animal hospital (much of which is in plain view for visitors to see), the center provides information on animal research and conservation programs.

Just outside Conservation Station is a small petting zoo, which features a hands-on encounter with goats, sheep, pigs, cows, and donkeys.

Before you leave Rafiki's Planet Watch, check out the enormous beautiful mural on the wall when you enter the Conservation Station. Take a look at the eyes of the frog, ostrich, squirrel, owl, and possum; there are a few hidden Mickeys for you.

As you leave Harambe, more animals and even more adventure await you in the majestic land of **Asia**. Here, Disney created another village, **Anandapur,** a town similar to yet different from Harambe.

Anandapur is similar in that its identity and story line are created by Disney. The fictional village is an amalgamation of places that can be found throughout Asia—most notably Nepal, India, and Thailand.

It's different from Harambe in that it depicts a unique lifestyle, atmosphere, and scenery. While Harambe is a bit more urban and contemporary, Anandapur resembles a rural, simple, yet spiritual existence at the foothills of the Himalayas.

One of the more prominent spiritual details Disney included throughout parts of Asia are the colorful ribbons hanging about. These ribbons are symbolic of a prayer left by someone. If a prayer ribbon is removed, that prayer will be negated, so they are left in place until Mother Nature decomposes them. In contrast, where you see a bell hanging, that means the prayer was answered.

Many of these prayer ribbons are found at **Kali River Rapids**, which is our first stop in Asia. But before we get there, take note of a few things.

Up first in Asia is the restaurant **Yak & Yeti.** The food here is good and quite tasty. Take a look at the sign above the entrance. Look at the writing above the word "restaurant"; this is Sanskrit, the language of Anandapur, which translates into "place of all delight."

Sanskrit is an ancient language that belongs to the Indo-Aryan group and is the root of many but not all Indian languages. You'll see more Sanskrit writing throughout the area.

The other sight to see before you embark on your river-rapid trip is the fifty-foot-tall towers and temple ruins that are habitats for gibbons. Anandapur is home to two distinctive species of gibbons, siamangs and white-cheeked.

You may notice some of the white-cheeked gibbons for the white fur on their cheeks and the siamangs for their large size; they can be twice the size of other gibbons.

As you approach the Kali River Rapids, there is a large structure with a roof and signage for the attraction. There are Fastpass kiosks here, themed as podiums, as if to stamp or review your passport before a journey.

This is an important little building, as it starts to set the stage for your journey down the Chakranadi River, which is Sanskrit for "river that flows in a circle."

More importantly, if you're facing it, this spot is a great landmark to remember where you dropped off your belongings before your trip down the rapids, since you're going to get wet on this ride—maybe even drenched!

Take a look to the left of this building; find a locker that's available, and put some of your belongings in there to keep them dry.

With your belongings safely stowed, it's time to walk the path toward the attraction. The original concept for this ride was for it to be like a safari on the river.

The proposed name was Tiger Rapids Run, and it would have featured a rapids trip past tigers and live animals. This concept was ultimately nixed and replaced with the theme and story we see today, conservation and deforestation with a splash of adventure—literally!

Walking through the queue for the attraction, you will eventually come upon a centuries-old temple, which is home to animal shrines and hand-painted murals. The ceiling through this part of the queue was hand-painted by a seventy-six-year-old artisan from Bali and was inspired by scenes from *Jataka Tales*, a collection of sacred Buddhist stories.

This area is packed with interesting items to observe and to help tell the story, not only of the area of Anandapur but of the logging and deforestation you're about to encounter on your trip.

As you stroll through the shops and offices here, there are more than five thousand items to grab your attention. Look for the paddles that were signed by Imagineers who helped design and develop the attraction.

As you make your way to the wooden pagoda and circular loading platform, get ready to board your twelve-passenger raft and take a trip up a ninety-foot incline to start your journey. Look around for the image of the tiger on the rock wall as you approach the top of the lift.

Now, you may be preoccupied and worried about who's going to get wet on this excursion, but don't fret—everyone will! So relax, take a deep breath, and enjoy the scents of jasmine and ginger that linger in the air.

When you make your way down the rapids, the story of logging starts to unfold. *The Imagineering Field Guide to Disney's Animal Kingdom* gives us the lowdown.

> As with the rest of the Park, even our grandest adventures are delivered with a conservation message woven into them. Here the issue is that of deforestation. We hear hints of the problems in the distant sounds of chainsaws echoing through the queue. There are signs touting the value of the wilderness and warning against deforestation. We begin our travels through this mystical place and are immediately drawn to it.
>
> When the raft enters the burn zone, where a logging company has been unethically stripping the trees off the top of the mountain, we feel a palpable sense of loss. We see the erosion eating away at the banks of the river. We can't understand how people could go into such a magical, inspirational wilderness and do what they've done. The process is so far out of balance that this environment is no longer sustainable. However, in this case, nature has the last word.
>
> The environment is fighting back against this intrusion. The logging truck is teetering on the brink of falling into the rapids because of the erosion of the barren banks. The loggers are not able to continue their efforts. We are thrown down the great drop and expelled from the area, as we imagine the loggers have been as well.

When you exit the ride, go over to the bridge that overlooks the rapids and check out the "Elephant Squirters." Press the button and try to soak the rafters who you think didn't get wet enough!

Our next stop in Asia is located right next to the rapids. The **Maharajah Jungle Trek** is a self-guided walking tour featuring tigers, gibbons, Eld's deer, blackbuck, Komodo dragons, Malayan flying foxes, water buffalo, and more than fifty species of birds.

The backstory says this area was once the hunting grounds of several generations of wealthy Maharajas (Sanskrit for "great king" or "great ruler").

Today, it's a nature and wildlife preserve, as Mother Nature has reclaimed the hunting grounds, leaving the centuries-old palace and monuments in ruins, illustrating that planet Earth has the last word over humans.

As you make your trek, the story of the Maharajas plays out before your eyes, as remnants and reminders are still very much present in the form of murals and bas reliefs. When you walk into the aviary, notice the floor tiles and columns; this area was once a ballroom for the royal family.

When viewing the gibbons, you can see forty-foot carved monument poles that are traditionally built to honor royalty or deities. Today, they are habitats.

Who would want to look at deteriorating murals when you could view the powerful and beautiful tigers? Well, if you approach the tiger-viewing rotunda and there are no tigers in the area, take a look at the four wall murals of the kings of Anandapur. They each offer a different story and perspective of their time spent at their royal hunting grounds.

Naturally, since this is Walt Disney World, there are a few hidden Mickeys to spot.

Pay attention to the earrings worn by the Maharajas. In the tiger-viewing area, look at the first mural on your right and then the mural opposite this mural on the left. Hidden Mickey earrings are on these royal gentlemen.

After your visit with the tigers, it's time to track down another creature. This creature, like the tiger, is powerful and elusive, but most of all, it's mysterious and legendary. The thrilling search is on for the Yeti, which will take us to **Expedition Everest—Legend of the Forbidden Mountain**.

Bigfoot, Sasquatch, the Abominable Snowman, and the Yeti—different parts of the world have different names and varied cultural stories linked to the beast. We've all heard the lore about this this larger-than-life creature. Is it a monster? Is it real? Is it fantasy? The world may never know. But for your time spent in the village of Serka Zong in the Himalayas, here in central Florida, the Yeti is very much real.

Disney's backstory on the Yeti parallels some of the traditional folklore and regional beliefs that still stand today. For many of the cultures in the Himalayas, the Yeti is the protector of the forest and is a real creature. Disney takes this premise and weaves their own story line around the story of this area and its protective beast.

According to Disney's website:

> Folklore has it that a fierce guardian monster protects the Forbidden Mountain. For years, the Royal Anandapur Tea Company shipped its tea by train through the Forbidden Mountain pass.
>
> After a series of mysterious accidents were blamed on the dreaded Yeti monster, the railroad closed. Today, the railway is operating again, thanks to a group of local entrepreneurs—Himalayan Escapes, Tours and Expeditions—who offer curious travelers transportation to the base camp on the scenic mountain.
>
> Yet there are some who believe the legend to be true and that the Yeti will do everything in its power to protect the sacred realm of the Himalayas. Visitors beware.

During your journey toward the enormous mountain that has been looming large during your stay in the area, watch for the changes in the imprints of the walkways.

You'll see footprints, plant imprints, animal prints, and bicycle tracks. But as you get closer to Mount Everest and into the village of Serka Zong, the bicycle tracks will cease, as these modes of transportation wouldn't be able to traverse the landscape.

Expedition Everest wasn't an opening-day attraction in April 1998; the thrill ride debuted in April 2006. Disney spent an estimated $100 million to make this ride and its environment a reality, and their Imagineers spent several months traveling the Himalayas.

After several trips and months spent in Nepal, Tibet, and China to study life, culture, and architecture in the Himalayas, Joe Rohde and his team of researchers and designers started to collect props and artifacts to display at their attraction.

More importantly, they also collected and recorded the local legends, stories, and sightings of the mythical beast by the villagers.

As Joe explains:

> "Our story was really about the culture and the people, the areas where there is human habitation," said Rohde.

> It took jets, helicopters and donkeys to deliver Disney's creative team past slippery, narrow roads, and to a 1,000 year old monastery to study the Himalayan culture.

> The team stayed there three days and gathered information and local beliefs about the Yeti.

> "The detail is there to make you believe in the reality of the story you're immersed in," said Rohde, lead designer of Animal Kingdom.

> "You need not think, Wow, that rock looks realistic. You

need to think, that is a rock. Detail at the Everest level is there to define. You're not in Kansas anymore. We created an environment that immerses guests deep into the story of Expedition Everest so they feel transported to a different place and adventure." (Associated Press, February 23, 2006)

The 6.2-acre area that defines Disney's Everest and village is packed with architectural and cultural authenticity.

As you trek through the village to board the train, you'll notice a variety of colors adorning the weathered and aging structures.

Red, black, and white paint combinations are placed on the buildings for balance and protection; red around the corners of buildings and openings of doorways is specific to protection.

A yellow candle-drip effect over one village home signifies the residence of an old, well-established family, and firewood stacked on the roof indicates wealth, as wood is an often scarce and valued commodity in the Himalaya region.

The architectural style of the buildings is a hybrid between Tibetan and Nepalese and is supposed to appear between fifty and three hundred years old.

Most of the buildings appear weathered and distressed. Some buildings even appear to be sinking or sloping.

Florida naturally has building codes, so all of these structures were built soundly. The appearance of sloping windows is a construction trick designed to give the appearance of a sinking building, in reality, the windows aren't built in a straight line.

The contents and props for the buildings of Serka Zong are filled with over eight thousand items, some of which have actually made the climb to the top of Everest, as some of the climbing gear on display was purchased from outfitters in Nepal when Disney's research team went to the base of Mount Everest.

Often, to get enough merchandise on their trips to bring back, Disney's buyers would buy out entire stores or would befriend local villagers and offer to buy their used items. After the locals sold their items, such as scissors or egg baskets, Disney would purchase new items as replacements for them.

On one trip, a prop buyer bought one vendor's year's supply of handmade nails. These are actually used to hang items on the walls in and around this part of the park.

Enough of the details about the village. Here's some information about the attraction. Every sixty seconds or so, thirty-four passengers per train take a three-minute trek along a nearly one-mile track, which rises one hundred feet and will plunge eighty feet at speeds of nearly fifty miles per hour and will twist and spiral up a sixty-degree angle—whereas most coasters twist and spiral down.

For a few brief seconds, you too may become a believer in the Yeti, as you encounter a nearly twenty-five-foot-tall, twenty-thousand-pound beast powered by hydraulic cylinders with more potential thrust than a 747 jetliner.

But remember, as local legend says, the Yeti is not to be feared, as he is the protector of the environment.

If you feel as though the Yeti you had a brush with is remarkable, you're right. He is, but so is the creation of the ride experience and the mountain.

Expedition Everest is actually made up of three separate structures. The Yeti is one structure, the coaster track is the second, and the outdoor mountain is the third. Each of these reaches all the way down to ground level and into the foundation without touching the others.

The ability to have this mountain created this way was thanks to a piece of 4-D scheduling software Disney created, so they could plan and then visualize with 3-D graphics how everything will come together at any given time during construction. It did, however, take twenty-four clay models to come up with the perfect mountain before the software could be used.

While the computer programs may have made the design work more efficient, to construct this behemoth, good old-fashioned hard work and labor went into bringing the mountain to Walt Disney World.

Much as we saw throughout Magic Kingdom, Mount Everest here in central Florida uses forced perspective to make roughly two hundred feet seem like twenty-nine thousand feet. In and around certain parts of the area, tall bamboo and pines were planted, along with swaying reeds used to blur the horizon, so the mountain seems more distant.

All in all, twenty million pounds of concrete, thirty-eight miles of rebar, five thousand tons of bolted structural steel, and two thousand gallons of paint (aluminum foil was applied to the concrete to create texture and sculpt the mountain) come together to provide a very realistic and fun theme park ride.

Let's keep moving through the park and head over to our final destination, DinoLand USA, and see if something there can top the Yeti.

Visitors to Walt Disney World are often surprised at the number of attractions with an educational undertone. Ssshhh, don't tell the kids they are secretly experiencing some edutainment!

The Magic Kingdom has the Hall of Presidents and, the look back on the evolution of home technology with the Carousel of Progress. Epcot is practically bursting with cultural discovery, and, as you've just experienced, the Animal Kingdom is rife with lessons in conservation and animal knowledge.

Here at **DinoLand USA**, educational theming or lessons aren't below the surface (as dinosaur bones are) but at the forefront of the story line. As Disney explains it on its website:

> It's a land where prehistoric beasts stalk primeval forests, great fossils are unearthed and guests venture back in time to discover living, breathing survivors of a magnificent era some 65 million years ago. It's a kaleidoscope of dino-kitsch with whimsical rides and a midway teeming with Cretaceous craziness.
>
> It's a place where bone-searching professors and grad students inhabit wooden cabins, rec halls and Quonset huts, over time forming a quaint and playful, albeit slightly peculiar, celebration of America's fascination with dinosaurs.
>
> For over 50 years, the story goes, the fossil-rich site has been inhabited by scientists, volunteers and grad students who have left a paper trail around the site of notes, theories, questions and answers about the lives of the vanished creatures. With a palpable sense of humor and rebelliousness, the site is open to the public as a "fossil discovery park" under the ownership of The Dino Institute.
>
> The paper trail of paleontologists' notes, sketches and findings leads deeper into DinoLand USA. and The Dino Institute, to those long-lost giants of 65 million years ago in the park's high-speed, heart-pounding adventure, DINOSAUR.

Let's begin our adventure in DinoLand where Disney's story line left off—at the signature thrill ride in this area, **DINOSAUR**, which is located at the back of DinoLand USA. Just look for the thirteen-foot-tall, forty-foot-long Tyrannosaurus Rex reproduction that is on display.

Now, this T-Rex on display isn't just *any* T-Rex; this is Dino-Sue, the largest and most complete T-Rex skeleton ever found. Fossil hunter Sue Hendrickson (hence the name "Sue") discovered her back in 1990 in the Black Hills of South Dakota.

In the early 1990s, Chicago's Field Museum purchased Sue for $8.4 million at auction. Some of the funds the museum used for the purchase were donated by Walt Disney World.

After the purchase was complete, the museum sent half of Sue's bones along with a team of paleontologists to complete their fossil preparations in full view of visitors to DinoLand.

Once the preparations were complete, Disney sent her bones back to the museum, where Sue is proudly on display. In appreciation for Disney's contributions, DinoLand has one of three complete replicas of Sue.

If Sue doesn't wow you, take a stroll inside the Dino Institute and travel back in time to experience a few animatronic dinosaurs.

Don't let the exhibits and museum-like stuffiness fool you. Once you pass into the research control center, you'll start to see what DINOSAUR is all about. As the story goes, this secret research facility requires you to go back in time and rescue an iguanodon before the meteor that wiped out the dinosaurs strikes.

This attraction features some of the largest audio-animatronics ever built. And if you've been to Disneyland and taken a ride on Indiana Jones Adventure: Temple of the Forbidden Eye, the ride technology featured on Indy is used here on DINOSAUR, which is something Disney invented and patented.

From the patent abstract (US Patent 5,623,878):

> A dynamic ride vehicle for executing a sequence of distinct motion patterns and for providing unique ride experiences in an amusement park attraction or other environment includes a movable chassis and a body having a passenger seating area.
>
> As the vehicle travels along the path, articulation of the body and appropriate steering of the vehicle enables the vehicle to execute, in cooperation with the motion apparatus, a sequence of distinct motion patterns. Execution of the motion patterns enhances the passengers' sensation of vehicle movement that is actually taking place, as well as the sensation of a realistic moving ride vehicle experience that is actually not happening.

Translation: get ready for a bumpy ride! Basically, the lower portion of the ride vehicle motors along like a traditional vehicle, but the upper portion, where you're seated, moves all over the place to simulate different terrain and experiences.

Here's a little fun fact about DINOSAUR: it was originally called Countdown to Extinction. The name change happened on May 1, 2000, to correspond with a movie Disney released on May 19, 2000, with the same name.

DINOSAUR and It's Tough to Be a Bug! are two Animal Kingdom attractions that had a presence in the park before their related movies hit the big screen. And don't forget to smile (or scream), as you're going to have your picture taken during your adventure.

As you're leaving the attraction, take one last look at the building. If you look past the green domelike feature on the roof, you should see a few trees around it.

Believe it or not, those trees are actually on the roof of the building. This is a little trick Disney does to try to hide the appearance and size of a building. This gives the illusion that the building is much smaller than it is, as you're tricked into believing those trees are actually on land.

Let's leave the land before time (sorry, wrong entertainment company reference) and head over to a mini-land within a land, owned by proprietors Chester and Hester.

In an effort to capitalize on the tourism in the area due to the fossil boom, these two guys turned their property into a roadside attraction—think Route 66, except here, as the sign says, it's Route 498, which is a reference to the park's opening month and year, 04/98.

Chester and Hester's Dinosaur Treasures has so much funky decor and signage in and around their building, it's hard to take it all in and appreciate the kitschy trinkets, knickknacks, and nostalgia. It's an "emporium of extinction."

Do look out for the few subtle dinosaur and gasoline references throughout the area—get it? Fossil fuels! See if you can find a portrait on the wall of the shop featuring the proprietors themselves.

Across the way from the shop, the tribute to roadside Americana continues with the tight turns and short drops of **Primeval Whirl**, the tilting, spinning dinos of **TriceraTop Spin** and **Fossil Fun Games**. If you enjoy whack-a-mole, you'll love Whac-a-Pachycephalosaur.

As you walk through this area, look down at the ground. It appears as though this little carnival popped up right in the middle of an old parking lot, as you can still see some of the painted lines through the cracked asphalt. It's actually painted, treated, and sandblasted concrete, as real asphalt heats up with the sun and softens, which doesn't make for a good walking experience!

After the mini dinosaur carnival, kids ten and under can dig at the **Boneyard** playground. Young paleontologists in training can participate in prehistoric discoveries and learn more about the world of dinosaurs.

They can climb atop rocks, cross rickety rope bridges, roam mysterious caves, and hurl down twisting slides. They can navigate a maze of dinosaur bones, unearth the remains of a wooly mammoth in a nearby sandpit, or excavate fossils from a triceratops and a Tyrannosaurus Rex. There are lots of interactive exhibits for the kids to enjoy.

All that work and play may leave you hungry, so go across the way and dig in at **Restaurantosaurus**, which continues the dino-themed humor and story line of student paleontologists living and working at this fossil site.

Restaurantosaurus is now a commissary and dorm for the grad students. See the Airstream trailer outside the restaurant? It was purchased from Imagineer Todd Beeson's grandparents!

We've talked a lot about Joe Rohde throughout this chapter, and you see his ideas and design work throughout the Animal Kingdom. Take a look at the large dinosaur painting on the wall in the counter service area; this was done by the man himself.

The visit to Restaurantosaurus brings to a close DinoLand USA, the Animal Kingdom, and the actual theme park experiences at Walt Disney World.

Hopefully, you enjoyed your visit, and whether this was your first visit or you've experienced the magic of the property hundreds of times, I hope *The Wonders of Walt Disney World* provided a great tour and opened your eyes to some of the details and backstory that lie just underneath the surface of the world's most visited theme parks.

Seeing as this is the official wrap-up regarding the ride experiences, I thought I would take a quick look at what Disney does for safety after hours.

Quoting from the "Walt Disney Parks and Resorts Reports on Safety":

> It is crucial that a ride be mechanically and structurally sound. That is why our rigorous maintenance efforts— which total thousands of hours of maintenance and inspection every day are an integral part of our daily routine.
>
> Every night after our parks close, maintenance teams review each attraction. Rides are not authorized for operation the

next day until scheduled preventive and corrective maintenance procedures have been performed.

In addition to these nightly inspections, ride vehicles are regularly taken out of operation for scheduled service, where parts are inspected, tested and replaced as needed.

This entire attraction maintenance program is managed through a computer-based system that tracks daily, weekly, monthly and yearly maintenance requirements for all our attractions and generates management tools such as work orders and checklists. This system is central to a scheduling and staffing process designed to facilitate the proper and timely completion of all our maintenance activities.

Even after the maintenance team has completed its inspections, our attractions cannot open without final review and approval from the operations team. Once confirmation is received that the nightly maintenance routine has been completed, ride operators use a detailed list taken from each attraction's operating guide to perform pre-opening checks of key ride components, such as seating restraints, video monitors and ride control systems.

To give Cast Members enough time to complete this important process in a thoughtful and thorough way, ride operators typically begin their shifts hours before the first Guest enjoys the attraction.

According to the safety report, here's a day in the life of the attraction maintenance team.

> 12:00 a.m.: Shift supervisor goes over assignments and work orders.

> 12:30 a.m.: Inspectors walk the ride tracks and inspect equipment.

> 1:15 a.m.: Engineering staff and maintenance evaluate equipment for wear and condition.

2:30 a.m.: Quality Assurance partners with Maintenance to verify that parts meet requirements for safe operations.

2:45 a.m.: Maintenance conducts inspection of each ride vehicle.

3:30 a.m.: Skilled technicians torque ride wheels to verify compliance with specifications.

6:15 a.m.: Maintenance powers up the ride to begin pre-opening inspections.

7:00 a.m.: Maintenance shift supervisor turns ride over to Operations team.

7:30 a.m.: Operators initiate ride startup and perform daily pre-opening checks.

9:00 a.m.: Ride opens to guests.

Chapter Five

Tidbits + Morsels

> *I don't believe there's a challenge anywhere in the world that's more important to people everywhere than finding solutions to the problems of our cities. But where do we begin? How do we start answering this great challenge? Well, we're convinced we must start with the public need.*
>
> —Walt Disney

According to industry estimates (Disney doesn't release official numbers) in 2016, 20,395,000 people visited the Magic Kingdom at Walt Disney World. This number breaks down to an average of 55,877 people a day. Figure in the unique visitors to Epcot, Hollywood Studios, Animal Kingdom, shopping, water parks, and a large portion Disney's 73,000 cast members staffing the parks, and Walt Disney World has a daily population soaring to well over 150,000 people.

Looking at these daily numbers, it appears as though Walt Disney did achieve his dream of having a vibrant community or town of his own in central Florida, albeit different from his original plans.

Nonetheless, just as in any other town, folks need to eat, drink, and sleep, and Disney has plenty of options for all three.

Across Walt Disney World, there are nearly four hundred restaurants to satisfy every diet and palate. With roughly thirty thousand hotel rooms, sleeping accommodations range from campgrounds to deluxe presidential suites. Let's have a look at Disney's on-site hospitality.

When the Walt Disney World Resort opened in 1971, hotel options were limited to just two locations on-site, Disney's Contemporary Resort and Disney's Polynesian Village Resort. These two resorts are not only nostalgic favorites for folks who've visited Walt Disney World since the resorts' inceptions, but they are still unique and very much in-demand luxury hotels.

Both resorts are in Disney's Deluxe category and are serviced by the monorail. Additionally, they have carved their own little niche in America's pop culture history.

Our first Disney hotel pop-culture event is with President Richard Nixon, at Walt Disney World's Contemporary Resort on November 19, 1973.

President Nixon was no stranger to the world of Disney. Over his career in politics as president and vice president of the United States, Nixon and Walt Disney became quite familiar with each other.

Not long after Disneyland opened in 1955, then vice president Nixon visited the park with his family and was presented with a ceremonial key to Disneyland. In 1959, he returned to help inaugurate the Disneyland Monorail. In 1969, after Walt's death, Nixon awarded Walt's widow and family the Walt Disney Commemorative Medal—Walt received the Presidential Medal of Freedom in 1964, but President Johnson bestowed that honor upon him.

President Nixon is, of course, also present at Walt Disney World's Hall of Presidents. But perhaps his most memorable Disney performance took place at a Disney hotel when he addressed hundreds of members of the Associated Press Managing Editors Association.

During this meeting, Nixon was embroiled in the Watergate scandal, and he "wanted the facts out, because the facts will prove that the president is telling the truth."

As the president tried to clear his name during a heated question-and-answer situation with the press, he gave this legendary quote: "In all of my years in public life I have never obstructed justice…People have got to know whether or not their president is a crook. Well, I'm not a crook."

On August 9, 1974, Richard Nixon resigned as president of the United States.

Now, let us take a quick trip on the WDW monorail and head over to Disney's Polynesian Village during Christmastime of 1974.

Just before the new year of 1975, one of the members of the Fab Four broke hearts everywhere when he crushed any hope of the Beatles getting back together.

May Pang, who at the time was dating John Lennon, chronicled the moment in her book *Instamatic Karma.* John was originally supposed to sign the legal documents dismantling the legendary band in New York City.

After commenting that the "stars weren't right," John skipped the meeting in New York and headed to Florida. On December 29, 1974, the band's lawyers traveled to WDW and met John at WDW's Polynesian Village. Lennon signed his name to the documents ending the band's reign.

There is another interesting story to share. Disney offers Value, Moderate, Deluxe, Deluxe Villas, and Disney Vacation Club (their version of a timeshare) resorts on their property.

Off of Walt Disney World property, Disney has a program called Good Neighbor Hotels. These hotels aren't owned by Disney but meet a certain criterion or standard to be included in this category.

They have to be AAA-approved, meet Disney standards for quality and service, and be convenient and close, usually within one to fourteen miles of Disney property.

Note that last little caveat: within one to fourteen miles of Disney property. Well, there are a couple of Good Neighbor Hotels much closer than one mile. They are actually surrounded by Disney property, within Disney's property, yet not on Disney property. It's quite a unique story.

If you motor along Buena Vista Drive through the Walt Disney World Resort, not too far from Disney's Caribbean Beach Resort, there's a 480-acre tract of land officially called the Bonnet Creek Nature Preserve. It's home to a few hotels, most notably the luxurious Waldorf Astoria. This property is surrounded by Disney property on three sides, and the fourth side is Interstate 4.

When Walt Disney was purchasing the twenty-seven

thousand–plus acres for his "Florida Project," he was able to secure all the land he wanted in this area except for the Bonnet Creek parcel.

As the story goes, Disney was unable to get in touch with the owners of the property but proceeded to purchase everything around it.

As the years went on, the stories grew about who actually owned the land and why Disney wasn't able to purchase it.

Finally, in the early 2000s, *Orlando Sentinel* reporter Tim Barker got to the bottom of the story. From the August 17, 2000, edition of the *Sentinel*:

> It's one of those stories that's too good to be true, and it's been circulating in Central Florida for decades. It's the one about former nationalist Chinese leader Chiang Kai-shek beating Walt Disney to the punch on a land purchase in what would become one of the world's busiest tourist corridors.
>
> As the story goes, the 480 acres were bought in 1962 and managed by a Taiwanese man—Ling Kai Kung—on behalf of the famous leader.
>
> The rumors sprang back to life recently when developers revealed plans to build hotels on what is now called Bonnet Creek Resort, which is bordered on three sides by Walt Disney World.
>
> But it appears that Chiang Kai-shek's only connection to the property was through his marriage into a wealthy Chinese family in 1927. Ling was his nephew by marriage. "All the mystery behind it really isn't all that mysterious," said Alan Ytterberg, the attorney who represented Ling's estate.
>
> Ytterberg insists that Ling purchased the land on his own as an investment, without any involvement from his uncle, a pivotal figure in the development of modern China and Taiwan.
>
> The land, between Interstate 4 and Disney's Caribbean

Beach Resort, was purchased by Ling with an eye toward several uses—at least two of which suggested he may not have actually seen the property before buying it.

Aside from a site for warehouses, Ling, who died in 1992, thought it might be useful to the shipping and space industries—despite its distance from Cape Canaveral and the coast.

The site's proximity to Disney's empire should make it ideal for development, with plans calling for construction of 3,000 hotel rooms, 1,600 time-share units and a 250,000-square-foot conference center. There is no timetable for the project.

This is exactly what happened to the parcel in 2004, when the first hotel opened adjacent to Disney's land.

> *We evolved by necessity. We did not sit down and say to ourselves, "How can we make a big pile of dough?" It just happened.*
>
> **—Walt Disney**

The shopping and dining extravaganza at Walt Disney World known today as Disney Springs has had several name changes over the decades.

While the area's identity has largely been the same—a place to visit without a price of admission—the area's name has changed quite a bit. Before it was Disney Springs, it was known as Downtown Disney (with an adjacent area called Pleasure Island, which for a hot minute back in 2010 was going to transform into something called Hyperion Wharf, a plan Disney abandoned). And before it was Downtown Disney, it was called Disney Village Marketplace. And before that, it was called Walt Disney World Village, and before that, it was known as Lake Buena Vista Shopping Village.

Despite the multitude of name changes and expansion over the decades, at its core, what appears today is by and large the same concept as Lake Buena Vista Shopping Village in 1975—waterfront shopping and dining.

The original incarnation of this area and some of the land adjacent to it was actually going to be something different, as in truer to the word "village."

With the success of Walt Disney World, in a January 1972 article in the *New York Times*, Disney announced they were going to build homes "to alleviate traffic" to the park. The original plan was to construct

> a model residential-commercial community on 4,000 acres that could eventually move the corporation into national real-estate development.
>
> Designed as a "second home" composed of condominiums and townhomes ranging in cost from $28,000 to $80,000, the community would incorporate features of a "living environment" that would lessen the dependence on the automobile.

By October of 1972, the plans were already underway for the housing sites.

> Lake Buena Vista, the already-started condominium town on the site bills itself as the "host community" to Walt Disney World. The project is the Disney organization's first, cautious attempt to try its hand at providing residential facilities, before it goes whole-hog with Epcot city.
>
> Lake Buena Vista's aim is more modest than Epcot's: it's merely a community of second homes for the wealthy, and a special attempt is being made to interest corporations in leasing houses as places to entertain clients. 80 homes, at prices ranging up to $100,000, will be occupied by November.
>
> The attached row-houses are generally arranged in clusters around golf courses, waterways and common green spaces.
>
> Disney will be "mini-Epcoting" some transportation experiments here; residents of Lake Buena Vista will be able to

travel throughout the town via a system of electric carts and boats, and no automobiles will be necessary.

As we've seen several times through the course of the book, what Disney announces isn't necessarily what Disney is going to create.

This became the situation with owning a home at Lake Buena Vista Village. By the time press started up again in late 1974 and early 1975 to announce the upcoming debut of the village, gone were any prospects of actually owning a home on Disney property.

Instead, when the village debuted, it was a waterfront European-style shopping village featuring twenty-nine shops and restaurants.

Adjacent to the shopping center was a golf course, additional hotels, and an office building. There would be no home ownership, but there were 133 one-, two-, and three-bedroom vacation villas, in addition to 32 tree-house villas, available to rent. From its opening day, the "village" was very successful, and, over the decades, it continues to be.

The area evolved, and Disney revamped it when they deemed it necessary or when the trends of the day have dictated, most notably when it came to food—wait, there wasn't a gluten-free and vegan bakery there in 1975, as there is today?

Regardless of the area's name or the wares the merchants are peddling, it is still an excellent place to enjoy away from the parks.

APPENDIX

AND

BIBLIOGRAPHY

NOTABLE IMAGINEERS MENTIONED IN THE BOOK:

Tony Baxter

Tony Baxter has played a key role in the design and creation of many Disney attractions and theme parks of the last 45 years, including *Big Thunder Mountain Railroad*, EPCOT Center, The original *Star Tours, Splash Mountain, the Indiana Jones™ Adventure*, and the overall creative role for Disneyland Paris. He is a 49-year veteran and most recently was Senior Vice President of Creative Development at Walt Disney Imagineering, where he was responsible for providing imaginative ideas and input for Walt Disney's original theme park. Tony is currently Creative Advisor to Walt Disney Imagineering where he continues to provide input on new projects and helps to mentor the next generation of Imagineers.

Rolly Crump

Words may not fully describe designer and Imagineer Rolly Crump. So to get a handle on this spirited, multitalented Disney designer, think: Leonardo da Vinci's Universal Man.
A true "original," even among Imagineers, Rolly drew forth genius in others. Disney Concept Designer John Horny observed, "Rolly has a knack for bringing out the best in others. Trusting their talent, he encourages artists to push their creativity to the limits. It's a rare creative person who can let others run with the ball." Show writer Jim Steinmeyer added, "The idea is king with Rolly. It doesn't have to be his vision, as long as it works."

Born Roland Fargo Crump on February 27, 1930, in Alhambra, California, Rolly took a pay cut as a "dipper" in a ceramic factory to join The Walt Disney Studios in 1952.

To help pay bills, he built sewer manholes on weekends. He served as an in-between artist and, later, assistant animator, contributing to *Peter Pan*, *Lady and the Tramp*, *Sleeping Beauty*, and others.

In 1959, he joined show design at WED Enterprises, now known as Walt Disney Imagineering. There, he became one of Walt's key designers for some of Disneyland's groundbreaking new attractions and shops, including the *Haunted Mansion, Enchanted Tiki Room*, and Adventureland Bazaar.

Rolly served as a key designer on the Disney attractions featured at the 1964-65 New York World's Fair, including *it's a small world*, for which he designed the Tower of the Four Winds marquee. When the attraction moved to Disneyland in 1966, Rolly designed the larger-than-life animated clock at its entrance, which sends puppet children on parade with each quarter-hour gong.

After contributing to the initial design of the Magic Kingdom at Walt Disney World in Florida, and developing story and set designs for NBC's *Disney on Parade* in 1970, Rolly left the Company to consult on projects including Busch Gardens in Florida and California, the ABC Wildlife Preserve in Maryland, and Ringling Brothers & Barnum and Bailey Circus World in Florida, among others.

He returned in 1976 to contribute to EPCOT Center, serving as project designer for The Land and the Wonders of Life pavilions. He also participated in master planning for an expansion of Disneyland until 1981, when he again departed to lead design on a proposed Cousteau Ocean Center in Norfolk, Virginia, and to launch his own firm, the Mariposa Design Group, developing an array of themed projects around the world, including an international celebration for the country of Oman.

In 1992, Rolly returned to Imagineering as executive designer, redesigning and refurbishing The Land and Innoventions at Epcot Center. Rolly "retired" from The Walt Disney Company in 1996, but continued to work on a number of creative projects. He released his autobiography, *It's Kind of a Cute Story*, in 2012. (courtesy of D23.com)

Marc Davis

Animator, artist, Imagineer. Marc Davis dedicated his creative genius to helping Walt Disney realize his dreams, from helping perfect the animated story to creating Disneyland, the world's first theme park. About his years at Disney, Marc once said, "I rarely felt confined to the animation medium. I worked as an idea man and loved creating characters, whether they be for animation or any other medium."

Marc is probably best known as the father of some of Disney's most memorable animated women, including Cruella De Vil from *One Hundred and One Dalmatians*, Maleficent from *Sleeping Beauty*, and Tinker Bell from *Peter Pan*. When once asked to choose a favorite among his bevy of grand Disney dames, he replied, "Each of my women characters has her own unique style; I love them all in different ways."

The only child of Harry and Mildred Davis, Marc was born on March 30, 1913, in Bakersfield, California, where his father was engaged in oil field developments. Wherever a new oil boom developed, the family moved with Harry and, as a result, Marc attended more than 20 different schools across the country while growing up.

After high school, he enrolled in the Kansas City Art Institute, followed by the California School of Fine Arts in San Francisco and Otis Art Institute in Los Angeles. While studying, Marc spent hours at the zoo drawing animals, which became one of his specialties.

His story drawings for *Bambi* are considered some of the finest studies of animal characters ever created at the Disney Studio.

Marc joined Disney in 1935 as an apprentice animator on *Snow White and the Seven Dwarfs* and moved on to story sketch and character design on *Bambi* and *Victory Through Air Power*. Over the years, he animated on classic Disney features such as *Song of the South*, *Cinderella*, and *Alice in Wonderland*, as well as shorts, including *African Diary*, *Duck Pimples*, and *Toot, Whistle, Plunk, and Boom*.

He later transferred to Disney's design and development organization, today known as Walt Disney Imagineering. As one of Disney's original Imagineers, Marc contributed whimsical story and character concepts for such Disneyland attractions as the *Enchanted Tiki Room*, *It's a Small World*, *Pirates of the Caribbean*,

Haunted Mansion and *Jungle Cruise*.

After 43 years with the Studio, Marc retired in 1978, but continued to lend his expertise to the development of Epcot Center and Tokyo Disneyland. He and his wife, Alice, who designed costumes for the *Audio-Animatronics®* characters featured in *Pirates of the Caribbean* and *it's a small world,* were also longtime supporters of the California Institute of the Arts, which was founded by Walt Disney.

Marc Davis passed away on January 12, 2000, in Glendale, California. (courtesy of D23.com)

John Hench

John Hench was Disney's Renaissance artist. Imagineer, philosopher, animator, designer, storyteller, voracious reader (52 magazines a month!), and teacher, John was always quick to share the lessons he learned from his own mentor—Walt Disney.

He recalled one of those lessons: "Walt always said, 'You get down to Disneyland at least twice a month and you walk in the front entrance, don't walk in through the back. Eat with the people. Watch how they react to the work you've done down there.' This made an enormous difference in how we approached our work."

As senior vice president of Walt Disney Imagineering, John carried on Walt's ideals and standards. Sandy Huskins, his assistant and confidante for more than 25 years, once said:

"Sometimes John says, 'Tomorrow, we're going to the Park,' and we'll go down, stand in line, and pretend we're guests. I always come back with a full load of notes."

Born in Cedar Rapids, Iowa, in 1908, John attended the Art Students League in New York City and received a scholarship to Otis Art Institute in Los Angeles. He also attended the California School of Fine Arts in San Francisco and Chouinard Art Institute in Los Angeles.

In 1939, he joined Disney as a sketch artist in the story department, working first on *Fantasia*. Always eager to learn, John accepted a variety of tasks over the years, including painting backgrounds on *Dumbo* and creating layouts for *The Three Caballeros*. His other film credits include art supervision on *Make Mine Music*, cartoon art treatments for *So Dear To My Heart*, color and styling for *Peter Pan*, and animation effects for *The Living Desert*.

In 1954, his special effects work on *20,000 Leagues Under the Sea* earned John an Oscar*. That same year, he left the Studio to work at what is today known as Walt Disney Imagineering. His first assignment was to design attractions for the original Tomorrowland in Disneyland.

Later, in 1960, John worked closely with Walt in developing the pageantry for the opening and closing ceremonies and daily presentations for the VIII Winter Olympic Games at Squaw Valley, as well as designing the iconic Olympic Torch. John worked on attractions for the 1964–65 New York World's Fair, before going on to help master plan Walt Disney World and Tokyo Disneyland. He was a key figure in the conceptualization and creation of Epcot Center, and developed ideas for theme parks including Disney's California Adventure, Animal Kingdom, and Tokyo DisneySea.

John was also Mickey Mouse's official corporate portrait artist, having painted Mickey's portrait for his 25th (1953), 50th (1978), 60th (1988), 70th (1998), and 75th (2003) birthdays.

In 2004, John celebrated his 65th year with the company. He passed away on February 5, 2004, in Burbank, still working full-time for Disney at age 95. (courtesy of D23.com)

Tom Morris

Tom began his Disney career in 1973, selling balloons at Disneyland. He transferred to Disneyland Operations four years later, and worked as a ride operator for Tomorrowland attractions. In 1979, Morris transferred to Imagineering as a draftsman and for his first assignment, he contributed to the *Journey into Imagination* attraction for EPCOT Center. Morris has worked on dozens of prestigious theme park projects, including Disneyland Paris's Fantasyland, Hong Kong Disneyland, Disney California

Adventure's Cars Land, and Euro Disneyland (now Disneyland Paris Resort). Tony Baxter applauded Morris's work, saying, "Tom successfully led teams of artists, architects, writers and engineers in the four-year development of a new version of the symbolic Disney castle and a fairy tale village that translates European fables and classic Disney animation into three-dimensional reality." Tom recently retired from Walt Disney Imagineering as an Executive Creative Director.

Joe Rohde

Artist, Designer, Writer, Executive, Speaker, sometime media personality.

Lead large integrated teams on large complex projects.

Currently a Creative Portfolio Executive at Walt Disney Imagineering.

Member of The Explorer's Club '10. Recently completed expedition to Western Mongolia to raise money for Snow Leopard conservation efforts.

With over thirty years at Walt Disney Imagineering, Joe Rohde has established himself as a respected veteran in the themed entertainment industry. He has led the conceptualization, design, and production of Disney's Animal Kingdom and all subsequent installations in that park, inducing the current "Avatar" project, as well as "Aulani, A Disney Resort and Spa."

Joe travels extensively for work and pleasure and has visited some of the most remote corners of the globe, most recently returning from Mongolia, where his Explorer's Club Flag Expedition, "The Leopard in the Land" has him painting large scale plein air landscapes in snow leopard habitat to raise money and awareness for these endangered cats. (courtesy of Linkedin.com)

Marty Sklar

As former vice chairman and principal creative executive of Walt Disney Imagineering (WDI), Marty Sklar stood as a dedicated torchbearer of Walt Disney's philosophy since first joining the

Company a month before Disneyland opened in 1955.

He helped express and preserve Walt's spirit of optimism, happiness, and hope for the future through attractions and special exhibitions in Disney theme parks around the world.

For more than 50 years, Walt's inspiration has burned in Marty. He once said, "Working with Walt Disney was the greatest 'training by fire' anyone could ever experience. Our training was by Walt, who was always there pitching in with new ideas and improving everyone else's input. The fire was that we were constantly breaking new ground to create deadline projects never attempted before in this business. That, I'm proud to say, has never stopped in my years at Disney."

Born Martin A. Sklar on February 6, 1934, in New Brunswick, New Jersey, Marty attended the University of California at Los Angeles where he served as editor of the *Daily Bruin* campus newspaper. In July 1955, the student editor was recruited to create an 1890-themed tabloid newspaper, *The Disneyland News*, which sold on Main Street during the Park's debut year. After completing his education, Marty returned to Disneyland publicity and marketing. There, he established *Vacationland* magazine.

He joined WDI in 1961 as part of a team assigned by Walt to develop industry-sponsored shows and pavilions for General Electric, Ford, Pepsi-Cola and UNICEF, and the State of Illinois at the 1964-65 New York World's Fair. Ever since, Marty served as a key representative working with American industry in developing and sponsoring attractions for Disney parks and resorts around the globe.

During his early years at Disney, Marty not only learned Walt's philosophy firsthand, but metabolized and translated it into materials he wrote for the master showman which were used in publications, television appearances, and special films. Among them was a 20-minute movie devoted to communicating Walt's vision of EPCOT, his Experimental Prototype Community of Tomorrow, originally intended to help resolve the urban challenges found in American cities.

Marty first became an Imagineering officer in 1974 when appointed vice president, concepts and planning, a role in which he guided creative development of Epcot Center at the Walt Disney World Resort in Florida. In 1979, he was named vice president of creative development, followed by executive vice president in 1982. He served as president and vice chairman from 1987 to 1996.

As vice chairman, Marty provided leadership for the Imagineering creative staff, delivering breakthrough entertainment concepts for Disney parks and resorts including Disneyland Paris, the Tokyo Disney Resort, and Hong Kong Disneyland. Imagineering is also responsible for all Disney resort hotels and the Disney Cruise Line ships, and has created concepts for restaurants, children's museums and hospitals, traveling shows, and exhibitions.

In 2001, the Company honored Marty with a special award for 45 years of service and leadership. After the 50th anniversary of Disneyland in 2005, he transitioned into a new role as Imagineering's international ambassador. He is the only person to have attended the grand openings of all Disney parks. He retired from Disney on July 17, 2009, after 53 years with the Company.

Martin A. "Marty" Sklar passed away in his Hollywood Hills home on Thursday July 27, 2017. (courtesy of D23.com)

Walt Disney Imagineering (WDI) is the creative force that imagines, designs and builds all Disney theme parks, resorts, attractions and cruise ships worldwide. Imagineering's unique strength comes from its diverse global team of creative and technical professionals, who build on Disney's legacy of storytelling to pioneer new forms of entertainment.

Founded in 1952 as WED Enterprises to design and build the world's first theme park—Disneyland—WDI is where imagination and creativity combine with cutting-edge technology to create unforgettable experiences. The Imagineers who practice this unique blend of art and science work in more than 100 disciplines to shepherd an idea all the way from "blue sky" concept phase to opening day.

Bibliography By Chapter:

INTRODUCTION:

[1] Jo, Sophie. "The Horses of History: Walt Disney's King Arthur Carrousel." *The Walt Disney Family Museum*, 26 Sept. 2017, waltdisney. org/blog/horses-history-walt-disney-s-king-arthur-carrousel.

[2] Bevil, Dewayne. "Disney World was announced 50 years ago this week." OrlandoSentinel.com. November 15, 2015. Accessed November 03, 2017. http://www.orlandosentinel.com/travel/attractions/theme-park-rangers-blog/os-disney-world-announced-50-years-ago-20151115-post.html.

[3] Patterson, James. *Miracle on the 17th Green*. New York, NY : Hachette, 2012.

CHAPTER 1:

[1] "Access." D23. Accessed November 03, 2017. https://d23.com/walt-disney-quote/i-dont-want/.

[2] "Walt Disney's Love of Trains Lives On at Walt Disney World Resort." Walt Disney World News. Accessed November 03, 2017. http://wdwnews.com/releases/walt-disneys-love-of-trains-lives-on-at-walt-disney-world-resort/.

[3] "Harmony Barber Shop, a Cut Above the Rest for Walt Disney World Resort Guests." Walt Disney World News. Accessed November 03, 2017. http://wdwnews.com/releases/harmony-barber-shop-a-cut-above-the-rest-for-walt-disney-world-resort-guests/.

[4] Udell, Erin. "The story of Disneyland's Main Street and Old Town Fort Collins." Coloradoan. November 11, 2016. Accessed November 03, 2017. http://www.coloradoan.com/story/life/2016/11/11/disneyland-main-street-old-town-fort-collins/93120656/.

[5] Wright, Alex. *The Imagineering Field Guide to the Magic Kingdom at Walt Disney World: An Imagineers-Eye Tour*. New York:

Disney, 2010. Page 24

[6]Heimbuch, Jeff. *Main Street Windows*. S.1.: Orchard Hill Press. 2014.

[7]"Joe Potter." D23. Accessed November 03, 2017. http://d23.com/walt-disney-legend/joe-potter.

[8]*Epcot Center Today*, Volume 1, Number 2, 1981.

[9] "Mail Services." Walt Disney World. Accessed November 03, 2017. https://disneyworld.disney.go.com/guest-services/mail-services/.

[10]"Cinderella Castle at Walt Disney World Resort Fact Sheet." Walt Disney World News. Accessed November 03, 2017. http://wdwnews.com/fact-sheets/2013/03/16/cinderella-castle-at-walt-disney-world-resort-fact-sheet/.

[11]Wright, Alex. *The Imagineering Field Guide to the Magic Kingdom at Walt Disney World: An Imagineers-Eye Tour*. Page 84. New York: Disney, 2010.

[12]"D23 Quotes." D23. Accessed November 03, 2017. https://d23.com/walt-disney-quote/the-only-problem/.

[13]Wright, Alex. *The Imagineering field guide to the Magic Kingdom at Walt Disney World: an imagineers-eye tour*. Page 112. New York: Disney, 2010.

[14]"Space Mountain Sends Magic Kingdom Guests Speeding Past the Stars at Walt Disney World Resort." Walt Disney World News. Accessed November 03, 2017. http://wdwnews.com/releases/space-mountain-sends-magic-kingdom-guestsspeeding-past-the-stars-at-walt-disney-world-resort/.

[15]"Storybook Circus: Big Fun Under the Big Top for New Fantasyland Guests." Walt Disney World News. Accessed November 03, 2017. http://wdwnews.com/releases/storybook-circus-big-fun-under-the-big-top-for-new-fantasyland-guests-2/.

[16]"Under the Sea ~ Journey of the Little Mermaid Fun Facts."

Walt Disney World News. Accessed November 03, 2017. http://wdwnews.com/releases/under-the-sea-journey-of-the-little-mermaid-fun-facts/.

[17]"New Fantasyland Immerses Guests in Classic Disney Stories, Magical Places." Walt Disney World News. Accessed November 03, 2017. http://wdwnews.com/releases/new-fantasyland-immerses-guests-in-classic-disney-stories-magical-places/.

[18]"Fairy Tale Elegance, French-Inspired Cuisine Celebrated At Be Our Guest Restaurant in Fantasyland." Walt Disney World News. Accessed November 03, 2017. http://wdwnews.com/releases/fairy-tale-elegance-french-inspired-cuisine-celebrated-at-be-our-guest-restaurant-in-new-fantasyland/.

[9]"Seven Dwarfs Mine Train: A Rocking, Rollicking Family-Friendly Roller Coaster Crowns New Fantasyland." Walt Disney World News. Accessed November 03, 2017. http://wdwnews.com/releases/seven-dwarfs-mine-train-a-rocking-rollicking-family-friendly-roller-coaster-crowns-new-fantasyland/.

[20]"'its a small world' Attraction in Fantasyland at Magic Kingdom." Walt Disney World News. Accessed November 03, 2017. http://wdwnews.com/releases/it/.

[21]Surrell, Jason. *The Haunted Mansion Imagineering a Disney Classic*. Los Angeles: Disney Editions, 2015. Pages 36-37.

[22]"Haunted Mansion Full of Fun and Fright for Guests in Magic Kingdom at Walt Disney World Resort." Walt Disney World News. Accessed November 03, 2017. http://wdwnews.com/releases/haunted-mansion-full-of-fun-and-frightfor-guests-in-magic-kingdom-at-walt-disney-world-resort/.

[23]Imagineers, The. *Walt Disney Imagineering: a behind the dreams look at making the magic real*. New York: Hyperion, 1998.

[24]Imagineers, The. *Walt Disney Imagineering: a behind the dreams look at making the magic real*. New York: Hyperion, 1998.

[25] *Walt Disney Imagineering: a behind-the-dreams look at making the magic real by the Imagineers.* New York: Hyperion, 1998. Page 48.

[26] "Big Thunder Mountain Railroad Whisks Riders on the Wildest Ride in the West." Walt Disney World News. Accessed November 03, 2017. http://wdwnews.com/releases/big-thunder-mountain-railroad-whisks-riders-on-the-wildest-ride-in-the-west/.

[27] Ghez, Didier. "Interview with Tony Baxter." Interview with Tony Baxter. May 31, 1995. Accessed November 03, 2017. https://web.archive.org/web/20120206025902/http://www.pizarro.net/didier/_private/interviu/baxter.html.

[28] Noland, Claire. "Dallas McKennon dies at 89; actor gave voice to many animated characters." Los Angeles Times. July 18, 2009. Accessed November 03, 2017. http://www.latimes.com/local/obituaries/la-me-dallas-mckennon18-2009jul18-story.html.

[29] Wright, Alex. *The Imagineering field guide to the Magic Kingdom at Walt Disney World: an Imagineers-eye tour.* Page 48. New York: Disney, 2010.

[30] Ghez, Didier. "Interview with Tony Baxter." Interview with Tony Baxter. May 31, 1995. Accessed November 03, 2017. https://web.archive.org/web/20120206025902/http://www.pizarro.net/didier/_private/interviu/baxter.html.

[31] Wright, Alex. *The Imagineering field guide to the Magic Kingdom at Walt Disney World: an imagineers-eye tour.* Page 48. New York: Disney, 2010.

[32] "Pirates of the Caribbean Takes Walt Disney World Guests On Swashbuckling Adventure in Sacked Seaport." Walt Disney World News. Accessed November 03, 2017. http://wdwnews.com/releases/pirates-of-the-caribbean-takes-walt-disney-world-guests-on-swashbuckling-adventure-in-sacked-seaport/.

[33] "Pirates of the Caribbean Takes Walt Disney World Guests On

Swashbuckling Adventure in Sacked Seaport." Walt Disney World News. Accessed November 03, 2017. http://wdwnews.com/releases/pirates-of-the-caribbean-takes-walt-disney-world-guests-on-swashbuckling-adventure-in-sacked-seaport/.

[34]Wright, Alex. *The Imagineering field guide to the Magic Kingdom at Walt Disney World: an Imagineers-eye tour*. Page 48. New York: Disney, 2010.

Chapter 2:

[1]Hench, John, Peggy Van Pelt, Frank Gehry, and Martin A. Sklar. *Designing Disney: Imagineering and the art of the show*. New York: Disney Editions, 2008.

[2]"Highway in the Sky: Walt Disney World Resort Monorail Fact Sheet." Walt Disney World News. Accessed November 03, 2017. http://wdwnews.com/releases/highway-in-the-sky-walt-disney-world-resort-monorail-fact-sheet/.

[3]"Highway in the Sky: Walt Disney World Resort Monorail Fact Sheet." Walt Disney World News. Accessed November 03, 2017. http://wdwnews.com/releases/highway-in-the-sky-walt-disney-world-resort-monorail-fact-sheet/.

[4]"About Fuller." Spaceship Earth | The Buckminster Fuller Institute. Accessed November 03, 2017. https://www.bfi.org/about-fuller/big-ideas/spaceshipearth.

[5]Hench, John, Peggy Van Pelt, Frank Gehry, and Martin A. Sklar. *Designing Disney: Imagineering and the art of the show*. New York: Disney Editions, 2008.

[6]Kavesh, Laura. "Project's creator still finding small stuff that needs polish." *The Orlando Sentinel*, October 24, 1982.

[7]"Epcot Fact Sheet." Walt Disney World News. Accessed November 03, 2017. http://wdwnews.com/fact-sheets/2016/07/01/epcot-fact-sheet/.

[8]Crump, Rolly, and Jeff Heimbuch. *Its kind of a cute story*. Place of

publication not identified: Bamboo Forest Publishing, 2012. Page 128

[9]Crump, Rolly, and Jeff Heimbuch. *Its kind of a cute story*. Place of publication not identified: Bamboo Forest Publishing, 2012. Page 128

[10]"Disney relaunches Mission: SPACE ride at Epcot with revised NASA cameos | collectSPACE." CollectSPACE.com. Accessed November 03, 2017. http://www.collectspace.com/news/news-081317a-disney-mission-space-epcot-nasa.html.

[11]"Epcot Guests Design Their Dream Wheels, then Buckle Up for Fun at the Re-Imagined Test Track Presented by Chevrolet." Walt Disney World News. Accessed November 03, 2017. http://wdwnews.com/releases/epcot-guests-design-their-dream-wheels-then-buckle-up-for-fun-at-the-re-imagined-test-track-presented-by-chevrolet-2/.

[12]Wright, Alex. *The Imagineering field guide to Epcot at Walt Disney World: an Imagineers -eye tour*. New York: Disney Editions, 2010.

[13]Rasmussen, Nate. "Vintage Walt Disney World: Fountain of Nations Dedication at Epcot." Disney Parks Blog. October 24, 2013. Accessed November 03, 2017. https://disneyparks.disney.go.com/blog/2013/10/vintage-walt-disney-world-fountain-of-nations-dedication-at-epcot/.

[14] "Walt Disney World Fun Facts." Walt Disney World News. Accessed November 03, 2017. http://wdwnews.com/releases/walt-disney-world-fun-facts/.

[15] "Walt Disney World Fun Facts." Walt Disney World News. Accessed November 03, 2017. http://wdwnews.com/releases/walt-disney-world-fun-facts/.

[16] "Walt Disney World Fun Facts." Walt Disney World News. Accessed November 03, 2017. http://wdwnews.com/releases/walt-disney-world-fun-facts/.

[17]Klein, Jeffrey S. "Splashing Through Disney Tour of Sea's Wonders." *The Orlando Sentinel*, February 16, 1986. Accessed November 3, 2017.

[18]Jackson, Jerry. "Lab To Stimulate Growth in Plants, Interest At Epcot." *The Orlando Sentinel*, October 8, 1988. Accessed November 3, 2017.

[19]Powers, Scott. "Biotech thrives in Epcot's secret garden." *The Orlando Sentinel*, September 15, 2007. Accessed November 3, 2017.

[20]"Soarin' Around the World Takes Flight at Epcot." Walt Disney World News. Accessed November 03, 2017. http://wdwnews. com/releases/soarin-around-the-world-takes-flight-at-epcot/.

[21]Ghez, Didier. "Interview with Tony Baxter." Interview with Tony Baxter. May 31, 1995. Accessed November 03, 2017. https:// web.archive.org/web/20120206025902/http://www.pizarro. net/didier/_private/interviu/baxter.html.

[22]Phillips, Lynn. "Sales team goes on the road again to find more sponsors for attractions." *The Orlando Sentinel*, October 24, 1982.

[23]"Canadian Pavilion Celebrates Our Neighbor to the North." Walt Disney World News. Accessed November 03, 2017. http://wdwnews.com/releases/canadian-pavilion-celebrates-our-neighbor-to-the-north/.

[24]"Spectacular Scenes Surround Epcot Audiences in Canadian Film." Walt Disney World News. Accessed November 03, 2017. http://wdwnews.com/releases/spectacular-scenes-surround-epcot-audiences-in-canadian-film/.

[25]"United Kingdom Brings Old World Charm To World Showcase." Walt Disney World News. Accessed November 03, 2017. http://wdwnews.com/releases/united-kingdom-brings-old-world-charm-to-world-showcase/.

[26]*The Imagineering field guide to Epcot at Walt Disney World ; an*

imagineers-eye tour. Page 119. New York: Disney Enterprises, 2006.

[27] *The Imagineering field guide to Epcot at Walt Disney World ; an imagineers-eye tour*. Page 108. New York: Disney Enterprises, 2006.

[28] *The Imagineering field guide to Epcot at Walt Disney World ; an imagineers-eye tour*. Page 119. New York: Disney Enterprises, 2006

[29] "Classic French at Monsieur Paul Restaurant at Epcot World Showcase France Pavilion." Walt Disney World News. Accessed November 03, 2017. http://wdwnews.com/releases/classic-french-at-monsieur-paul-restaurant-at-epcot-world-showcase-france-pavilion/.

[30] Defendorf, Richard. "Morocco now part of Epcot's world." *The Orlando Sentinel*, September 14, 1984. Accessed November 3, 2017.

[31] Stewart, Laura. "Morocco ." *The Orlando Sentinel*, May 27, 1984.

[32] *The Imagineering field guide to Epcot at Walt Disney World ; an imagineers-eye tour*. Page 102. New York: Disney Enterprises, 2006.

[33] "Centuries of Culture Come to Life in Epcot Japan Pavilion." Walt Disney World News. Accessed November 03, 2017. http://wdwnews.com/releases/centuries-of-culture-come-to-life-in-epcot-japan-pavilion/.

[34] "The great Torii." The great Torii | Miyajima Official Website - Japan. Accessed November 03, 2017. http://visit-miyajima-japan.com/en/culture-and-heritage/spiritual-heritage-temples-shrines/le-torii-flottant.html

[35] Kurtti, Jeff. *Since the world began: Walt Disney World, the first 25 years*. New York: Hyperion, 1996

[36] Gholdston, Sharon, and Lynn Phillips. "Disney unveils dazzling

voyage to Future World." *The Orlando Sentinel*, October 3, 1978.

[37]"Behind the Scenes at The American Adventure." Walt Disney World News. Accessed November 03, 2017. http://wdwnews.com/releases/behind-the-scenes-at-the-american-adventure/.

[38]*The Imagineering field guide to Epcot at Walt Disney World ; an imagineers-eye tour.* Page 93. New York: Disney Enterprises, 2006.

[39]*The Imagineering field guide to Epcot at Walt Disney World ; an imagineers-eye tour.* Page 90. New York: Disney Enterprises, 2006.

[40]"Epcot Fact Sheet." Walt Disney World News. Accessed November 03, 2017. http://wdwnews.com/fact-sheets/2016/07/01/epcot-fact-sheet/.

[41]""Re-Discovering America: Family Treasures from the Kinsey Collection" Gallery at Epcot." Walt Disney World News. Accessed November 03, 2017. http://wdwnews.com/releases/epcot-expands-re-discovering-america-family-treasures-from-the-kinsey-collection-gallery-this-spring/.

[42]"Behind the Scenes at The American Adventure." Walt Disney World News. Accessed November 03, 2017. http://wdwnews.com/releases/behind-the-scenes-at-the-american-adventure/.

[43]"Behind the Scenes at The American Adventure." Walt Disney World News. Accessed November 03, 2017. http://wdwnews.com/releases/behind-the-scenes-at-the-american-adventure/.

[44]"Behind the Scenes at The American Adventure." Walt Disney World News. Accessed November 03, 2017. http://wdwnews.com/releases/behind-the-scenes-at-the-american-adventure/.

[46]"Behind the Scenes at The American Adventure." Walt Disney World News. Accessed November 03, 2017. http://wdwnews.com/releases/behind-the-scenes-at-the-american-adventure/.

[47] *The Imagineering field guide to Epcot at Walt Disney World ; an imagineers-eye tour*. New York: Disney Enterprises, 2006.

[48] *The Imagineering field guide to Epcot at Walt Disney World ; an imagineers-eye tour*. New York: Disney Enterprises, 2006.

[49] "Epcot Fact Sheet." Walt Disney World News. Accessed November 03, 2017. http://wdwnews.com/fact-sheets/2016/07/01/epcot-fact-sheet/.

[50] "'IllumiNations: Reflections of Earth' is Nightly Epcot Finale." Walt Disney World News. Accessed November 03, 2017. http://wdwnews.com/releases/illuminations-reflections-of-earth-is-nightly-epcot-finale/.

[51] "Epcot World Showcase Presents Sweeping Spectacle of Nations." Walt Disney World News. Accessed November 03, 2017. http://wdwnews.com/releases/epcot-world-showcase-presents-sweeping-spectacle-of-nations/.

[52] "Epcot World Showcase Presents Sweeping Spectacle of Nations." Walt Disney World News. Accessed November 03, 2017. http://wdwnews.com/releases/epcot-world-showcase-presents-sweeping-spectacle-of-nations/.

[53] Phillips, Lynn. "Taiwanese reveal Epcot plans." *Sentinel Star*, February 2, 1978.

[54] Services, Star. "Disney in contact with China as possible Epcot sponsor." *Star Sentinel*, January 25, 1980.

[55] Blumenstyk, Goldie. "Disney won't display chunk of marble sent by city in Taiwan ." *The Orlando Sentinel*, May 12, 1983.

[56] *The Imagineering field guide to Epcot at Walt Disney World ; an imagineers-eye tour*. Page 84. New York: Disney Enterprises, 2006.

[57] *The Imagineering field guide to Epcot at Walt Disney World ; an imagineers-eye tour*. Page 84. New York: Disney Enterprises, 2006.

[58]"Stave church - See the unique Norwegian stave churches." Fjord Norway. Accessed November 03, 2017. https://www.fjordnor-way.com/things-to-do/culture-and-heritage/stave-churches.

[59]Vaughn, Vicki. "Next at Epcot: Norway and Vikings." *The Orlando Sentinel*, June 13, 1985.

[60]"Norway Pavilion Brings Excitement of Scandinavia to Epcot." Walt Disney World News. Accessed November 03, 2017. http://wdwnews.com/releases/norway-pavilion-brings-excitement-of-scandinavia-to-epcot/.

[61]"Sail Through the Kingdom of Arendelle on Frozen Ever After." Walt Disney World News. Accessed November 03, 2017. http://wdwnews.com/releases/sail-through-the-kingdom-of-arendelle-on-frozen-ever-after/.

[62]*The Imagineering field guide to Epcot at Walt Disney World ; an imagineers-eye tour*. Page 76. New York: Disney Enterprises, 2006.

[63]"Walt Disney World Epcot Salutes Mexico's Heritage." Walt Disney World News. Accessed November 03, 2017. http://wdwnews.com/releases/walt-disney-world-epcot-salutes-mexicos-heritage/.

CHAPTER 3:

[1]*Walt Disney Imagineering: a behind-the-dreams look at making the magic real by the imagineers*. New York: Hyperion, 1998.

[2]Hench, John, Peggy Van Pelt, Frank Gehry, and Martin A. Sklar. *Designing Disney: Imagineering and the art of the show*. New York: Disney Editions, 2008.

[3]Martino, Alison. "In Memory of the Pan-Pacific Auditorium." Los Angeles Magazine. November 23, 2016. Accessed November 03, 2017.http://www.lamag.com/citythinkblog/memory-pan-pacific-auditorium/.

[4]Martino, Alison. "In Memory of the Pan-Pacific Auditorium."

Los Angeles Magazine. November 23, 2016. Accessed November 03, 2017.http://www.lamag.com/citythinkblog/memory-pan-pacific-auditorium/.

[5]"Los Angeles Conservancy." Chapman Plaza | Los Angeles Conservancy. Accessed November 03, 2017. https://www.laconservancy.org/locations/chapman-plaza.

[6]Wright, Alex. *The Imagineering field guide to Disney's Hollywood Studios at Walt Disney World: an Imagineers-eye tour*. NY, NY: Disney Editions, 2010.

[7]Wright, Alex. *The Imagineering field guide to Disney's Hollywood Studios at Walt Disney World: an Imagineers-eye tour*. NY, NY: Disney Editions, 2010.

[8]"Los Angeles Conservancy." Chapman Plaza | Los Angeles Conservancy. Accessed November 03, 2017. https://www.laconservancy.org/locations/chapman-plaza.

[9]Wright, Alex. *The Imagineering field guide to Disney's Hollywood Studios at Walt Disney World: an Imagineers-eye tour*. NY, NY: Disney Editions, 2010.

[10]Wright, Alex. *The Imagineering field guide to Disney's Hollywood Studios at Walt Disney World: an Imagineers-eye tour*. NY, NY: Disney Editions, 2010.

[11]Malmberg, Melody. *Walt Disney Imagineering: a behind the dreams look at making the magic real*. New York: Disney Ed., 2010.

[12]Eisner, Michael, and Tony Schwartz. *Work in progress*. New York: Hyperion, 1999.

[13]Malmberg, Melody. *Walt Disney Imagineering: a behind the dreams look at making the magic real*. New York: Disney Ed., 2010.

[14]"Disney's Hollywood Studios Fact Sheet." Walt Disney World News. Accessed November 03, 2017. http://wdwnews.com/fact-sheets/2016/07/01/disneys-hollywood-studios-fact-sheet/.

[15]"20 Facts For The Twilight Zone Tower of Terror's 20th Anniversary." Disney Parks Blog. Accessed November 03, 2017. https://disneyparks.disney.go.com/blog/2014/07/20-facts-for-the-twilight-zone-tower-of-terrors-20th-anniversary/.

[16]"20 Facts For The Twilight Zone Tower of Terror's 20th Anniversary." Disney Parks Blog. Accessed November 03, 2017. https://disneyparks.disney.go.com/blog/2014/07/20-facts-for-the-twilight-zone-tower-of-terrors-20th-anniversary/.

[17]"Random Ride Sequences Turn Up the Thrills For Guests on Tower of Terror." Walt Disney World News. Accessed November 03, 2017. http://wdwnews.com/releases/random-ride-sequences-turn-up-the-thrills-for-guests-on-tower-of-terror/.

[18]"Rock 'n' Roller Coaster Starring Aerosmith - Fast Facts." Walt Disney World News. Accessed November 03, 2017. http://wdwnews.com/releases/rock-n-roller-coaster-starring-aerosmith-fast-facts/.

[19]"Aerosmith Rocks, Guests Roll at Disney's Hollywood Studios Thrill Ride." Walt Disney World News. Accessed November 03, 2017. http://wdwnews.com/releases/aerosmith-rocks-guests-roll-at-disneys-hollywood-studios-thrill-ride/.

[20]"Rock 'n' Roller Coaster Starring Aerosmith Turns 15 at Walt Disney World Resort." Disney Parks Blog. Accessed November 03, 2017. https://disneyparks.disney.go.com/blog/2014/07/rock-n-roller-coaster-starring-aerosmith-turns-15-at-walt-disney-world-resort/.

[21]Wright, Alex. *The Imagineering field guide to Disney's Hollywood Studios at Walt Disney World: an Imagineers-eye tour*. NY, NY: Disney Editions, 2010.

[22]Wright, Alex. *The Imagineering field guide to Disney's Hollywood Studios at Walt Disney World: an Imagineers-eye tour*. NY, NY: Disney Editions, 2010.

[23]Wright, Alex. *The Imagineering field guide to Disney's Hollywood*

Studios at Walt Disney World: an Imagineers-eye tour. NY, NY: Disney Editions, 2010.

[24]"Indiana Jones Is Better Than Ever at Disney's Hollywood Studios." Walt Disney World News. Accessed November 03, 2017. http://wdwnews.com/releases/indiana-jones-is-better-than-ever-at-disneys-hollywood-studios/.

[25]Eisner, Michael, and Tony Schwartz. *Work in progress.* New York: Hyperion, 1999.

[26]"'Star Tours - The Adventures Continue' Brings Star Wars™ Thrills in 3-D to Disney's Hollywood Studios Theme Park." Walt Disney World News. Accessed November 03, 2017. http://wdwnews.com/releases/star-tours-the-adventures-continue-brings-star-wars-thrills-in-3-d-to-disneys-hollywood-studios-theme-park/.

[27]"A Galaxy of Star Wars Experiences Awaits Guests at Disney's Hollywood Studios." Walt Disney World News. Accessed November 03, 2017. http://wdwnews.com/releases/star-wars-experiences-at-disneys-hollywood-studios/

[28]"Disney Deal: Kermit Goes For The Big Bucks." Forbes. February 18, 2004. Accessed November 03, 2017. https://www.forbes.com/2004/02/18/cx_da_0218ton.html.

[29]Wright, Alex. *The Imagineering field guide to Disney's Hollywood Studios at Walt Disney World: an Imagineers-eye tour.* Page 106. NY, NY: Disney Editions, 2010.

[30]Malmberg, Melody. *Walt Disney Imagineering: a behind the dreams look at making the magic real.* New York: Disney Ed., 2010.

[31]"Walt's Quotes." D23. Accessed November 18, 2017. https://d23.com/walt-disney-quote/i-only-hope/.

[32]"Toy Story Midway Mania Opens at Disney's Hollywood Studios." May 31, 2008. Accessed November 03, 2017. https://d23.com/this-day/toy-story-midway-mania-opens-at-disneys-hollywood-studios/.

[33]"Immersive Experiences Starring YOU at Walt Disney World Resort." Walt Disney World News. Accessed November 03, 2017. http://wdwnews.com/releases/immersive-experiences-starring-you-at-walt-disney-world-resort/.

[34]"Immersive Experiences Starring YOU at Walt Disney World Resort." Walt Disney World News. Accessed November 03, 2017. http://wdwnews.com/releases/immersive-experiences-starring-you-at-walt-disney-world-resort/.

[35]Barnes, Brooks. "Will Disney Keep Us Amused?" The New York Times. February 09, 2008. Accessed November 03, 2017. http://www.nytimes.com/2008/02/10/business/media/10ride.html.

[36] "Water Animation and Fireworks Combine For Fantasmic! Show at Disney's Hollywood Studios." Walt Disney World News. Accessed November 03, 2017. http://wdwnews.com/releases/water-animation-and-fireworks-combine-for-fantasmic-show-atdisneys-hollywood-studios/

CHAPTER 4

[1] Disney, Oh My. "Disney Goes Wild | Insider." Oh My Disney. April 15, 2016. Accessed November 18, 2017. https://ohmy.disney.com/insider/2012/04/24/disney-goes-wild/.

[2] "In Walt's Own Words: Plussing Disneyland." The Walt Disney Family Museum. October 09, 2015. Accessed November 03, 2017. https://www.waltdisney.org/blog/walts-own-words-plussing-disneyland.

[3] "Disney's Animal Kingdom Fact Sheet." Walt Disney World News. Accessed November 03, 2017. http://wdwnews.com/fact-sheets/2016/07/01/disneys-animal-kingdom-fact-sheet/.

[4] "Disney's Animal Kingdom Fun Facts." Walt Disney World News. Accessed November 03, 2017. http://wdwnews.com/releases/disneys-animal-kingdom-fun-facts/.

[5]"Animal Kingdom Fun Facts." Walt Disney World News. Accessed November 03, 2017. http://wdwnews.com/releases/disneys-animal-kingdom-fun-facts/.

[6]Malmberg, Melody. *The making of Disney's Animal Kingdom Theme Park*. New York: Hyperion, 1998.

[7]Malmberg, Melody. *The making of Disney's Animal Kingdom Theme Park*. New York: Hyperion, 1998.

[8]Lancaster, Cory. "Mixing it up--Part Zoo, Part Fantasy." *The Orlando Sentinel*, April 19, 1998.

[9]Spitz, Jill Jorden. "Disney's Discovery Island Zoo May Face Springtime Extinction." *The Orlando Sentinel*, December 11, 1997.

[10]Barker, Tim. "Disney To Close Its Struggling Discovery Island." *The Orlando Sentinel*, March 26, 1999.

[11]Hinman, Catherine. "Discovery Island Deserted." *The Orlando Sentinel*, April 9, 1999.

[12]Malmberg, Melody. *The making of Disney's Animal Kingdom Theme Park*. New York: Hyperion, 1998.

[13]*The Imagineering field guide to Disney's Animal Kingdom at Walt Disney World: an imagineers-eye tour*. New York: Disney Enterprises, 2007.

[14]*The Imagineering field guide to Disney's Animal Kingdom at Walt Disney World: an imagineers-eye tour*. New York: Disney Enterprises, 2007.

[15]*The Imagineering field guide to Disney's Animal Kingdom at Walt Disney World: an imagineers-eye tour*. New York: Disney Enterprises, 2007.

[16]Malmberg, Melody. *The making of Disney's Animal Kingdom Theme Park*. New York: Hyperion, 1998. Page 38

[17] ""It's Tough to be a Bug!" Even at Disney's Animal Kingdom." Walt Disney World News. Accessed November 03, 2017. http://wdwnews.com/releases/its-tough-to-be-a-bug-

even-at-disneys-animal-kingdom/.

[18]Malmberg, Melody. *The making of Disney's Animal Kingdom Theme Park*. New York: Hyperion, 1998. Page 38

[19]"Disney's Animal Kingdom All Aglow with New Rivers of Light Show." Walt Disney World News. Accessed November 03, 2017. http://wdwnews.com/releases/rivers-of-light/.

[20]"Walt Disney Parks and Resorts to Give up to $1 Million to Protect and Restore Wildlife Habitats in Celebration of the Opening of Pandora – The World of Avatar." Walt Disney World News. Accessed November 03, 2017. http://wdwnews.com/releases/walt-disney-parks-and-resorts-to-give-up-to-1-million-to-protect-and-restore-wildlife-habitats-in-celebration-of-the-opening-of-pandora-the-world-of-avatar/.

[21]"Disney Dedicates Pandora – The World of Avatar, a New Land of Other-Worldly Sights, Sounds and Experiences at Disney's Animal Kingdom Theme Park." Walt Disney World News. Accessed November 03, 2017. http://wdwnews.com/releases/pandora-dedication/.

[22]"Pandora – The World of Avatar at Disney's Animal Kingdom: Explore the Magic of Nature in a Distant World Unlike Any Other." Walt Disney World News. Accessed November 03, 2017. http://wdwnews.com/releases/pandora-the-world-of-avatar-at-disneys-animal-kingdom-explore-the-magic-of-nature-in-a-distant-world-unlike-any-other-2/.

[23]"Inside Pandora – The World of Avatar How Walt Disney Imagineering Brought Pandora to Life ." Walt Disney World News. Accessed November 03, 2017. http://wdwnews.com/releases/inside-pandora-the-world-of-avatar-how-walt-disney-imagineering-brought-pandora-to-life/.

[24]"Awe-Inspiring Adventure! Avatar Flight of Passage is Thrilling Centerpiece on Pandora – The World of Avatar at Disney's Animal Kingdom." Walt Disney World News. Accessed November 03, 2017. http://wdwnews.com/releases/

avatar-flight-of-passage/.

[25]"Wonderment and Unforgettable Encounters Await Disney's Animal Kingdom Guests with the new Na'vi River Journey on Pandora – The World of Avatar." Walt Disney World News. Accessed November 03, 2017. http://wdwnews.com/releases/navi-river-journey/.

[26]*Walt Disney Imagineering: a behind-the-dreams look at making the magic real by the imagineers.* New York: Hyperion, 1998.

[27]"Wonderment and Unforgettable Encounters Await Disney's Animal Kingdom Guests with the new Na'vi River Journey on Pandora – The World of Avatar." Walt Disney World News. Accessed November 03, 2017. http://wdwnews.com/releases/navi-river-journey/.

[28]"The Culinary Story on Pandora – The World of Avatar at Disney's Animal Kingdom." Walt Disney World News. Accessed November 03, 2017. http://wdwnews.com/releases/the-culinary-story-on-pandora-the-world-of-avatar-at-disneys-animal-kingdom/.

[29]Delgado, Lauren. "Two Disney culinarians named top pastry chefs in America." OrlandoSentinel.com. July 28, 2017. Accessed November 03, 2017. http://www.orlandosentinel.com/food-restaurants/foodie-blog/os-et-disney-pastry-chefs-20170728-story.html.

[30]*The Imagineering field guide to Disney's Animal Kingdom at Walt Disney World: an imagineers-eye tour.* New York: Disney Enterprises, 2007.

[31]*The Imagineering field guide to Disney's Animal Kingdom at Walt Disney World: an imagineers-eye tour.* New York: Disney Enterprises, 2007.

[32]Malmberg, Melody. *The making of Disney's Animal Kingdom Theme Park.* New York: Hyperion, 1998. Page 115

[33]Malmberg, Melody. *The making of Disney's Animal Kingdom*

Theme Park. New York: Hyperion, 1998. Page 108

[34]Malmberg, Melody. *The making of Disney's Animal Kingdom Theme Park*. New York: Hyperion, 1998. Page 88

[35]Malmberg, Melody. *The making of Disney's Animal Kingdom Theme Park*. New York: Hyperion, 1998. Page 116

[36]Malmberg, Melody. *The making of Disney's Animal Kingdom Theme Park*. New York: Hyperion, 1998. Page 133

[37]*The Imagineering field guide to Disney's Animal Kingdom at Walt Disney World: an imagineers-eye tour*. New York: Disney Enterprises, 2007

[38]Malmberg, Melody. *The making of Disney's Animal Kingdom Theme Park*. New York: Hyperion, 1998.

[39]"Historic British Trains Live Again on Wildlife Express." Walt Disney World News. Accessed November 03, 2017. http://wdwnews.com/releases/historic-british-trains-live-again-on-wildlife-express/.

[40]*The Imagineering field guide to Disney's Animal Kingdom at Walt Disney World: an imagineers-eye tour*. New York: Disney Enterprises, 2007.

[41]*The Imagineering field guide to Disney's Animal Kingdom at Walt Disney World: an imagineers-eye tour*. New York: Disney Enterprises, 2007.

[42]*The Imagineering field guide to Disney's Animal Kingdom at Walt Disney World: an imagineers-eye tour*. New York: Disney Enterprises, 2007.

[43]Staff. "Asia Tour Should Come Roaring Back Next Month." *The Orlando Sentinel*, January 11, 1999.

[44]Lancaster, Cory. "Open With A Roar." *The Orlando Sentinel*, March 12, 1999.

[45]Staff. "Orient Yourself to Asia." *The Orlando Sentinel*, May 10, 1999

[46]Staff. "Rapids Ride Quenches Visitors Thirst For Thrills." *The Orlando Sentinel*, July 7, 2000.

[47]*The Imagineering field guide to Disney's Animal Kingdom at Walt Disney World: an imagineers-eye tour*. New York: Disney Enterprises, 2007.

[48]Meitner, Sarah Hale. "Disney officials head to Himalayas." *The Orlando Sentinel*, May 6, 2005.

[49]Powers, Scott. "Imagineers traveled far for details." *The Orlando Sentinel*, January 25, 2006.

[50]Powers, Scott . "Disney's $100 Million Gamble." *The Orlando Sentinel*, January 22, 2006.

[51]Powers, Scott. "Disney Rides Everest To New Popularity." *The Orlando Sentinel*, April 5, 2007.

[52]"Himalayan Village an Architectural Wonder That Welcomes Expedition Everest Adventurers." Walt Disney World News. Accessed November 03, 2017. http://wdwnews.com/releases/himalayan-village-an-architectural-wonder-that-welcomes-expedition-everest-adventurers/.

[53]"Landscape Architects Create Authentic Scenery to Heighten Storyline at Expedition Everest At Walt Disney World Resort." Walt Disney World News. Accessed November 03, 2017. http://wdwnews.com/releases/landscape-architects-create-authentic-scenery-to-heighten-storyline-at-expedition-everest-at-walt-disney-world-resort/.

[54]Garcia, Jason. "Disney 'yeti' loses its ferocity." *The Orlando Sentinel*, July 31, 2010.

[55]"Expedition Everest Fast Facts." Walt Disney World News. Accessed November 03, 2017. http://wdwnews.com/releases/expedition-everest-fast-facts/.

[56]Randolph, Eleanor, and JOHN J. GOLDMAN | TIMES STAFF WRITERS. "Museum Snaps Up T. Rex in Historic Sale." Los Angeles Times. October 05, 1997. Accessed November 03, 2017.

http://articles.latimes.com/1997/oct/05/news/mn-39658.

[57] "Fossil Fever! Dino Sue, Disney's Oldest 'Cast' Member, Greets Guests at Disney's Animal Kingdom." Walt Disney World News. Accessed November 03, 2017. http://wdwnews.com/releases/fossil-fever-dino-sue-disneys-oldest-cast-member-greets-guests-at-disneys-animal-kingdom/.

[58] "Fun with Fossils! Rides, Slides and Cretaceous Creatures Highlight DinoLand U.S.A." Walt Disney World News. Accessed November 03, 2017. http://wdwnews.com/releases/fun-with-fossils-rides-slides-and-cretaceous-creatures-highlightdino-land-u-s-a/.

[59] The Imagineering field guide to Disney's Animal Kingdom at Walt Disney World: an imagineers-eye tour. New York: Disney Enterprises, 2007.

CHAPTER 5:
[1] "Theme Index." Http://teaconnect.org. Accessed November 18, 2017. http://www.teaconnect.org/Resources/Theme-Index/

[2] Emerson, Chad. Four decades of magic: celebrating the first forty years of Disney World: a collection of essays. Ayefour Publishing, 2011.

[3] Emerson, Chad. Four decades of magic: celebrating the first forty years of Disney World: a collection of essays. Ayefour Publishing, 2011.

[4] Barker, Tim . "East Meets West Just Off Disney Land." Tribunedigital-orlandosentinel. August 17, 2000. Accessed November 04, 2017. http://articles.orlandosentinel.com/2000-08-17/business/0008170125_1_chiang-kai-shek-ling-walt-disney.

CHAPTER 6:
[1] Nordheimer, Jon. "Town Is Planned At Disney World." The New York Times, January 26, 1972.

2 "Disney Springs: Fast Facts, Fun Facts." Walt Disney World News. Accessed November 04, 2017. http://wdwnews.com/fact-sheets/2016/11/15/disney-springs-fast-facts-fun-facts/.

3 "Disney's Blizzard Beach Fact Sheet." Walt Disney World News. Accessed November 04, 2017. http://wdwnews.com/fact-sheets/2014/10/31/disneys-blizzard-beach-fact-sheet/.

4 "Typhoon Lagoon Fact Sheet." Walt Disney World News. Accessed November 04, 2017. http://wdwnews.com/fact-sheets/2014/10/31/typhoon-lagoon-fact-sheet/.

About the Author

Aaron Goldberg is an alumnus of the University of Pennsylvania, having graduated with bachelor's and master's degrees in anthropology. He is the author of the best-selling book *The Disney Story: Chronicling the Man, the Mouse and the Parks.*

Aaron and his book have been mentioned in stories about Disney in the *Los Angeles Times* and the Huffington Post. He's active on Twitter @aaronhgoldberg and has visited the Walt Disney World Resort more times than his wallet cares to remember!

Other Great Books by Aaron.

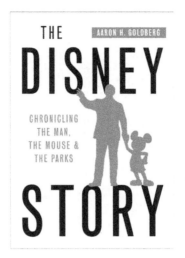

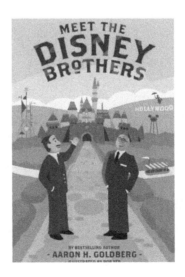

aaronhgoldberg.com

CPSIA information can be obtained
at www.ICGtesting.com
Printed in the USA
LVHW031457110220
646576LV00010B/768